Finding My Way

The Salty Key Inn Series
Book - 2

Judith Keim

BOOKS BY JUDITH KEIM

THE HARTWELL WOMEN SERIES:

The Talking Tree – 1
Sweet Talk – 2
Straight Talk – 3
Baby Talk – 4
The Hartwell Women – Boxed Set

THE BEACH HOUSE HOTEL SERIES:

Breakfast at The Beach House Hotel – 1
Lunch at The Beach House Hotel – 2
Dinner at The Beach House Hotel – 3
Christmas at The Beach House Hotel – 4
Margaritas at The Beach House Hotel – 5
Dessert at The Beach House Hotel – 6
Coffee at The Beach House Hotel – 7
High Tea at The Beach House Hotel – 8 (2024)

THE FAT FRIDAYS GROUP:

Fat Fridays – 1
Sassy Saturdays – 2
Secret Sundays – 3

THE SALTY KEY INN SERIES:

Finding Me – 1
Finding My Way – 2
Finding Love – 3
Finding Family – 4
The Salty Key Inn Series . Boxed Set

THE CHANDLER HILL INN SERIES:

Going Home – 1
Coming Home – 2
Home at Last – 3
The Chandler Hill Inn Series – Boxed Set

SEASHELL COTTAGE BOOKS:

A Christmas Star
Change of Heart
A Summer of Surprises
A Road Trip to Remember
The Beach Babes

THE DESERT SAGE INN SERIES:

The Desert Flowers – Rose – 1
The Desert Flowers – Lily – 2
The Desert Flowers – Willow – 3
The Desert Flowers – Mistletoe and Holly – 4

SOUL SISTERS AT CEDAR MOUNTAIN LODGE:

Christmas Sisters – Anthology
Christmas Kisses
Christmas Castles
Christmas Stories – Soul Sisters Anthology
Christmas Joy

THE SANDERLING COVE INN SERIES:

Waves of Hope – 1
Sandy Wishes – 2
Salty Kisses – 3

THE LILAC LAKE INN SERIES

Love by Design – 1
Love Between the Lines – (2024)
Love Under the Stars – (2024)

OTHER BOOKS:

The ABC's of Living With a Dachshund
Once Upon a Friendship – Anthology
Winning BIG – a little love story for all ages
Holiday Hopes
The Winning Tickets (2023)

PRAISE FOR JUDITH KEIM'S NOVELS

THE BEACH HOUSE HOTEL SERIES

"Love the characters in this series. This series was my first introduction to Judith Keim. She is now one of my favorites. Looking forward to reading more of her books."

BREAKFAST AT THE BEACH HOUSE HOTEL is an easy, delightful read that offers romance, family relationships, and strong women learning to be stronger. Real life situations filter through the pages. Enjoy!"

LUNCH AT THE BEACH HOUSE HOTEL – "This series is such a joy to read. You feel you are actually living with them. Can't wait to read the latest one."

DINNER AT THE BEACH HOUSE HOTEL – "A Terrific Read! As usual, Judith Keim did it again. Enjoyed immensely. Continue writing such pleasantly reading books for all of us readers."

CHRISTMAS AT THE BEACH HOUSE HOTEL – "Not Just Another Christmas Novel. This is book number four in the series and my introduction to Judith Keim's writing. I wasn't disappointed. The characters are dimensional and engaging. The plot is well crafted and advances at a pleasing pace. The Florida location is interesting and warming. It was a delight to read a romance novel with mature female protagonists. Ann and Rhoda have life experiences that enrich the story. It's a clever book about friends and extended family. Buy copies for your book group pals and enjoy this seasonal read."

MARGARITAS AT THE BEACH HOUSE HOTEL – "What a wonderful series. I absolutely loved this book and can't wait for the next book to come out. There was even suspense in it. Thanks Judith for the great stories."

"Overall, Margaritas at the Beach House Hotel is another wonderful addition to the series. Judith Keim takes the reader on a journey told through the voices of these amazing characters we have all come to love through the years! I truly cannot stress enough how good this book is, and I hope you enjoy it as much as I have!"

THE HARTWELL WOMEN SERIES:

"This was an EXCELLENT series. When I discovered Judith Keim, I read all of her books back to back. I thoroughly enjoyed the women Keim has written about. They are believable and you want to just jump into their lives and be their friends! I can't wait for any upcoming books!"

"I fell into Judith Keim's Hartwell Women series and have read & enjoyed all of her books in every series. Each centers around a strong & interesting woman character and their family interaction. Good reads that leave you wanting more."

THE FAT FRIDAYS GROUP :

"Excellent story line for each character, and an insightful representation of situations which deal with some of the contemporary issues women are faced with today."

"I love this author's books. Her characters and their lives are realistic. The power of women's friendships is a common and beautiful theme that is threaded throughout this story."

THE SALTY KEY INN SERIES

FINDING ME – *"I thoroughly enjoyed the first book in this series and cannot wait for the others! The characters are endearing with the same struggles we all encounter. The setting makes me feel like I am a guest at The Salty Key Inn...relaxed, happy & light-hearted! The men are yummy and the women strong. You can't get better than that! Happy Reading!"*

FINDING MY WAY- "Loved the family dynamics as well as uncertain emotions of dating and falling in love. Appreciated the morals and strength of parenting throughout. Just couldn't put this book down."

FINDING LOVE – "I waited for this book because the first two was such good reads. This one didn't disappoint.... Judith Keim always puts substance into her books. This book was no different, I learned about PTSD, accepting oneself, there is always going to be problems but stick it out and make it work. Just the way life is. In some ways a lot like my life. Judith is right, it needs another book and I will definitely be reading it. Hope you choose to read this series, you will get so much out of it."

FINDING FAMILY – "Completing this series is like eating the last chip. Love Judith's writing, and her female characters are always smart, strong, vulnerable to life and love experiences."

"This was a refreshing book. Bringing the heart and soul of the family to us."

THE CHANDLER HILL INN SERIES

<u>*GOING HOME*</u> *– "I absolutely could not put this book down. Started at night and read late into the middle of the night. As a child of the '60s, the Vietnam war was front and center so this resonated with me. All the characters in the book were so well developed that the reader felt like they were friends of the family."*

"I was completely immersed in this book, with the beautiful descriptive writing, and the authors' way of bringing her characters to life. I felt like I was right inside her story."

<u>*COMING HOME*</u> *– "Coming Home is a winner. The characters are well-developed, nuanced and likable. Enjoyed the vineyard setting, learning about wine growing and seeing the challenges Cami faces in running and growing a business. I look forward to the next book in this series!"*

"Coming Home was such a wonderful story. The author has a gift for getting the reader right to the heart of things."

<u>*HOME AT LAST*</u> *– "In this wonderful conclusion, to a heartfelt and emotional trilogy set in Oregon's stunning wine country, Judith Keim has tied up the Chandler Hill series with the perfect bow."*

"Overall, this is truly a wonderful addition to the Chandler Hill Inn series. Judith Keim definitely knows how to perfectly weave together a beautiful and heartfelt story."

"The storyline has some beautiful scenes along with family drama. Judith Keim has created characters with interactions that are believable and some of the subjects the story deals with are poignant."

SEASHELL COTTAGE BOOKS

A CHRISTMAS STAR – *"Love, laughter, sadness, great food, and hope for the future, all in one book. It doesn't get any better than this stunning read."*

"A Christmas Star is a heartwarming Christmas story featuring endearing characters. So many Christmas books are set in snowbound places...it was a nice change to read a Christmas story that takes place on a warm sandy beach!" Susan Peterson

CHANGE OF HEART – *"CHANGE OF HEART is the summer read we've all been waiting for. Judith Keim is a master at creating fascinating characters that are simply irresistible. Her stories leave you with a big smile on your face and a heart bursting with love."*

Kellie Coates Gilbert, author of the popular Sun Valley Series

A SUMMER OF SURPRISES – *"The story is filled with a roller coaster of emotions and self-discovery. Finding love again and rebuilding family relationships."*

"Ms. Keim uses this book as an amazing platform to show that with hard emotional work, belief in yourself and love, the scars of abuse can be conquered. It in no way preaches, it's a lovely story with a happy ending."

"The character development was excellent. I felt I knew these people my whole life. The story development was very well thought out I was drawn [in] from the beginning."

THE DESERT SAGE INN SERIES:

<u>THE DESERT FLOWERS – ROSE –</u> "The Desert Flowers - Rose, is the first book in the new series by Judith Keim. I always look forward to new books by Judith Keim, and this one is definitely a wonderful way to begin The Desert Sage Inn Series!"

"In this first of a series, we see each woman come into her own and view new beginnings even as they must take this tearful journey as they slowly lose a dear friend. This is a very well written book with well-developed and likable main characters. It was interesting and enlightening as the first portion of this saga unfolded. I very much enjoyed this book and I do recommend it"

"Judith Keim is one of those authors that you can always depend on to give you a great story with fantastic characters. I'm excited to know that she is writing a new series and after reading book 1 in the series, I can't wait to read the rest of the books."!

<u>THE DESERT FLOWERS – LILY</u> – "The second book in the Desert Flowers series is just as wonderful as the first. Judith Keim is a brilliant storyteller. Her characters are truly lovely and people that you want to be friends with as soon as you start reading. Judith Keim is not afraid to weave real life conflict and loss into her stories. I loved reading Lily's story and can't wait for Willow's!

"The Desert Flowers-Lily is the second book in The Desert Sage Inn Series by author Judith Keim. When I read the first book in the series, The Desert Flowers-Rose, I knew this series would exceed all of my expectations and then some. Judith Keim is an amazing author, and this series is a testament to her writing skills and her ability to completely draw a reader into the world of her characters."

THE DESERT FLOWERS – WILLOW – "*The feelings of love, joy, happiness, friendship, family and the pain of loss are deeply felt by Willow Sanchez and her two cohorts Rose and Lily. The Desert Flowers met because of their deep feelings for Alec Thurston, a man who touched their lives in different ways.*

Once again, Judith Keim has written the story of a strong, competent, confident and independent woman. Willow, like Rose and Lily can handle tough situations. All the characters are written so that the reader gets to know them but not all the characters will give the reader warm and fuzzy feelings.

The story is well written and from the start you will be pulled in. There is enough backstory that a reader can start here but I assure you, you'll want to learn more. There is an ocean of emotions that will make you smile, cringe, tear up or outright cry. I loved this book as I loved books one and two. I am thrilled that the Desert Flowers story will continue. I highly recommend this book to anyone who enjoys books with strong women."

Finding My Way

The Salty Key Inn Series
Book - 2

Judith Keim

Wild Quail Publishing

wildquail.pub@gmail.com
www.judithkeim.com

Published in the United States of America by:

Wild Quail Publishing
PO Box 171332
Boise, ID 83717-1332

ISBN# 978-1-959529-90-3

Dedication

For all the dreamers who hope one day to write a book.
It's a long, bumpy ride, but you have my encouragement.
Storytellers are born to write!

CHAPTER ONE

DARCY

Darcy Sullivan crossed the lawn of the Salty Key Inn in Sunset Beach on the west coast of Florida, her thoughts still on the challenge her Uncle Gavin had given her and her two sisters in his will. They'd each been left a one-third share of the hotel—a share that might or might not mean a large amount of money in the future. Right now, it meant nothing but a ton of work and a lot of uncertainty.

She couldn't take her mind off the special message Uncle Gavin had written at the end of his letter to her: "Darcy, you are not who we think you are."

"What in the hell does that mean?" Darcy mumbled to herself. Uncle Gavin Sullivan, or the "Big G," as he was sometimes called, had been a mystery to her and her sisters. Even though they were related, he hadn't been much of a presence in her life. She had a vague memory of a big man with a big voice, but because her father never got along with his brother, she'd rarely seen Gavin. That's why his crazy scheme for them to renovate the hotel in a year's time in exchange for a lot of money was so weird.

"You are not who we think you are." Whoa! She, more than her sisters had her shit together, didn't she? Her older sister, Sheena, was still making her way through motherhood with a family who'd all but taken away her self-esteem. And her younger sister, Regan, the family beauty, was still learning she was a lot smarter than she'd always thought. As for herself,

Darcy intended to see this project through, get the money, and take off for exciting destinations. Perhaps her uncle's genes were playing a part, but like him, she wanted to have adventures and see the world.

On this bright, sunny morning in May, Sheena strode across the hotel property toward Darcy with confident steps that swung her auburn hair back and forth above her shoulders. The young mother of two teenagers, she was an attractive woman ... and still the so-called "perfect one" in the family.

"Darcy! You're just the person I want to see!" said Sheena. "I've made an appointment for you to meet with a reporter from the local newspaper. They're going to run a story on the Salty Key Inn and what we're trying to do here. Nick Howard is the reporter's name. I told him you'd call to confirm a meeting as soon as possible."

Darcy rolled her eyes. *What was it about big sisters that made them so damn bossy?* "Okaaay, I'll do it." As she said the words, Darcy felt a tingling sensation like the imprints of a long-legged spider cross her shoulders. Ever since she was a kid, her secret desire was to become either a newspaper reporter or the famous author of the world's favorite novel. She'd ended up doing computer programming because that's where the money was, and she needed to be able to pay back student loans. But now, the idea of traveling while writing the perfect novel was her dream.

Darcy eagerly accepted Sheena's note with Nick's name and phone number. Somehow, she'd have to put a positive spin on the situation she and her sisters found themselves in. When they'd been told of their inheritance, Darcy had thought she'd be rich and sitting on the beach sipping margaritas. What a bad joke!

###

Inside her office, Darcy punched in the number for the newspaper reporter.

"Hello?" The man at the other end spoke in a deep, rich voice that reminded Darcy of the heavy-set actor whose well-known bass voice made even mundane television commercials seem sexy.

"Hi, Nick? This is Darcy Sullivan. My sister, Sheena Morelli, spoke to you about doing a newspaper article about our hotel, the Salty Key Inn."

"Ah, yes. Sounds interesting."

"I'd like to set up a meeting with you. If you're able, we'd like you to be our guest for lunch at Gracie's, the restaurant at the hotel."

"Sounds good. Why don't we do that today?"

"Perfect. Let's say one o'clock. I'll meet you outside."

"See you then," said Nick.

As she hung up the phone, Darcy wondered about the man behind the voice. The dating scene in Florida hadn't worked well for her. First, she'd made a fool of herself over Brian Harwood, the guy next door, and her one other date had been a huge flop. Her date had actually reunited with his ex, leaving Darcy high and dry. If Nick Howard looked anything like his voice sounded, this might be a good time to try dating again. She had to prove to herself she wasn't that much of a loser.

For the rest of the morning, the issues of installing a wi-fi system in the two guest-rooms buildings took over Darcy's attention. As tight as their budget was, all three sisters had agreed in today's world, having wi-fi was essential. With the help of Chip Carson, a young guy eager to do the work for a reasonable price, they were making good progress.

Just before one, Darcy left her office in the main building, which fronted Gulf Boulevard, and hurried across the hotel grounds to the suite she was sharing temporarily with Regan.

She wanted to freshen up before her luncheon appointment with Nick.

Before she reached the building, she stopped and stared at what once had been a small, pink-clapboard house. It was where Uncle Gavin had intended for her to live with her two sisters for an entire year. After a terrible fire, the house was now being torn down because the insurance adjuster had called it a hazard and a liability. She and her sisters were grateful the cost of rebuilding it would not come from their skimpy renovation budget but from the fire insurance settlement. Any extra funds needed would come from Uncle Gavin's estate. But with their living in their suites, it did mean a possible loss of revenue. They wouldn't be able to rent out those rooms until the new building was done.

Sighing at the problems they faced, Darcy hurried along and into her room.

As she was washing up, Darcy heard Regan enter the suite and then cross the hall into Darcy's bathroom.

Wearing cut-off jeans and an old T-shirt spotted with blue paint, Regan looked as beautiful as ever with her long, dark hair and violet-blue eyes. Some people said she was a Liz Taylor look-alike, a real stunner.

"Hey! What are you doing? You're all dressed up," said Regan giving her a good, hard look.

"I'm meeting a reporter for lunch. Sheena made arrangements for me to do an interview for a newspaper article on the Salty Key Inn and us."

Regan smiled. "Nice. A good way for us to get started on our advertising program."

Darcy nodded, but inside she was thinking it might be a good way for her to start being a creative writer, not only for the hotel project but for the novel she hoped to write.

After checking herself in the mirror, Darcy ran a hand

through her red curls and brushed off an imaginary spot on her simple, dark-green, sleeveless dress. "Guess I'm as ready as I ever will be." It seemed so easy for her sisters to look put together while she had to really work at it.

Once more, Darcy hurried across the hotel grounds.

A blur of blue feathers headed toward her.

"No, Petey! Go away!" Darcy cried. She began to charge the pesky peacock that ruled the area.

When the big bird realized that Darcy was serious, he emitted a raucous squawk and strutted away, dragging his tail feathers behind him.

Damn bird!

Darcy's steps slowed as she approached the restaurant. Standing outside the entrance was a tall, broad-shouldered, heavy-set man with white hair and a white beard that contrasted with his tanned skin. *Was this Nick Howard?*

Darcy looked around to see if anyone else was nearby, and when none appeared, she approached the man.

"Nick?"

He bobbed his head and grinned at her. "Darcy?"

Darcy held out her hand. "For a minute, I didn't know whether to call you St. Nick or Ernest Hemingway."

His laughter was hearty, almost a ho-ho-ho as if he practiced it at Christmastime.

Delighted, Darcy chuckled.

Nick ended his handshake and, with twinkling eyes, said, "I like a woman with a good sense of humor. How old are you, Darcy?"

"Twenty-six," she replied, wondering why he wanted to know. *Was he one of those older guys who like to have a "niece" on his arm for social occasions?* "Shall we go inside?"

He patted his stomach. "Definitely. I have to confess I've heard of Gracie's. It has a very good reputation in these parts.

I sometimes do restaurant reviews for the paper, but let's not tell anyone who I am or why I'm here. Okay?"

"Sure," she said.

They entered the restaurant run by Gracie Rogers and the rest of the group everyone called Gavin's people. Gavin had helped these eight people he'd known in his life—giving them a free place to live in exchange for what they could do working at the hotel. When they'd inherited them, along with the hotel, Darcy and her sisters had continued this arrangement.

Lynn Michaels waved to her as they walked into the restaurant and came right over to them.

"Good afternoon. Nice to see you." She led them outdoors to a table under an umbrella on the patio.

Maggie O'Neill hurried over to greet them, holding menus in her hand.

"Good afternoon." She smiled at Darcy and then turned her attention to Nick.

"Can I get you anything to drink besides water?"

Nick glanced at Darcy. "How's the iced lemonade?"

"Delicious. But I'm having sparkling water. Would you like some of that?"

"Sure," said Nick. He accepted a menu from Maggie and began studying it.

After Maggie left, Darcy said, "Right now, Gracie's serves only breakfast and lunch. She may apply for a wine and beer license and serve dinner in the future."

Nick nodded. "I see. The menu looks pretty impressive. There are several things I'd love to try." He frowned when his cell phone buzzed, but he lifted it out of the pocket of his blue-plaid shirt.

Darcy watched him as he studied a message and then thumbed a rapid reply.

"Sorry about that." Nick gave her an embarrassed look as

he slipped the phone back into the shirt pocket. "It was my wife, checking on me to make sure I'm sticking to the diet she put me on."

At the guilty expression that crossed his face, Darcy hid a laugh.

He leaned across the table and whispered, "You won't tell on me if I order something not on her list, will you?"

Darcy couldn't help laughing now. "No, I promise. You give the restaurant a good rating, and I'll keep your secret."

"Deal," he said, straightening with a smile. "It's hell being married to someone who wants to take care of you all the time. But I love her."

After a few more moments of studying the menu, Nick set it down.

Maggie noticed and hurried over to the table. "Are we ready to order?"

Nick glanced at Darcy and then smiled up at Maggie. "Thought I'd sample a couple of things. Chicken wings, grouper sandwich, and tomato salad."

Maggie's eyes widened, but she maintained a smile. "How about you, Darcy?"

"I'll have my usual. Chicken salad."

After Maggie left, Darcy shook a finger at Nick playfully. "Can't wait to read your review."

They laughed together and then Nick grew serious. "Tell me about the hotel. I see you've done work on it already. Some years ago, it was one of the best family places around with its great location and beach access. I understand from Sheena that your uncle left it to you and your sisters."

Darcy nodded. "We were so surprised when we were told about the hotel, and totally shocked when we saw it. But my sisters and I are determined to meet my uncle's challenge to get it up and running for guests within one year. We've all had a lot to learn about the hotel business."

While she was talking, their food came. Between bites, Darcy continued speaking. "And we've learned a lot about each other."

Nick listened intently, even when smacking his lips with pleasure over his meal.

"Working with your sisters isn't always easy. When a fire destroyed our house and put Sheena's children in danger, Sheena, my oldest sister and the strong one, wanted to quit, believing she was making her family unhappy and putting them in jeopardy. And ..." Darcy suddenly realized how long she'd been talking and stopped, feeling her cheeks grow hot. "I didn't mean to prattle on and on."

Nick studied her. "Have you ever thought of writing? You have such a natural way of telling a story."

Darcy blinked in surprise. "Actually, I have. As a kid, I wanted to be a newspaper reporter, and then later, I thought I'd like to try my hand at writing a novel. But, so far, I haven't had the time to do either."

Nick leaned forward. "How would you like to be the restaurant reviewer for the *West Coast News*? I'd help you, of course, and it would get my wife off my back."

Darcy laughed and sat back in her chair to study him. "You're serious?"

"Yes. And who knows? Maybe later, you could work your way into a weekly column of some kind. I like you, Darcy. We could use someone like you at the paper—someone with a fresh, new look at things."

A rush of excitement filled Darcy. This could be the beginning of her dream. She could already see herself on a tropical island, sprawled in a beach chair, reading a book or plotting out her prizewinning novel.

"Okay, I'll do it." As she spoke, she recalled the tingly

feeling she'd had saying those very words earlier. Maybe this was all part of a bigger plan, she thought, suddenly nervous.

"All right," said Nick, resting his gaze on her. "What would you say about your meal?"

Darcy took a deep breath, conjuring up the best words she could use. "My chicken salad was tasty, with exotic additions of melon and ginger, topped with crisply browned almond slices, and flavored with a lemony dressing that blended the ingredients perfectly."

Nick grinned. "I knew it." He reached across the table and offered his hand. "You're hired."

She accepted his hand and gave it a firm shake. "I'll take the job. How much do I get paid?"

He laughed. "In addition to free food?"

"Oh, I get it," said Darcy, realizing how small this local newspaper was for her to be even considered for the job. "Even so, I'll do it. But, Nick, I want that newspaper column."

"Good. We'll talk about that in a couple of months." He smiled. "Now, let's order dessert. The food here is dynamite, and I want to see if their pies and cakes are just as good."

As she waited for Nick to finish tasting the Key Lime Pie and the Orange Chocolate Cake, Darcy studied him. He seemed to be such a happy, pleasant guy. *Maybe*, she thought, *that's what I've been missing in the dating scene.* Her dates had always seemed uptight and eager to prove something. Sheena had told her to relax, that she'd find someone someday. And perhaps now, with her new part-time position at the paper, she'd stop worrying about having a man in her life and take each day as it came—with or without a boyfriend.

After Nick had taken the last bite of his meal, he winked at her. "Ready to give me a tour of the property?"

"Yes, but only if you understand we're still very much in the renovation process. If things go well with it, then after the first of the year, we'll be adding a lot more upgrades to the rooms as well as additional hotel facilities."

"Gotcha. Let's do it." Nick stood and helped her out of her chair.

As Darcy showed Nick the property, including the bayfront dock area and the pool, she described plans for how they intended to improve them. And when she took him inside the Egret guest-rooms building and showed him a bedroom being fixed up, a real sense of pride filled her. The painted furniture, sitting atop a sand-colored, commercial carpet, looked wonderful. Shabby-chic is how Regan described the stressed finish of the wooden pieces. In time, they'd find soft goods and other furniture to complete the room.

"Very nice job," said Nick to Regan, after Darcy made the introductions. "You have a real good eye for this."

Darcy was pleased to see the expression of delight that crossed Regan's face. Of them all, Regan was the one who was happiest about their effort to meet Uncle Gavin's challenge. She was already a much different person with a lot more self-confidence.

They left the building and headed toward the parking lot by Gracie's.

Sheena emerged from the restaurant, waved, and crossed the lawn toward them. She'd fought her family to participate in this challenge of Gavin's, and Darcy was glad she had. Smart and willing to work the numbers, Sheena was a great asset, even if she was a bit bossy.

"Nice to meet you, Nick," Sheena was saying. "I hope you give us a lot of good publicity."

Nick grinned. "Believe me; I will. Gracie's deserves a five-star rating as the best place around for lunch." He clapped a hand on Darcy's back. "And Dee Summers, here, is going to help me do restaurant reviews."

Sheena and Darcy exchanged questioning looks.

"Dee Summers?" said Darcy.

Nick let out a belly laugh. "That's going to be your name at the paper. You can't do reviews under your real name. And I have a special column idea in mind."

"What are you talking about?" asked Sheena, giving them a puzzled frown.

"Like Nick says, I'm going to help him with some restaurant reviews. And then, I might get my own weekly newspaper column." Darcy couldn't hide the wonder in her voice. It was a dream come true. Well, maybe not the ultimate one she wanted of writing a novel, but it was a beginning.

Sheena gave her a thoughtful nod. "Good for you, Darcy."

After she walked away, Darcy looked over at Nick. "I think I will call you St. Nick. I feel as if I've just opened a Christmas package."

He grinned. "Okay, Dee. See you around. I'll be in touch."

CHAPTER TWO

SHEENA

Sheena approached the pink house that she and her sisters were supposed to have lived in. As she stood in the warm sun gazing at the scorched remnants of it, a tremor went through her. Several weeks ago, her children had been in the house when the gas line to the kitchen stove had burst, causing an explosion. Watching the flames, knowing they were inside, had been a terrifying experience—one that continued in her nightmares. Even now, inhaling the odor of burnt wood, Sheena's stomach turned, and she grew dizzy at what she might have lost.

She'd wanted her children to come to Florida to experience what she was going through at the hotel so they'd realize that her leaving Boston for a year would be well worth it. At almost fifteen, Meaghan had needed a dose of reality and kindness. Now seventeen, Michael was also a teenager who thought he was entitled to the good things he had been given. Between the work Sheena had made them do around the hotel and the close call in the fire, their attitudes had changed dramatically. But it was her husband, Tony's, change of heart that touched her more than anything. With his encouragement, he'd given her a reason to stay at the hotel to try to make it a success.

Before going on her way, Sheena waved to the workmen clearing the remnants of the house. In a few weeks, the kids would return to Florida for good. Tony might be with them. He was thinking of setting up a separate plumbing business in

Florida. In the meantime, he had a job anytime he wanted working for Brian Harwood, the young man Gavin had entrusted to help them renovate the hotel.

Sheena entered the suite she and her sisters had fixed up as a temporary residence for her and her family. At one time, the three of them had thought they'd renovate the suites first. But with the necessity of living there, they were concentrating instead on renovating the twenty guest rooms on the first floor of the Egret Building. Then, if they had enough money, they would tackle the twenty rooms on the second floor.

Sheena sat at the small wooden kitchen table they'd rescued from the furniture collection in the original rooms. They planned to replace all the furniture in the suites, but until they'd done the rooms in the Egret Building and had even more revenue, that would have to wait.

Staring at the numbers on her computer screen, Sheena let out a sigh. Unless a miracle happened, they wouldn't be able to get the suites ready for guests for some time. There were many things they needed—furnishings, soft goods, pool and patio furniture, televisions, phones, and on and on. She did an on-line search for hotel suppliers to see what sales they could find. They'd already picked up some artwork and lamps from one hotel renovation sale. Surely there would be others.

Her cell rang. Sheena checked her screen and smiled. *Meaghan.* There'd been a time when her daughter had refused to speak to her because she'd been angry Sheena had left Boston. Now, she wanted to talk all the time, like the fourteen-year-old she was.

"Hi, sweetheart! What's up?"

"It's Lauren. Now that she knows you own a hotel she wants to be friends again."

"And?" prompted Sheena.

"And I don't know what to do," admitted Meaghan. "She's

one of the popular girls. Or was. Shelby doesn't like her anymore."

"Meaghan, it's important to be friendly to everyone, but equally as important to choose close friends wisely. Remember how cruel Lauren was to you? I'd keep only a friendly distance if I were you."

"Guess what! Tommy asked me if I wanted to go to the End of School Dance. I told him I'd think about it."

"Think about it?" Sheena shook her head. At one time her daughter would do anything to go anywhere with Tommy Whitehouse.

"Yeah, because I'm hoping Danny Sawyer will invite me," Meaghan said.

"Just remember to be kind," warned Sheena.

"I know, Mom. You don't have to tell me," Meaghan huffed with exasperation.

Sheena bit back a reply. Dealing with a teenager was difficult at times, especially when it was your daughter, who was discovering that boys found her attractive. That was both good news and bad.

They chatted about the dress Meaghan wanted for the dance, and then Sheena hung up with a promise to look at the photograph of the dress that Meaghan was to email to her.

Darcy knocked on the door and entered. "Here's the final bill from Chip for installing the wireless system in all the buildings."

Sheena accepted the paper Darcy handed her and studied the figures. "Higher than I thought, but it's still reasonable. We'll have to juggle dollars on the televisions for the guest rooms."

"You got a bargain on the carpeting for all forty rooms, though, right?" said Darcy.

Sheena nodded. "That helped our budget. Thank goodness,

someone ordered an extra few rolls for a job they were doing, and we could get it for remnant pricing."

Darcy gave her a long look. "After showing Nick around, I got to thinking. With the new publicity he might give us, we need to open those rooms as quickly as possible. I think we should have a meeting with Regan."

"Sounds good. We need to talk about patio furniture and any other facilities and amenities to offer our guests. Even if we have only twenty rooms open, we need to have it right." Sheena couldn't help asking, "You're really going to do restaurant reviews for the *West Coast News*?"

Darcy grinned. "Hey, it's a beginning. Right? And Nick is a great guy. It shouldn't take up too much time. A few evenings out."

"Well, if you ever need anyone to accompany you, I'll do it."

Darcy laughed. "We'll see."

That evening, Sheena fixed a simple green salad topped with cold shrimp for herself and her sisters. Darcy poured a chilled pinot grigio, and Regan sliced the French bread Gracie had donated.

Sheena placed the salads in front of her sisters and turned to Darcy. "Hey! Don't write about this. The *West Coast News* is *not* doing a review of my cooking."

"We'll see," Darcy replied, smiling.

Regan frowned. "What are you two talking about?" "I'm going to be doing restaurant reviews for the *West Coast News*," Darcy announced proudly. "Nick Howard asked me if I would help him, and if things go well, I might even be given a weekly column to write."

Regan's eyes widened. "Wow, Darcy! That's great!" Her expression suddenly grew serious. "But it won't take away from the advertising campaign for the hotel, will it?"

Darcy shook her head. "No, but I'm worried that with the article Nick is doing for us, people will ask to make room reservations. I wanted to talk to you and Sheena about moving our schedule up."

"You're the one in charge of guest rooms, Regan. So, in many respects, you're in charge of the operation," said Sheena.

"Yeah, we need to know what you think," added Darcy.

Regan covered her face with her hands.

Sheena and Darcy glanced at each other.

"You okay, Regan?" Darcy asked.

When Regan lifted her face, Sheena was surprised to see tears in Regan's eyes. "What's wrong, hon?"

"It's the first time you two have ever told me I could be in charge over you. Do you have any idea what that means to me?" Regan's voice was quivery.

Darcy raised her glass of white wine. "Here's to sisterhood!"

Regan grinned and lifted her glass. "Here's to us!"

"The Sullivan sisters!" said Sheena, feeling love for her sisters swell inside her.

They hadn't always gotten along, but working on this project had brought them together. Uncle Gavin had hoped his challenge would be a life lesson for each of them. It appeared class was in session.

"We need a complete update of the rooms," said Sheena. "What has been done, what needs to be done, and a schedule for each."

"Okay, big sis, after dinner, let's go into the living room and discuss it," said Regan.

"And we need to put together a list of things we need to buy," Darcy said.

"After you give me the information, I'll be able to do a complete update of our budget. I might be able to convince Blackie Gatto to move some of those items into reasonable, pre-opening hotel expenses so that our ridiculous renovation budget of one hundred fifty thousand dollars can work. We've spent a lot of money already."

"No more dinner meetings with Blackie. Keep it to coffee, okay?" said Darcy.

Sheena couldn't help the frown she felt. "It was a business meeting. Remember?" When her husband Tony had discovered she was out to dinner with Blackie, he'd been furious. It had taken her some time to convince him it was only a business thing.

"I think we should invite Blackie to our grand opening," said Regan, dispelling the uneasy moment.

"Good idea," said Sheena. "In the meantime, we need to convince him some of the cost of doing this should come out of Gavin's estate and not our budget."

Regan talked about the progress on the guest rooms. She'd taken a lot of the original dressers, end tables, and headboards from the guest rooms and, with a special technique of using chalk paint, had refreshed them into pale blue pieces with a shabby-chic finish. The walls had been painted and new carpeting put in. But finishing touches—the more expensive ones of window treatments and electronic equipment—still needed to be added to the rooms.

"What about the bathrooms?" asked Sheena. "We haven't done much to them."

"We've tried to clean them with normal products," sighed Regan, "but I think we should hire professionals to clean them with special chemicals and bleach out the tile floors, too. Someone told me that, if necessary, tubs can be resurfaced. And I think the grout just needs cleaning, not replacement."

"Should we bother trying to make them look like new?" asked Darcy.

"Yes. It makes a big difference. And I have an idea for the vanities. If we replace the old, wooden cabinets with a laminate countertop with twin basins, we can add an open shelf below to store towels and other supplies. That will make it more attractive for families too. Tony did that for a small property in New Hampshire, and it worked well and for little cost."

"Let's ask Tony to work on that with Brian," said Darcy.

At the idea, Sheena's lips curved. That would give Tony a good excuse to return to Florida—without the kids.

"How are we going to get people to book rooms here when we're still renovating?" asked Regan.

"I have a plan," said Sheena.

Darcy shot her a wicked smile. "Of course, you do. Let's hear it."

"Okay. What if we give every person who stays here for two nights or more, fifty percent off on two nights booked in the next six months. That's a win-win for everyone. Right?"

"That's brilliant!" gushed Darcy. "We can run an ad in the local newspapers, and I can put it up on our website."

"There's another issue," said Regan. "We need to get at least one room finished before we can take promotional pictures of it for the website and other media."

"Okay," said Sheena. "I'll take care of calling a cleaning company, getting Tony ready to come down, and dealing with Brian on installing the countertops and shelves in the bathrooms. We'll aim to get the bathrooms done on the first floor as soon as possible. We'll take out the sinks in the second-floor bathrooms and use them to make identical twin sinks in the new vanities. But by doing that, we'll have the additional cost to replace the sinks on the second floor when we redo those rooms."

"What about the patio furniture?" said Darcy. "We need some for each of the twenty rooms and the pool area, too."

Sheena gave them a devilish grin. "Leave that up to me. Anyone want to join me for coffee with Blackie?"

CHAPTER THREE

REGAN

Regan arose early, quietly dressed in clothes that were becoming more and more paint-spattered, and left the suite for Gracie's. She was to meet with two of Brian Harwood's men who were helping her complete the renovation of the guest rooms. As much as she tried to avoid Brian, she needed to talk to him about bathroom fixtures and hardware. He should be able to get what they needed at a discount through his construction company. She wanted new shower curtain rods, the curved kind that gave people more room in the shower. And maybe he knew of another hotel sale for small things like reversible mirrors and soap holders.

As she entered Gracie's, she was met by smiles. The restaurant was due to open for the day soon, and the staff was gathered at tables, sipping coffee and eating breakfast before the restaurant became a whirl of activity.

"Coffee?" asked Lynn.

Regan gave her a grateful nod. "Sounds wonderful."

"How about some eggs?" said Bertha Baker, better known as Bebe. A heavy-set woman with gray hair pulled back into a bun, she looked like the typical cook one might see in a child's picture book. She was quieter than some others in Gavin's group, but Regan liked her a lot.

"Thanks. Scrambled eggs and an English muffin would be great."

Bebe laughed. "I knew you'd order that." She hefted herself

to her feet. "Be back in a minute."

"What's going on?" asked Gracie, walking into the room. The delicious food she cooked was the reason the restaurant had been named after her.

"We're trying to finish up the guest rooms as soon as possible so we can open the hotel for business," said Regan. "We're hoping to get enough of them ready for guests in a couple of months."

"Sounds like a ton of work," said Rocky Gatto. Blackie's brother was a pirate look-alike with his dark, curly hair, hooked nose, and large gold earring. To complete the image, all he needed was a red bandana, a shiny sword, and a parrot perched on his shoulder.

"Yeah, but we need to start making money to fulfill the challenge," said Regan. "Has anyone seen Brian? I need to talk to him."

"He should be along soon," said Maggie O'Neil. In her forties and the youngest of Gavin's people, Maggie was an attractive woman who had an air of vulnerability that Regan had always noticed. Regan, like her sisters, didn't know much about the group, but she was sure Maggie had a bigger story beyond getting caught with drugs in the hospital where she once had worked as a nurse.

Bebe returned with Regan's eggs. "Here you go, sweetie."

Regan dug in. If she was lucky, she'd be through eating and out of the restaurant before Brian arrived. She realized she didn't want to face him in front of the others because he created so many confusing feelings inside her—feelings she wouldn't be able to hide from him or anyone else.

After finishing her meal, Regan rose. "Thanks, everyone. Have a good day. Tell Brian I'll be working in the Egret Building."

Regan hurried out of the restaurant and headed across the

lawn. When a small lizard ran across the grass in front of her, she stopped and fought back a squeal. She still wasn't used to the creatures, but she'd been told how valuable they were because, even as small as they were, they ate a lot of the little bugs that flitted about.

Petey strutted toward her, his peacock feathers gleaming blue in the sunlight.

"Hi, handsome," Regan crooned. She smiled when he lifted his tail feathers and spread them half-heartedly. "Aw, you need someone to love, don't you?"

"Everyone needs someone to love," came a deep voice behind her.

Regan whirled around. At the sight of the handsome man in front of her, her cheeks grew hot. "Hi, Brian."

"Hi. I saw Clyde outside the restaurant. He said you wanted to see me."

She reminded herself not to stare. "Yes. Sheena was going to call you, but I need to talk to you about the bathrooms—what fixtures we need to order for the new design we want. Want to come take a look at what we have in mind?"

Brian gazed into her eyes. "Sure."

As they walked toward the building together, Regan's hand accidentally touched Brian's arm. She bit back a gasp at the jolt the brief contact with him sent through her system. She couldn't deny the attraction between them, but, as always, she told herself to be careful. In the past, men had been interested in her only for her looks. And when they discovered she wasn't interested in the same things they were—especially when she wouldn't give them the sexual favors they wanted, they took off, calling her a tease or worse. She was convinced Brian Harwood was like them. Women all but drooled over him, and he seemed to like it. In a drunken state, Darcy had even asked him to be friends with benefits. How bizarre was that?

Regan shook her head. No more devastating experiences like that for her.

"Anything wrong?" Brian asked her.

"No, no," Regan quickly replied. Better to keep things on a purely professional basis.

They entered the building and walked into one of the downstairs rooms.

Regan led Brian into the bathroom. "We want to hire professionals to clean the tile floors and tub/shower surrounds and to refinish any tubs that need it. Know of anyone?"

Brian grinned. "Sure. One of my guys can do it."

Regan couldn't help laughing. Brian and the crew in his construction company could, apparently, do anything. "Okay, talk to Sheena about it. And we need to get shower curtain rods and replace wall mirrors for a good price, maybe even at a hotel sale."

"What's the new design you talked about?" Brian said.

"Instead of this outdated cabinet for the sink, we want to install a new counter with twin sinks and open shelving underneath. We plan to take the sinks from the second-floor rooms because they match these. We'll then replace those with new ones later. We thought Tony could help with that."

"Good idea. He can handle the plumbing too. I'll see how we can fit it into our schedule and let Sheena know."

"Uh, that's just it. We want it done quickly. We're trying to open the rooms on this floor within a couple of months or so. Can you do it?"

A rush of tenderness filled his face as he continued to stare at her.

She knew he wanted to kiss her and stepped back, bumped into the bathtub, and felt herself falling.

Strong arms gripped her. "Steady, now."

As Brian drew her up into her arms, she started to make a sound of protest. But when his lips came down on hers, her body rebelliously responded. She loved the feel of his lips, the taste of him, the safe way she felt in his embrace.

Common sense took over.

She broke away. "Sorry, I don't know what happened to me."

Brian gave her a steady look that reached deep inside her. "You don't?"

Regan shook her head firmly. "I'm not interested."

A teasing smile crossed Brian's face. "You will be because I'm not giving up. But don't worry, I'll give you plenty of time to change your mind."

Regan swallowed hard. If she was going to be interested in anyone, it might be Brian. But she had too much responsibility on her shoulders to think about dating for the foreseeable future. For the first time in her life, her sisters and everyone else thought she was smart.

Brian gazed at her and sighed. "Okay, I'll talk to Sheena, and we can try to get the bathroom project rolling. See you later." He turned and walked out of the bathroom, leaving Regan to wonder if she was so smart after all.

CHAPTER FOUR

DARCY

Darcy stood alongside Sheena in Blackie Gatto's office in St. Petersburg, waiting for him to join them. "Nice office," she whispered, gazing at the attractive furniture and then looking out the large window to the inlet below, where several boats were tied up.

Sheena smiled. "He's very smart, very successful. We're lucky to have him on our side when it comes to dealing with Gavin's lawyer in Boston. Archibald Wilson wouldn't be nearly as creative about making things an ordinary, pre-opening hotel expense not covered by our ridiculously low budget."

Darcy heard a noise outside the door, and then Blackie Gatto strode into the room. She'd always thought he looked like a younger George Clooney. She wondered, as she had before, how two brothers could give someone such opposite feelings. Rocky Gatto frightened her with his deep, dark, mysterious eyes and his knowing smiles. But Blackie wasn't scary at all.

"Ah, Sheena, good to see you again, my dear. And how is Tony?"

Sheena laughed. "Feeling a little sheepish about the way he acted toward you."

Blackie grinned. "He's a good man." He turned to Darcy. "And you are Darcy, right?"

Darcy bobbed her head. "Yes. The middle sister." Saying it

made her feel insignificant. But then, being compared to her sisters had always made her feel that way.

Blackie studied her and smiled. "Gavin was always interested in what you were up to. He had a strong feeling that you were going to fool everyone by doing something different, unexpected."

A rush of pleasure filled Darcy. "Well, actually I am starting on something that's new for me."

Blackie's eyebrows lifted. "Oh?"

"It's got to be hush-hush, but I'll be doing some restaurant reviews in the area. And maybe I'll end up with a weekly column at the *West Coast News*." Darcy couldn't hide the sense of pride she felt.

"Interesting," said Blackie. "I think Gavin would be pleased."

Darcy couldn't hide her unease. "How well did you know my uncle?"

"Gavin and I go back a long way. He was one of my first clients. As I told Sheena, he loved the three of you girls. With no viable children of his own, you meant a lot to him."

"But he hardly knew us," protested Darcy.

"He knew a lot more than you think," Blackie answered.

"He and Mom were close," Sheena said to Darcy. "Even though Dad didn't want much to do with him, she kept in touch with him."

Darcy let that idea settle in her mind. She knew her parents hadn't had the happiest of marriages, but she'd always thought it was because her mother was often sick in bed with debilitating migraine headaches.

"Please, have a seat," said Blackie to them.

As Blackie sat behind his desk, Darcy settled in a brown-leather chair next to Sheena.

"So, what can I help you with today?" Blackie asked,

studying each of them a moment.

"We need a better definition of what can be considered pre-opening expenses as opposed to those our renovation budget is supposed to cover," said Sheena. "We need to seek as much financial help with this project as possible to meet the challenge. I'm sure you understand that."

"I see," said Blackie in a non-committal tone.

"We need to talk about patio furniture, in particular," Sheena said, giving Darcy a sly wink as Blackie busied himself with paperwork.

"We need to abide by your uncle's will," said Blackie.

"Yes, but I'm sure Uncle Gavin wouldn't mind being a little creative," Sheena responded.

Blackie grinned. "You're right. Let's see what we can do."

Sheena and Blackie went back and forth, trying to come up with a fair plan for all. Listening to her sister, Darcy grew more and more impressed. Sheena was smart and inventive.

When at last she was satisfied with his answers, Sheena simply said, "Thank you."

"Well, I think that does it for now," said Blackie. "Gavin would be proud of you, Sheena. You sure have inherited the Sullivan genes for bargaining."

Sheena laughed. "We're trying to make everything work. Certainly, patio furniture could be considered a normal pre-opening expense. We have to have some ability to use the pool deck, terraces, and balconies."

"And add at least one hammock," interjected Darcy.

"I'll call Archibald Wilson and get his approval and then get back to you," said Blackie. "But I say go ahead and see what bargains you can come up with for both the pool and the guest rooms."

They all shook hands, said their goodbyes, and then Darcy and Sheena left his office.

Outside, Darcy said, “Great job, Sheena. Now, I want to see the Vinoy. I’ve checked it out, and it’s right downtown here in St. Petersburg, on the bay.”

“Okay, let’s go. What did you find out about it?”

Darcy was happy to share what she’d learned. “The hotel opened in 1925 and had its golden years as a resort until 1942. It then went through a number of changes in use, from a training facility for military cooks during the war to a low-rent boarding house in the early ’70s until it closed outright in 1974 in a sad state of disrepair. In the ’90s, it experienced a rebirth. The website shows how beautiful it is after a more than a ninety-three-million-dollar restoration.”

“Wow! You really did do a lot of research on it.”

“Yes,” said Darcy. “It’s the kind of place where I’d love to be able to stay someday.”

Sheena checked her watch. “Let’s visit there and then have lunch. Sometime, I’d like to see the Salvador Dali Museum and some of the other cool stuff, but I don’t feel right about leaving Regan out.”

Darcy held back a groan. Sheena would never stop being the big sister and a mom.

Darcy parked the van along the street a short distance from the hotel, and she and Sheena walked up to the historic, salmon-colored structure.

Standing before it, Darcy let out a sigh of appreciation. It was gorgeous.

They walked into the lobby and explained they were merely looking around. The tall arches in the ceiling, the shiny brass fixtures, the subtly lit candles all bespoke of elegance and a richness Darcy had once dreamed of.

“Beautiful,” gushed Sheena. “And what a history.”

Darcy laughed. "The Salty Key Inn has its own history, but nothing like this."

They picked up some brochures and quietly left.

As they walked away from the hotel, Darcy's mind whirled. Maybe she'd look into the history of their hotel and use it for PR purposes. Nick had said their hotel at one time was a well-known place for families to stay.

Sheena turned to her and gave her a questioning look. "Why the grin?"

"I just thought of a way to advertise the Salty Key Inn. We'll be what it's always been—a super place for families."

"I like it," said Sheena. "We won't pretend to be more than we are. But, as a mother, I would want every convenience available for children. And that means we have to spend more money."

Darcy gave her a solemn nod. "Understood."

They settled on The Terrace, a small outdoor café, for lunch. As they sat in the shade, the warm air was pleasant. A cute, young waitress approached them. "Here are the menus." She plopped them down on the table and turned to go.

"Wait!" said Darcy. "Can you bring me a Diet Coke?"

"And I'd like a glass of water," said Sheena.

"Okay," said the waitress. "Be right back."

As she left, Darcy and Sheena gave each other looks of dismay.

"Can you imagine Gracie letting her waitresses get away with that kind of welcome?" said Sheena. "We're lucky to have Gavin's people there."

"I know. Let's see what's on the menu." Darcy's mouth watered as she studied the choices. "If the food is as good as it reads, I don't care how rude the waitress is."

Sheena laughed. "What are you having? I'm having the Southern Salad with fried chicken. I want to see how it compares to Gracie's."

"Okay. I'll order the Spinach Salad with the smoked gouda, snap peas, and warm bacon and apple vinaigrette." Darcy nudged Sheena. "I'm going to do a restaurant review on our experience and show it to Nick. For practice."

"Great. You have to be honest about the service, though."

"Oh, yes. I know." Darcy looked up and smiled at the waitress walking toward them with her diet drink.

The waitress handed the glass to Darcy. "Ready to order?"

Sheena placed her order, and Darcy followed. "And could we have water too?"

The waitress gave them a weak smile. "Sorry. I forgot."

Left alone, Darcy told Sheena. "I'll be right back. I'm going to check out the inside of this place."

The interior of the restaurant was done in a peach and green color scheme, keeping to a tropical look. Darcy counted fifteen tables inside and had already noted ten tables outside. Not a whole lot different from Gracie's inside except for the lack of customers here.

"Can I help you?" said a young guy coming out of the kitchen. He was wearing a white apron over what was a noticeably buff body beneath a white T-shirt. A baseball cap topped his dark curls. Green eyes studied her.

"No, thanks. I'm just looking around."

He shrugged and went back into the kitchen.

Darcy returned to the table outside and sat down beside Sheena.

"Well?"

"It's cute and about the same size as Gracie's," said Darcy. "But very few customers are inside." She gazed at the four occupied tables around them.

"Here comes our food," whispered Sheena.

Darcy sat back in her chair and watched as the waitress

placed a beautiful salad in front of her. After setting down another gorgeous salad in front of Sheena, the waitress handed them silverware wrapped in paper napkins.

"Anything else?" said the waitress.

"Our two glasses of water," Darcy said. "My sister has been waiting this whole time."

The waitress frowned. "Oh, yeah. I forgot. I got busy with our other customers."

"Well, we'd appreciate having some water," Darcy said in a deceptively calm voice that hid her irritation.

The waitress sighed. "Sure. Be right back."

"My salad looks wonderful," said Sheena. She lifted a fork and took a bite of the fried chicken pieces that topped the salad. "Mmm. Delicious."

Darcy dug into her spinach salad. "Wow! The warm bacon and apple dressing is to die for."

The waitress returned with their water and said, "How is everything?"

"Delicious!" Darcy and Sheena said together.

By the end of their meal, Darcy was convinced it was some of the best food she'd ever eaten. She'd tasted Sheena's salad, and it, too, was fabulous. Excitement curled through her. Her first ever restaurant review would be a good one. If, and it was a big 'IF,' Nick allowed her to post it.

When Darcy and Sheena returned to the Salty Key Inn, all thoughts of restaurant reviews died. The internet service was down, and things were in chaos. Darcy quickly called Chip to come help her.

As they worked together, Darcy realized that her duties at the hotel had to come before anything else. They were working hard to be able to open as soon as possible, and she needed everything to be running smoothly.

After the internet was up again, Darcy turned her attention to the website she was creating. She worked on a better description of the hotel as a place for families. She hadn't yet come up with a design for a logo, and without it, they couldn't move forward with any advertising campaign. She decided to call another meeting. Time for the Sullivan sisters to work together to create something unique.

CHAPTER FIVE

SHEENA

Sheena returned to her suite with a better appreciation for Darcy. Her sister could sometimes be impetuous and very outspoken, but she'd listened to Blackie and her discuss finances without interference. And going out to lunch with her had been fun, giving her more insight into Darcy's ambition for the future. Sheena couldn't wait to see what kind of restaurant reviews Dee Summers would come up with.

After changing her clothes, Sheena sat at the kitchen table to work on numbers. She'd made a list of items that she and Blackie had agreed constituted normal, pre-opening hotel expenses and another of costs that would have to come from their renovation budget.

Looking at the expenses they were responsible for, Sheena grimaced. New furniture was out of the question. It was time for another trip to a distributor of used hotel furniture for the couches, tables, desks, and chairs they needed. She and Darcy would have to meet with Regan again.

She punched in Regan's cell number.

"I'm on my way," said Regan. "Tell Darcy to be patient for once."

"What are you talking about?" said Sheena.

"Aren't you calling about a meeting? Darcy told me to meet her at your suite."

Sheena looked up to see Darcy entering the kitchen. Laughing, she told Regan, "See you soon."

She clicked off the call and turned to Darcy. "What's up?"

"We need a good definition of the Salty Key Inn. I can't do any advertising campaign without it."

Regan arrived out of breath. "Okay, what's so important that I have to come right away?"

"I want to talk to you about furniture," said Sheena.

"And we should talk about a logo and tagline for the hotel," said Darcy. "I'm trying to put together a website, and I need them. Nick told me that at one time the Salty Key Inn was known as a family place. Is that what we want here?"

"Have a seat you two," said Sheena. "Darcy and I have talked about it a little, and I think it's a good idea to develop this hotel as a place for families. But I don't want to leave singles or couples out of the equation."

Regan gave her a thoughtful look. "I don't see why we can't emphasize both. All the guest rooms in the Egret Building have connecting doors, so they can be used for either."

"Yes, but what single person or young couple is going to want to come here if it's packed with kids?" said Darcy.

"One of the things I like about this property is its quiet setting." Regan made a face. "Unless Petey decides to strut his stuff. Can't we please get rid of that bird?"

Sheena shook her head. "Not as long as Rocky is around. He rescued him from being picked on. Remember? Besides, it's sort of nice to have a 'guard bird' around."

Regan and Darcy laughed.

"I'd like to see the waterfront be a place where people could sit with a drink," said Regan.

"Or lie in a hammock," said Darcy. "We want families to feel welcome, but I don't want to give up the idea that it's a peaceful place."

"How about something like 'The Salty Key Inn, A Quiet Treasure?'" said Regan.

"Hmmm," said Sheena. "That would turn off families with a lot of kids without our saying so."

"I like it, especially with Treasure Island not that far away," said Darcy. "Now, how about a logo? Should we use a simple sun?"

"How about an outline of sunshine with a blue wavy line underneath it? We could ask Austin Blakely to help us. And then maybe he could make a carved wooden road sign for the hotel," said Regan.

Sheena smiled. "I love it. Let's move forward with it. Darcy, you'll take care of the website and work with Austin, won't you?"

"Sure. What are you going to be doing?"

"Besides working on numbers, I'll be addressing the refurnishing of rooms. We need to fill in some of the furniture voids. I propose going to the hotel resale dealer that I talked to last week. We need to find simple wooden desks, desk chairs, coffee tables, and pull-out couches. But we need to get them for a bargain basement price." Sheena glanced at Regan. "Will you be able to take that on?"

"Okay. I know what I want for the rooms. I just hope we can get them. And we need to go ahead with painting the walls of the other twenty rooms and redoing the furniture while we have people to help us. That will also minimize any disturbances to other guests once we open the ground floor rooms."

"Are the bathrooms downstairs coming along?" said Darcy.

"It's a slow process, but they're underway." She smiled at Sheena. "When is Tony coming?"

Sheena grinned. "He'll be here this weekend. I'm anxious to spend some alone time with him."

"Okay by me," said Darcy. "I'd like a little break too."

Regan frowned. "Uh, we're already behind the schedule I

set up. We all need to keep going if you want to open by the end of summer."

Sheena opened her mouth to protest and shut it. Regan was right. They couldn't slow down now. Her kids would be here in a few weeks and then, like it or not, her attention would be diverted.

As Sheena waited for Tony to show up at the airport in the baggage claim area, she felt like she used to a long time ago when Tony was about to pick her up for a date. With two teenagers in their lives, time alone with him was rare. And even then, they were often too tired for a lot of romance. Now, settled in the suite at the hotel, she was ready to enjoy her husband in a way that hadn't seemed possible not many months ago.

When Tony saw her, a smile crossed his face, lighting it with pleasure.

An image of the moment she first met him came back to her. She'd just started college and was to meet some friends in Somerville. As she walked into the bar, she caught sight of Tony. Their eyes met and, like in the most romantic of novels, the world around her melted away. From that moment, her life changed. Some months later, unexpectedly pregnant, she'd been forced to give up her idea of becoming a nurse as the role of mother and wife took over. Having lost the future she'd once dreamed of, she was now determined to meet Gavin's challenge. In the few months she'd been in Florida, she'd begun thinking of several new career possibilities associated with the hotel.

As Tony came closer, his smile widened. The light in his dark eyes sent warmth through her. She felt giddy. The chemistry between them was almost palpable.

"Hi," said Sheena, allowing herself to be swept up in Tony's arms.

"Good to be here," said Tony, nuzzling her neck.

Then, they stood apart and grinned at each other.

She grabbed hold of his hand. "C'mon, let's get your luggage and get out of here."

As they waited for his suitcase to appear on the conveyor belt, she said, "How are the kids?"

"It's amazing what the spring break stay here in Florida did for them. They have a very different attitude about things." His expression grew somber. "I can't believe we almost lost them in the fire. We had a close call."

Sheena shuddered. "I still dream about it—losing a child—children—is a parent's worst nightmare."

"A lot of things are happening at home. We can talk about it later. Right now, I want to enjoy being with my wife."

The sexy look he gave her sent another rush of heat through Sheena's body. She elbowed him playfully. "I've already told my sisters they are to leave us alone."

He laughed and squeezed her close. "Good girl."

At the hotel, Sheena showed Tony how she and her sisters had spruced up the suite they were to use temporarily. They'd used as much of the old furniture as they could, and though Rocky and crew had cleaned the carpet not once, but twice, it would be ripped out before any guests occupied the suite.

"It's the best we could do for the moment. We'll move into some of the guest rooms in the Egret Building as soon as we can so we can renovate the suites."

"It'll do," said Tony. "It's being with you that's important to me."

Sheena led him into the bedroom. "New mattress, new

bedding, everything nice here."

"Why, Sheena, what do you have in mind?" Tony teased. "*Moi?*"

Sheena laughed. He was right about that.

Later, lying next to Tony, Sheena stroked his strong body, loving the feel of his skin next to hers. Approaching forty, Tony was a healthy, handsome man who'd just proved to her that he hadn't lost the magic of his lovemaking. She trailed a finger across his cheek and then pressed her finger to his lips. "Should we go down to the beach for a walk? We can talk there."

Tony opened his eyes and smiled at her. "Let's go down to the bay. It's peaceful there. And it will give me a chance to take a look at what Michael is talking about. He's very pleased with the idea of being in charge of dock activities when that area is fixed up."

"Okay," said Sheena. "But if there are any snakes around, you're going to have to rescue me."

He laughed. "We'll chase them away."

Sheena got out of bed and headed into the bathroom, grateful the suite had a real shower. The pink house had contained one small, very old-fashioned bathroom with an ancient tub that had served as a shower too. It had been another of Uncle Gavin's challenges. That, a small, old kitchen, and three sisters living together.

As warm water sluiced over her body, Sheena recalled the few times she'd seen her uncle. Gavin had been a big man with a booming laugh. Though he and her father had fought like the incompatible brothers they were, she'd thought Gavin was wonderful. She was just a child when he'd given her a stuffed monkey. Later, when the monkey was worn from her hugs, a seam had opened up. Reaching inside with curious fingers, she'd pulled on the stuffing, and an old, gold coin fell out. And when Sheena showed it to her mother, she'd warned Sheena to say nothing about it and then tucked it away. It wasn't until after her mother died that Sheena found an envelope with her name on it stashed in a drawer. Inside was the gold coin and a note from her mother. The coin, which had been hidden from the moment she'd found it, still was a secret. No one else in her family knew about it.

Sheena closed her eyes and sighed as the water continued to caress her body. Life was sometimes such a surprise, she mused, thinking of all the changes that had taken place in the last few months. Gavin's challenge to the three of them had been very unexpected for her and her sisters. She and Tony had fought about her coming to Florida, but she'd held onto the belief that it was a way to help her family. Now, with her family's blessing, it wasn't the mistake they'd first thought. They were all learning more about themselves and each other. Sheena wasn't sure, but she'd begun to suspect Gavin might be her father, not the uncle everyone said he was. She'd discovered that he and her mother had loved one another. And even after Gavin was forbidden to come to the family home, her mother had secretly kept in touch with him.

Behind her, she heard the shower door open and close. Smiling, she turned around to face Tony.

He winked at her and, after filling his hand with liquid bath soap, began to stroke her body. "Haven't had the chance to do this in some time."

"Some time? Years," said Sheena, sighing happily at his touch.

Sheena and Tony strolled hand in hand toward the back of

their lot where a small dock sat on the bayfront. Clearing of the area had begun, but it still needed a lot of work. The removal of some of the undergrowth had opened up the entire eastern end of the property, expanding it by quite a bit. Here, they hoped to set up an area where guests could come to sit and have a refreshing drink or just relax. Uncle Gavin had even talked to Blackie Gatto about establishing a waterside restaurant there. Sheena was hesitant to do anything like that now or maybe even in the future. She wanted to wait and see how the hotel accommodated guests first.

"This area can be very nice," said Tony. "Even with activity at the dock, people can sit in the shade and unwind."

Sheena gave him a steady look. "Are you ready to talk about what's going on at home? Is it something I should be worried about?"

Tony shook his head. "Not at all. Is the dock safe? Can we sit and talk there?"

"It needs some work, but it's safe." Sheena held onto Tony's hand as they walked onto the wooden structure.

They sat on the decking and dangled their feet above the water. The sun peeked out from behind the gray clouds that filled most of the sky, sending beams of light onto the tips of the waves that rippled in the water, edging them with a golden hue. A great blue heron waded in the water, looking for its next meal. Sheena drew a deep breath, loving the scenery around her.

"Sheena?"

She turned to Tony.

"You ready to talk?" His expression was serious as he faced her. "A few days ago, Mom and Dad asked me to come over to their side of the duplex to discuss something important."

"Are they all right?" She loved her in-laws, Rosa and Paul Morelli.

"Yes. As a matter of fact, they're like kids again. They've decided to put the house on the market and move to Florida. Dad has already talked to a real estate agent in Boston. And they've put in a bid on a house in his friend's neighborhood right near here."

Sheena felt her jaw drop. Her staid, conservative father-in-law was leaving Somerville and Boston just like that? She would never have guessed he'd be willing to do it. This was a man who took his time over every little decision he made.

"And Rosa is fine with this?"

Tony grinned. "Mom can't wait to get to a place where they don't have to think of the high cost of heating that big house in cold, wintry weather."

"So, that puts us out on the street?" Sheena said, not at all unhappy with the idea.

"They know we can't afford to buy the house at fair market value, and they need the money to purchase their new home. Besides, I don't want it." He studied her. "Do you?"

Sheena shook her head. "I'm ready for something new. This experience at the hotel has made me realize how bound I've been by family tradition in Boston. I want something different, and I want our children to have new experiences."

Tony let out a long sigh. "Good, because I have more news to tell you." Tony's expression held both excitement and concern.

"Oh?" She cocked an eyebrow at him.

He gave her a smile that was almost shy. "I've talked to Brian about working with his company until I can qualify to take all the necessary exams to run my own plumbing-contracting company here in Florida."

"You want to move here too? Really?" Sheena threw her arms around him. "That would be wonderful! Simply wonderful! I think Darcy, Regan, and I are going to get this hotel fixed up and beat the challenge. And then we'll have enough money to take care of everything."

"Well, we're not destitute," Tony said with a bit of his old pluckiness. "John is serious about buying the business. He has someone in mind to be his partner, and Dave and Anna want a share of it too."

Sheena's mind raced. Her sister-in-law, Anna, had married a nice guy who had a natural talent for marketing. Dave had recently lost his job and had started working with Tony. John Larson had worked with Tony for years and had indicated he wanted to buy into the business a long time ago.

"Are you happy about turning things over to them? You, the both of us really, have worked very hard to build it up."

Tony stared out at the water, silent for a moment. When he turned back to her, there was a tenderness in his expression that hadn't been there. "Nothing is more important to me than my family. As you keep telling me, we're young. We can start fresh down here. And if the hotel doesn't work out, we can still live well while I build my new business." His lips curved. "It might be good to work under someone else for a while without worrying about how I'm going to make sure everyone who's working for me is well taken care of."

Sheena squeezed his hand. "We can do it, Tony. Together, as a family, we can make this new situation work for us. It'll be good for everyone."

Tony grinned. "Mom and Dad won't be far, but thank God we'll have a house of our own."

"What about seeing if we can buy the house that's being rebuilt here on the property?" Sheena said.

Tony shook his head. "No, Sheena. We'll find something close by if you want, but we're not living with a bunch of hotel guests."

"Yeah, I guess you're right."

"Tomorrow, I'm meeting with Brian and his partners to arrange a deal."

"Do the kids know yet?"

Tony shook his head. "We'll tell them together. A few months ago, they would have been upset about leaving Somerville. Now, I think they're ready. After talking to some other guys he's met here, Michael wants to play baseball. And Meaghan? Who knows?"

They laughed together. Their daughter would, no doubt, continue to be a challenge.

CHAPTER SIX

DARCY

Darcy punched in the number for Austin Blakely and waited for him to pick up. Regan had found one of his wood carvings in a garage sale, and they'd since become friends. Good-looking, Austin was a nice, all-around guy, easy to get along with, and fun to be around, but Darcy wasn't romantically interested in him. She merely hoped they could work together to come up with a logo design for the website and to use in a carved wooden sign for the hotel.

Once she could get some of the work done for the hotel, Darcy intended to focus on the role of restaurant reviewer. She'd put in a call to Nick Howard at the *West Coast News*, but he hadn't gotten back to her.

"Hello?"

"Hi, Austin?"

"Yeah. Who's this?"

"Darcy Sullivan, Regan's sister. I'm wondering if we can work together on coming up with a logo design and if I can talk to you about carving a wooden, roadside sign for the hotel."

"Okay. I'm almost done with the Sandpiper sign for the suites building. I'll be down to visit my grandparents next week. Do you want to meet up then?"

"Sure. We can have coffee here at the hotel or go out someplace else. Whatever you want. How are your grandparents?"

"My grandmother isn't doing well at all. The cancer isn't going away, and my grandfather is freaked out about being left alone after Grandma dies."

"I'm sorry," said Darcy sympathetically. "My mother died of cancer a year ago. It's not a fun time for anyone."

"Yeah, I promised my folks I'd check on my grandparents every couple of weeks. And I've promised my grandfather that, as soon as I finish dental school, I'll find a practice nearby."

"I know how much your family must appreciate you," said Darcy. "Thanks for agreeing to meet with me. Call me when you get into town."

She hung up and sighed. Austin was such a nice, comfortable guy, easy to talk to.

Sheena walked into the office. "What's up?"

Darcy told her about the phone call. "What's going on with you and Tony? You've been walking around with grins on your faces."

"You won't believe it!" said Sheena, taking a seat behind the other desk in the office. "The whole family is moving here—Tony, the kids and me, and his parents."

"Whaaat? His parents? But they've lived in Somerville forever."

A smile spread across Sheena's face. "I know. I can hardly wait to tell the kids about our move and all that's happening."

"They don't know? How are they going to take it?"

"I think they'll be fine. They're already looking forward to going to school here. And after one more year, Michael will be off to college. Meaghan, I'm sure, will be happy to leave the mean girls in Somerville."

Darcy gave her sister a questioning look. "And if the hotel doesn't make it? What will you do then?"

Sheena waved away her concern. "I'm not even going there.

We will make it—do or die."

Darcy stared out the window. An onshore breeze was stirring the fronds of a palm tree near the road. It was a sight that pleased her, but she wanted to experience so many more things. She'd been forced by financial circumstances to stay in Boston, but now the thought of traveling filled her mind. She turned back to Sheena. "If the hotel makes it and our challenge is over, I'm not going to stick around. I want to see as much of the world as I can. And maybe, just maybe, write about it."

"Really?" Sheena's look of surprise stung a bit. "I didn't know you wanted to do a lot of traveling. You were the middle sister who went to school in Boston and then stayed there."

"You're making a lot of changes. Why can't I?" Darcy said more defensively than she'd intended.

"Of course, you can," said Sheena calmly. "I just don't think of you not being settled somewhere. Why are you upset? Is everything all right?"

Darcy shook her head. "I called Nick about the restaurant review I wrote up. It's been days, and he still hasn't gotten back to me. You don't think he was lying to me about working for the paper, do you?"

"No, I don't. He seemed like a forthright man. Give him time."

Darcy sighed. "I know, but it's hard. You know it's a dream of mine to work for a newspaper. I want to get started because I need to do that for the training before I can tackle a novel."

"You don't need to work there in order to write a novel," said Sheena, giving her a steady look. "If you're really serious about it, you need to sit down in a chair and start writing every day."

"But I'm busy with hotel work," Darcy complained.

"I've read some articles by various authors, and they all say the same thing: Write. Read. Write." Sheena's expression softened. "Maybe you can put that idea to use in your spare time, reading or plotting out novels of your own."

Darcy thought about it and grinned. "Hmmm, maybe you're right. It's just damn scary to think of all those blank pages. You know?"

"I can imagine." Sheena checked her watch and rose. "I've got to go. I just wanted to tell you my good news. Tomorrow, Tony will begin working with Brian on the bathrooms for the guest rooms. In the meantime, I have a date with him."

At the look of excitement on Sheena's face, Darcy drew a deep breath. She hoped she'd one day meet some guy who made her feel the way Sheena looked when she talked about Tony. Brian Harwood was someone she'd once wanted to attract, but that didn't work out. And now she thought it was probably a good thing.

A week later, Darcy drove to St. Petersburg with a sense of urgency. She wanted to make the meeting with Austin short, so she could take some extra time to look around the city. With its museums and combined cultures, it was an intriguing place.

She found a parking spot not far from the Vinoy and, as agreed, headed to The Terrace cafe where she and Sheena had eaten. She still hadn't heard from Nick Howard about the restaurant review she'd done on it, and she wanted to check it out again to make sure she'd been fair.

As Darcy neared the restaurant, she saw Austin sitting at one of the outdoor tables. She waved, glad to see him.

When she approached the table, he stood. "Hi, Darcy. I was getting worried that I'd messed up the timing."

"Oh, sorry I'm late. I was held up by a problem at the hotel.

I hope you didn't have to wait long."

Austin smiled pleasantly. "I went ahead and ordered a cold beer. Want one?"

"Sure." She looked around. "Where's the waitress?"

"Inside, I think." He rose. "I'll go get her."

He returned with an older woman carrying a tray holding two glasses of beer and two glasses of water. In the other hand, she had menus. "I'm sorry for the delay," she said, giving Darcy a smile. "Our regular waitress is on break."

"A permanent one, hopefully," mumbled Darcy.

The woman looked at her with surprise. "You've been here before?"

Darcy's cheeks flooded with heat. "I'm sorry. I didn't mean for you to hear, but, yes, my sister and I ate here about ten days ago."

"I see," the woman said, giving her a cryptic look before turning away.

"If you've come back here, the food must be good," said Austin. "The menu is great. What are you going to have?"

Darcy grinned. "The Mexican salad. I almost chose it last time I was here. Another guest had it, and it looked delicious!"

"I'm going to have their Big Burger." Austin patted his stomach. "Don't have much time to enjoy a meal at school."

"When will you graduate?" Darcy asked. She didn't think he'd have any problems setting up a new practice—not with his pleasant, calm manner.

"Next January, I'll be through the course work unless I continue through the summer. Then, I'll be through by fall. I was considering taking the summer off and going on a charity trip to Central America to do some free dentistry, but I can't sign up until after things are settled with my grandparents. I promised Mom and Dad."

Darcy couldn't hide her curiosity. "Why aren't they the

ones helping your grandparents?"

Austin held up a hand. "Oh, they do when they can, but they travel all over the world for their business. Sometimes they're gone for weeks at a time. It's always been that way."

"What do they do?"

"They specialize in upscale travel arrangements for groups and individuals."

Darcy straightened in her chair. "After my year at the hotel is up, I want to travel all around the world. It sounds so exciting! Hey, maybe they could help me."

"Maybe."

In her eagerness, Darcy leaned closer. "Have you traveled a lot yourself? Where have you been?"

"Pretty much everywhere," Austin said. "The world is a fascinating place—a lot to see, a lot to do."

"You don't seem very excited about it," said Darcy.

"Oh, but I am, though you know the famous line: 'There's no place like home.'"

"Boring," teased Darcy.

"Not at all. As much as I like to go places, I like to come home," countered Austin. "But I wouldn't give up travel for anything. I still have a list of places I want to visit."

Darcy sat back in her chair and studied him. Of average height and with his chocolate-brown hair, bright-blue eyes, and solid build, he was good-looking in a wholesome way.

After their food came, the conversation ended as they dug into their meals.

Darcy took a bite of romaine lettuce coated with a spicy, tomato-based dressing and another of a slice of avocado and smacked her lips with satisfaction.

Austin smiled. "That good?"

Darcy laughed. "Yes, and yours?"

"Great," said Austin, taking another bite of his burger.

They ate in companionable silence. It felt good to Darcy that she didn't have to try to impress Austin. They were just friends.

The waitress appeared as they finished eating. "Care for another beer?"

Darcy and Austin glanced at each other and nodded.

"Okay, let's talk about the logo," said Austin. "You want to come up with a design that matches your tagline. Right?"

"Yes. 'A Quiet Treasure' is the tagline. So, we're thinking maybe a logo with a stylized sun and waves of blue water. The furniture in the bedrooms is painted an antique, soft blue. Maybe we can match that. We didn't want a palm tree, which wouldn't be that unique. What do you suggest?"

Austin took a pen and pad out of the notebook that was sitting in an empty chair beside him. "Let's try a few things."

Darcy watched him quickly sketch a number of choices and looked up when a young man wearing a white apron and a blue baseball cap made his way through the tables to them.

"How was the meal?"

"Delicious," she said.

His green eyes narrowed. "Weren't you here a week or so ago?"

She raised her hand. "Guilty as charged."

"So, you like the food?"

"The food is great."

"And the service?"

Darcy hesitated and then blurted out, "Not great. I thought the situation might change, but it hasn't."

His suspicious look drilled into her. "Are you some kind of restaurant reviewer or something?"

As Darcy opened her mouth to reply, Austin spoke up. "She may not be a reviewer, but she knows good service when she sees it. And today was just so-so."

"And the first time I was here, it was awful."

The guy's eyebrows narrowed to a V. "Careful! You're talking about my girlfriend and, today, my mother."

Their waitress appeared. "What's going on Graham?"

"These two are complaining about the service."

Embarrassed, Darcy said, "Oh no, Ma'am. You were so much better than ..." She paused and glanced up at Graham "... than his ... um ... the other one."

Graham's mother placed her hands on her ample hips. "I've told you over and over, Graham, that you should fire her. Uncle Nick thinks so too."

"Just because he does restaurant reviews, it doesn't make Uncle Nick an expert," grumbled Graham.

Darcy's eyes widened with surprise. "Are you talking about Nick Howard?"

"Yeah? What of it?" said Graham.

Darcy gulped. "I just happen to know him. That's all."

From inside, a man signaled Graham and said, "You'd better come. We're running behind."

Graham gave her a backward glance as he hurried inside the restaurant.

"I'm sorry," said Darcy to the waitress standing at their table. "I didn't mean to cause a problem."

Graham's mother patted Darcy on the shoulder. "No problem, dear. We've all complained about the service here. In fact, why don't I compliment your meal? And feel free to sit here as long as you like. As you can see, we only have a few tables filled."

After she left, Austin said, "You were right, Darcy. If the guy doesn't have good service, how can he succeed? Now let's talk about the logo."

After a few minutes of looking at Austin's sketches, Darcy knew exactly what she wanted. The sun from one sketch was perfect with the stylized waves of another. Simple, but tasteful.

She beamed at Austin. "You're really good, you know."

"Thanks. I enjoy it. I think of certain dentistry as artistic too. It's not quite as exciting as this, but it's a good way to have a life where I can travel and do my artwork."

"Very nice," she said, wishing her life would become something like his, with travel and writing.

As they left the restaurant, Austin said, "Do you want to head back to my car? I have the Sandpiper sign ready for Regan. We can pick it up, and I'll carry it to your car."

"Okay, thanks." Darcy had just stepped into the street when a speeding car rushed toward them.

Austin pulled her back so quickly she fell into his arms.

Nestled against his strong chest, Darcy felt her body relax for a moment before lust surged through her in unsettling waves. She realized what was happening and quickly straightened.

Shaken by the desire that still throbbed inside her, she stared at Austin. It had felt so safe, so right for her to be in his arms.

When she stepped away, Austin's blue gaze captured hers, sending a flush to her cheeks.

Another car roared past them.

"Better be careful," Austin said, taking her arm.

She nodded, too stunned by her reaction to him to speak.

CHAPTER SEVEN

REGAN

Enjoying a short coffee break, Regan sat with Sheena in her suite. Reaching across the table, Regan squeezed her sister's hand. "I'm happy you're moving to Florida. It makes our work here at the hotel seem worthwhile. Following our year of living together here, and even if we don't meet the challenge, I intend to stay too."

"I'm glad. After we're through here, Darcy wants to spend time traveling. I understand, but I'm disappointed."

Regan couldn't stop herself from saying, "But, if we succeed, we'll *all* need to be able to run the hotel for the foreseeable future."

"We'll work something out. Remember, Darcy's been working hard to get the computer systems under control. And now she's heading the advertising campaign."

"I know, but..."

Sheena raised her hand to halt the conversation.

"Okay. I'll stop complaining and go back to my room to check online for commercial-furniture sales for hotels."

Regan hadn't searched long before she found St. Pete Hotel Suppliers, Inc., a store in downtown St. Petersburg. And when she read that they were having an end-of-season sale, she hurried over to Sheena's suite to give her the news.

"I'm going to take Gavin's old car and go into town to take a look. Want to come?"

Sheena shook her head. "No, you go ahead. I'm busy here.

Meaghan said she'd call me. And this is my last night with Tony until the kids come down. We want to do something special."

"Like?" Regan teased, giving her sister a knowing look.

Sheena laughed. "None of your business."

Still chuckling, Regan grabbed the car keys for Gertie. Darcy had the van, and they'd been asked to take the car out occasionally. The red Cadillac convertible with a white top and white-wall tires was a classic from the 1950s. Regan usually left the driving of Gertie to Darcy, but she was too excited about the furniture sale to wait for her to return from her meeting with Austin.

As Regan headed toward St. Petersburg, she marveled at the palm trees, the warm weather and the tropical feel to the area. Boston was a beautiful city full of history and life, and her childhood in Dorchester had been a good one. But this part of Florida now felt like home to her.

At Treasure Island, she crossed the bridge onto the mainland and made her way to the outskirts of St. Petersburg. There, on the right side of the road, she saw the sign for the hotel suppliers. She pulled into the parking lot in front of the building, which looked more like a warehouse than a storefront. The two display windows, though, held attractively arranged settings of furniture.

She got out of the car and eagerly hurried inside. The building was long, wide, and open, filled with furniture and other items for hotels.

Seeing all the beautiful things, Regan drew in a breath of excitement. Surely, she could find something on sale for them to buy.

"Well, hello, sweetie! I saw you come in. How can I help you?"

At the thought of being typically hit on, Regan clenched her teeth and whirled around.

Her jaw dropped.

A thin man of less-than-average height faced her. He wore a pink, button-down shirt, a lime-colored bowtie, and gray slacks carefully creased above his brown tassel loafers. Lively, light-brown eyes sparkled at her from his brown face. His dark curly hair was carefully trimmed and gently greased. His bright smile lit his entire face. He was, well ... adorable.

"Hi," she said.

"I'm Mo Greene. Can I help you?"

Regan shook the hand he offered her. "Regan Sullivan. And, yes, I'm hoping you can help me find some things on sale. I've brought a list with me."

Mo studied her. "Let's sit down." He motioned her to a leather couch nearby. "After we're settled, why don't you tell me a bit about yourself and what you're looking for."

Regan eased herself onto the couch and waited while Mo found a seat at the far end of it.

"Okay, sweetie, let's talk."

Regan gave him a brief description of how she and her sisters had come to own the Salty Key Inn and the challenge they faced. "I've come up with a way for us to save money by repainting some of the case goods, and my sister and I were able to buy carpeting at a huge discount. Now we need to fill in with some additional pieces of furniture for the rooms on the first floor of the largest guest building. We can't afford to furnish the twenty rooms on the second floor yet. Not until we bring in some money."

"What are you looking for?"

"We need pull-out couches, desks, coffee tables, and chairs. We have the rest."

"And what color is your furniture?" he asked, giving her a thoughtful look.

"Antique blue." Regan explained about chalk paint and how one could make the wooden pieces look old. "I've kept to the beach scene theme with pale-yellow walls and textured, sand-colored carpeting."

He listened carefully. "Are you an interior decorator?"

She grimaced. "I wanted to be an interior designer, but I couldn't get into RISD."

He shook his head. "Neither could I. Not with those costs. But I did get a degree from FIU."

"FIU?"

"Florida International University. Someday I want to have my own interior design and decorating business."

"Sounds wonderful," sighed Regan. "I envy you." She handed him an Excel spreadsheet. "My sisters and I made a list of all the things we need. Our biggest requirements are simple, light-colored desks with chairs and standard, pull-out couches or two-seaters."

Mo held up a finger. "I think you've come to the right place. We got a return on a shipment of yummy, pull-out couches the original owners decided they didn't like. Come with me."

He led her through several collections of couches, desks, bureaus, and chairs to a back corner. He gave her a little bow. "Ta-dah! Others may not like it, but we know that butterscotch and baby blue play nicely with each other when they are arranged in a woven pattern like this."

Regan's eyes widened as she studied the couch, imagining it in one of the rooms. She clutched her hands together. "Please tell me you have twenty of these couches."

He grinned. "Actually, we have fifty. Feel the fabric. Sturdy but comfortable."

Regan trailed her fingers over the fabric, liking its softness, its strength. "Are all the couches in good shape?"

"Sweetie, if you buy them, I'll inspect each one before it's loaded on the truck. And if you take all fifty, I'll make you a deal you won't believe."

"Okay, let me take a couple of pictures with my phone and send them to my sisters."

"Sure," Mo said. He stood by while Regan withdrew her phone from her purse and took several pictures of the couch from different angles and sent them along to Sheena and Darcy.

"How about coffee tables, desks, and chairs?" she asked. "I want something in pine, or maple, or other light wood."

Mo cupped his chin with a hand. "Let me think. No, that one wouldn't do. Maybe the ones from Georgia? No ..." He snapped his fingers. "Come with me. They've been hanging around for a while. Probably because they're quite plain. But it might work with your scheme."

He led her farther into the building. Here, wooden furniture was displayed in a variety of scenes set up to look like guest rooms.

"What about this?" Mo said. He indicated a plain, pine table sitting next to the wall of one of the rooms.

Long and narrow, it had no drawers, but the surface would make a nice desk area and be long enough to hold other things. "Any chairs to go with it?" she asked.

"Are you talking about office chairs? If so, no. But our sister store carries those. You could find something there."

"What about ladder-back chairs in pine?"

Mo frowned, and then his expression brightened. "A motel in the North Georgia mountains ordered more than they needed. I think there were several chairs like that. Let me check the inventory, and if we don't have them, we can get them."

"How many pine tables do you have?"

"I'll check that too. I think it was plenty for what you need."

He walked her into a nearby display. "These coffee tables would be a perfect match."

Regan gripped her hands together again in a prayerful pose. "If this all works out, it would be wonderful."

Mo responded with a smile. "It's up to us to make it work. C'mon. Let's work up a deal."

Regan's phone pinged, and when she saw the message, she grinned and turned to Mo. "Sheena and Darcy liked what they saw. Sheena wants to know if we can have thirty now and have you hold the last twenty for six months."

Mo gave her an encouraging smile. "We can make that part of the deal."

Regan followed Mo to his office by the entrance and then sat in one of the wing-back, leather chairs in front of his desk. While he did some work on his computer, she looked around his office. He'd made it very attractive. Her gaze landed on the nameplate on his desk. "Moses?"

He looked up at her and laughed. "From the beginning, my mother had great aspirations for her son. Luckily, she has an open mind because I sure didn't turn out the way she thought I would."

Regan chuckled at his humor. "From what I've seen, she should be proud. It's obvious you know your work. And, Mo, you have excellent taste. Would you consider coming to the hotel to help us put finishing touches on the rooms?"

His smile reached his eyes. "I'd like that, Regan. I really would."

He went back to his computer. After a few minutes, he turned to her. "Okay, I think we can get you a very good deal on the couches. And we have some options on the chairs." He paused. "Do you really want ladder-backs? Maybe you'd like to look at something a little different?"

"Sure," Regan said.

"How about these?" He showed her a vinyl, cross-back one. The lines of the back of the chair gave it a more upscale look than she'd imagined.

"We can do this in a neutral color with a brown, cushioned seat," said Mo.

Regan turned to him with excitement. "I love it. But is it expensive?"

"Cheaper than the other," he said. "And remember, we're here to make a deal."

"Okay, let's talk about it. But, Mo, my sister Sheena is in charge of our budget. She's the one you're going to have to convince. But I'm behind you all the way."

"All right then. Let's make a package deal she can't refuse."

Mo's cell phone rang. He answered it and listened. "I'll have to call you back. I'm with an important client." He hung up and turned to her. "Sorry about that. My mother."

Regan couldn't help chuckling at Mo's sheepish look. "No problem."

He studied her. "We have a family event coming up this weekend. I know it may seem strange for me to ask, but are you free on Saturday? I need to make a quick appearance at my family's party. We won't have to stay long, I promise."

Regan's eyes widened. "You're asking me to be your date?"

"Not really. I'm just asking you to do something to help me out of a jam. It'll be totally safe, I promise you. My boss will be happy to give you references if you want."

Regan laughed. "If it were anyone else, I'd be insulted at such an outrageous proposal. But why not? I like you, and it's a good way to thank you for all you're doing for us."

"I knew you were special," he said, beaming at her.

Her sisters would think she was crazy for doing this, but she didn't care. She and Mo had made an instant connection. And, besides, maybe it was time to have a little fun.

CHAPTER EIGHT

DARCY

Darcy stood in front of her mirror telling herself to relax. She leaned forward and stared at her reflection. The sun had bleached her hair to a prettier, lighter-red color, and her blue eyes were clear and alert. Sheena told her she worried about her looks too much, but what was a girl to do with two sisters who were stunners? She'd always felt ugly around them.

Regan stuck her head into the room. Her violet-blue eyes sparkled. "Have fun tonight. See you later."

"You too. Can't wait to meet your new guy. You say he's coming to the hotel next week?"

"He's going to help me with some ideas for final touches for the guest rooms. By the way, I'm taking the van. I'm going to meet him rather than having him pick me up. It'll be a lot more convenient that way."

"Okay. Austin's picking me up in a few minutes."

Regan left, and Darcy pulled a brush through her hair, wondering why she had to be the sister with the red curls instead of straight, dark hair like Regan's or pretty, thick, smooth, auburn hair like Sheena's.

Sheena came into the room. "Austin's here." She smiled. "You look pretty, Darcy. Have fun. I'm going to hang around my room and enjoy a quiet evening."

"You miss Tony?"

"It's hard to have my family away from me." A mischievous

grin spread across her face. "But as long as I'm away from them, I might as well enjoy the peace and quiet."

Darcy laughed. "Don't stay up too late."

Sheena waved and left the room.

Darcy drew a deep breath and grabbed her purse.

Austin was waiting for her outside. Smiling, he approached her and then escorted her to his car—an old Volvo sedan. After helping her inside, he walked around the back of the car and slid into the driver's seat. He turned to her. "You look nice."

"Thanks," she said. Austin was only twenty-six, like her, but with all his good manners, he acted like a gentleman from a bygone era, like some of the heroes she'd read about in novels. She liked it. It made her feel ... well, worthy.

"I'm glad you called," said Darcy. "Where are we going?"

"There's a place in Clearwater that I've wanted to try. Tamales is a beachside bar that has interesting Mexican food. It's become the 'in' place to go. Good beer, good food, good music."

Darcy brightened. "It sounds like fun."

They drove in companionable silence. Darcy told herself to forget how great she'd felt in Austin's arms when he'd saved her from falling. She had a habit of making more of moments like that than was sensible. Besides, Austin wasn't the wild type she usually went for, and at this stage in her life, it was silly to think of becoming serious with anyone when she was involved with the hotel and about to embark on a new career.

They pulled into a parking lot.

"Tamales is a couple of blocks away, but we'd better park here. It's going to be jammed tonight. I'm told it's crowded every Saturday night."

"Fine with me," said Darcy. "The walk will be fine. I've been stuck behind a desk most of the week."

Austin parked the car and took care of paying for and

getting the parking ticket to leave on the dashboard. "Okay, let's go, Miss Sullivan." She smiled and took his arm.

As they got closer to their destination, music and the sound of people laughing and talking filled their ears.

Darcy's eyes widened when she saw their destination. The sign advertising Tamales flashed its name in bright pink.

As they neared it, she saw that every section of the two-story building was painted a different color. The blue, ground floor had nearby tables on the sidewalk filled with guests. A few steps up led to an orange deck, where a large bar was surrounded by people. A side staircase led to the green second-story. There, a white balustrade surrounded the decking and served as a guard rail for the customers leaning over it.

She took a closer look. Bright turquoise clapboards covered the sides of the building. Poles designed and painted to look like palm trees held up the roof over the second story.

"Shall we?" said Austin, indicating for her to climb the stairs.

At the top of the stairway, Darcy saw another large bar surrounded by people laughing and talking. The beat of the music was persistent but not so loud you couldn't be heard if you spoke up.

"Let's see if I can grab a high-top table by the rail," said Austin. "Follow me."

They made their way through the crowd. Darcy saw that a couple was just getting ready to leave and tugged on Austin's arm for attention. They walked over to them.

"Mind if we take the table after you?" asked Austin.

"Not at all. Here, better grab this chair before someone else takes it away," said the guy, giving Darcy an approving glance.

"Thanks," said Austin. "Pretty crowded tonight."

"Always is, but the food is great." The guy and his date

moved away.

Darcy sat down and stared at the scene below. People were milling about. Some were dancing on the white sand beyond the walkway. Others were sitting and eating at tables near the sidewalk. It felt good to be part of a fun, active scene. The hotel work had seemed duller each day as she'd waited to hear something from Nick Howard about the restaurant review she'd written.

As if his name had conjured up a ghost, his nephew, Graham, appeared through the crowd with a girl whom Darcy recognized as the young waitress at The Terrace restaurant.

She quickly turned her head, hoping Graham hadn't seen her.

"Hey, Graham!" Austin called and waved to him.

Darcy sighed and watched surreptitiously as Graham and his girlfriend came over to them. She heard Austin say, "Wanna join us? I think we got the last seats in the house."

"You're the guy from the restaurant. I hope you didn't bring ..." Graham stopped talking as Darcy turned around.

Darcy gave Graham a friendly smile. "Hi. Like Austin says, you're welcome to join us."

"Uh, Lacy Morris, this is Darcy Sullivan and Austin ..."

"Austin Blakely," he prompted.

Lacy glared at Darcy. "You told my future mother-in-law that I didn't do a good job at the restaurant. Thanks a lot, bitch."

Darcy blinked in surprise, then held up her hand. "Look, I'm sorry if I got you into trouble. I was just trying to be honest when she kept asking me about it."

"Well, pick on someone else. Come on, Graham. I refuse to stay here." She marched away.

Graham gave Darcy an apologetic look. "I fired her yesterday. She's still upset about it. But my mother said you were right to tell me, that if I wanted to be successful, I had to have competent help. Lacy might not like it, but you did me a favor." He saluted Austin and went after Lacy.

"Like they say, the truth sometimes hurts, but it's good to face facts," said Austin. "And hopefully it will help Graham's business. I like the guy, and the food is good."

"Yes, but I've realized that you have to be very careful how you talk to owners of the business," Darcy said. She'd learned a lesson. She just hoped she hadn't ruined her chances with Nick and the newspaper.

A waitress came, cleared their table, and then asked for their drink orders as she handed them menus.

After the waitress left, Darcy looked over her menu. "Everything looks delicious, but I'm going to have the special fish tacos."

"Okay. I'm going to try their cheese and meat tamales."

The waitress brought Austin his beer and Darcy her Texas margarita and left with their orders.

The sound of the band, the happy conversations around them, and people dancing on the sand brought back memories of earlier island vacations Darcy had taken with her roommates. She couldn't wait for the opportunity to travel again. It was another reason she shouldn't get seriously involved with Austin or any other man.

"What do you think of the place?" asked Austin.

Darcy gave him a thumbs-up. "I'm loving this. It reminds me of the Caribbean."

"Yeah, it feels good to relax. I've been studying for tests, and I need a break."

"Okay, let's just have some fun," said Darcy.

He laughed. "Sounds good."

Taking a sip of her drink, Darcy wondered how Regan's date was going.

CHAPTER NINE

REGAN

Regan stayed close to Mo's side as she made her way through the people gathered at his mother's house. Laughter rang out as the women greeted each other with hugs, and the men in the family shook hands or clapped each other on the back.

"Stick with me," Mo said as they approached the woman who was obviously the hostess.

"'Bout time you got here, Moses," his mother said, studying Darcy. "And who is this lovely-looking girl?"

Regan smiled and held out her hand. "I'm Regan Sullivan."

"A new ... girlfriend?"

Regan glanced at Mo, who rolled his eyes. "Regan, this is my mother, Marietta."

"Nice to meet you," said Regan, studying her as she held out her hand. Mo's mother was of average height with a plentiful girth that was appealing. Within a pretty face, her brown eyes sparkled with intelligence and good humor. Regan instantly liked her.

Marietta shook Regan's hand and then patted it. "You look like a nice girl, Regan."

"She is, Mom," said Mo. "I met her at the store, and she and I kind of get each other."

Marietta smiled. "That's good, son. Now, come do your duty and say hello to everyone."

"Do I have to?"

Marietta arched an eyebrow at him.

"Okay. C'mon, Regan. I'll put you to the test, and then I swear I will make it up to you, big time."

Regan laughed. She was fascinated by the large, happy group in the house. From where she stood in the hall, she could see a table in the dining room spread with delicious-looking food. While Regan was growing up, family gatherings at her home had been small and unusually quiet until after her father and two of his brothers had drunk a few beers. Then they stood outside on the back porch and roared at their own jokes, bringing some life to the group inside.

"Hi, Uncle Mo! Is this your girlfriend?" asked a shy, little girl who peered up at her from behind pink-rimmed eyeglasses. She sashayed back and forth, holding onto the hem of her sundress.

"Regan, this is Mercy," said Mo. "My goddaughter."

Regan knelt in front of her. "Hi, Mercy. How old are you?"

"Six," she answered.

"A very pretty six," said Regan, loving the way the front strands of curly dark hair had been woven into tiny braids and pulled back behind her head.

Mo offered Regan a hand, and Regan rose to her feet as a small, bent, gray-haired woman approached them, using a cane to help make her way through the crowd. People on either side of the woman parted to make a pathway for her as if she was royalty.

"My grandmother," whispered Mo, and Regan could hear a slight tremor in his voice.

"Well, Moses, you have appeared as requested," said the woman, eyeing Regan as she spoke.

"Hello, Grandmother," Mo said with reverence before hugging her. "I'd like you to meet Regan Sullivan, a friend of mine."

"Indeed," said his grandmother. She tapped her cane against Mo's leg.

Mo straightened. "Oh yes. Regan, this is my grandmother, Carlotta Beecher."

"How do you do?" said Regan, aware that this was what her mother would have called "an important, grand moment."

Carlotta stared at Regan. "Anyone ever tell you that you look like that actress ... you know the one. She played in *National Velvet* and was married more times than the fingers on my right hand."

"Elizabeth Taylor?" prompted Regan.

Carlotta nodded. "Yep. That's the one."

"Yes, people have mentioned it, but I don't think we're alike at all. She was a very talented woman."

Carlotta studied her. "And what do you do for a living?"

"Right now, I'm helping my family fix up the Salty Key Inn in order to open it."

A smile spread across Carlotta's face. "You're the decorator working with Moses?"

Regan hesitated, not sure how to answer. She'd like to be a decorator, but, in truth, she wasn't.

"Yes, she's got a good color sense, Grandmother." He grinned. "We see eye to eye on a lot of things."

Carlotta laughed. "Always joking, this guy." She patted Regan on the arm. "You take good care of him, hear?"

"Yes, Ma'am," Regan said, wondering exactly what Carlotta meant. Didn't she realize Mo was gay?

As Carlotta moved away from them, Mo took Regan's arm. "Let's get out of here."

They headed for the backyard. Before they could get outside, a man grabbed Mo. "Hey! Where you going? Don't you want to say hello to your Uncle Bob?"

Mo shook his head. "I've got to get Regan outside. She's not feeling well."

Regan hid her surprise and played along. "Thanks, Mo."

They emerged into the backyard, where a group of men was standing around a barbecue grill. In the grass, not far from them, several women sat in a circle of lawn chairs talking.

Regan turned to Mo. "What was that all about?"

"Uncle Bob gets mean when he's had too much to drink. Neither one of us needs that."

"Certainly not," said Regan. Feeling protective, she slung a casual arm over his shoulder. "I really liked your mom and your grandmother."

"Thanks," he said. "They're good people. Come meet my relatives. They'll like you."

Mo led her over to the circle of women. "Hey, people, I'd like you to meet Regan Sullivan. She and I are working together on a project. She's new to town."

"Hey! Come join us," said one of the younger women. "We're just catching up on what's going on in the area."

Regan sat down in an empty lawn chair.

"And bring her a drink, Mo," said another woman before turning to her. "Margarita? Beer?"

"Beer," Regan quickly said. She never wanted to taste tequila again after drinking too many margaritas with Darcy the night Tony surprised Sheena with a visit.

"So, tell us about yourself," said one of the women.

The others leaned forward in anticipation.

Regan accepted a beer from Mo, took a quick sip, and then said, "My sisters and I unexpectedly inherited the Salty Key Inn in Sunset Beach. So far, it isn't the glamorous thing we'd thought it'd be. We're struggling to get it ready to open. Mo is helping us."

"You must be something special, or Mo would never have brought you here," said one of the ladies.

"Thank you for being his friend," said another woman. "We love Mo. He's a doll."

Regan smiled. "I think so too." She looked up to find Mo hovering nearby, giving her an anxious look.

She waved to him, signaling she was fine.

He returned the wave and went inside.

"Tell me about yourselves," said Regan, warming to the women. Eleven others sat in the circle with her. Of different ages, two were white, the others in varying shades of brown. As each woman introduced herself, she was teased by the telling of additional stories about her. From the conversation, it was obvious they'd known each other for a long time. Regan sat back and listened to the banter, totally comfortable with them. She couldn't help thinking of her life in New York City and the indifferent people she'd known there. In the few months since she'd been in Florida, she'd found a comfortable home where she could be freer, happier. Being accepted by this group confirmed it. It made her wonder what other surprises were in store for her.

CHAPTER TEN

DARCY

Darcy finished her tacos and sat back in the chair, enjoying Austin's company and the views around her. Dressed in a tank top, denim skirt, and floppy sandals, she felt her body relax from the tension of working at the hotel. The warm air of the onshore breeze caressed her skin and tossed the red curls she'd carefully tamed. She didn't care. She just wanted a good time with a friend.

"Want to dance?" said Austin.

"Sure. Why not?" Darcy turned to the couple sitting next to them. "We'll be right back. Don't let anyone take our table. Okay?"

"Gotcha covered," the guy said, grinning.

Darcy followed Austin down the stairs and out to the strip of beach set aside for dancing. She took off her sandals and sighed. The light grains of sand felt cool on her feet.

Austin held out his hand. Darcy took it, then let it go as they moved to the beat of a hard rock song. Darcy loved to dance like this—free and easy. She glanced over at Austin and grinned. He was a great dancer!

When the music segued into a soft, slow number, she moved into his arms. Darcy's thoughts drifted along happily. When she felt Austin stop, she opened her eyes with surprise.

Graham Howard stood beside them. "May I cut in?" he asked.

Darcy glanced at Austin.

Austin stepped away.

Darcy adjusted her stance to fit Graham, who was taller than Austin by at least three inches.

"I wanted to talk to you," said Graham. "I've broken up with Lacy."

"But you were engaged," said Darcy.

Graham shook his head. "No, she wanted me to marry her, but I never even implied that that was going to happen. My mother and uncle didn't approve of her because of her lack of concern for others."

"Oh, I'm sorry to hear that," said Darcy, wondering why Graham was telling her all this.

"Uh, I'm wondering if I can take you out sometime. My Uncle Nick really likes you."

"He does?"

Graham nodded. "He said you might be doing some work for him and thinks we can help each other." He studied her. "What do you say?"

"Maybe someday. You just broke up with your girlfriend." Darcy's mind raced. Considering that Nick Howard was his uncle, it might be a good idea to find out more about him. Later.

"Okay, I guess I deserve that." Graham walked her to where Austin was standing, handed her back to him, and stepped away. "I'll call you, Darcy."

Austin took her in his arms again. "What was that all about?"

"I'm pretty sure it was a business deal," said Darcy, still rocked by the idea that Nick Howard wanted Graham and her to get together.

The slow music stopped.

"I'm ready for another beer," said Austin. "Let's go."

Darcy followed him back to their table, still confused by

Graham's actions. Was it right for someone to break up with an almost fiancée and immediately ask another girl out? She didn't like that.

Austin ordered another round of drinks, and they sat comfortably watching other dancers and laughing together at some of their moves.

Another slow song played.

Austin gave her a questioning look. "Dance?"

"Sure." Their first slow dance had been interrupted by Graham.

Darcy followed Austin out onto the sand once more. At this later hour, the mood was a little more mellow, and several couples danced around them as Austin took her in his arms.

"Nice night," he murmured.

"Yeah, it's been fun," Darcy responded, meaning it. She felt so comfortable with him that she hadn't worried all evening how she looked or if she'd said the right thing.

He drew her closer, and she lay her head on his shoulder, liking this friendship with him.

When the music stopped, they stared at each other a moment and then Austin said, "We'd better head on home. It's getting late."

"All right," Darcy said agreeably. "It'll be another busy day at the hotel. We're all pitching in to finish the painting of the furniture on the second floor. Even though we can't afford to furnish those rooms just yet, we're doing as much work on them as we can."

"Regan is very clever," said Austin. "I like what she's done."

Darcy nodded and told herself that her pang of jealousy was foolish.

On the trip back to the hotel, Darcy stared out the window. Palm trees framed a view of the beaches. The light-colored sand contrasted sharply with the dark water that splashed against the shore in rhythmic beats. Gray clouds hurried through the sky, blotting the moon in a pattern that signaled a new front coming into the area. Through the open window, the air already felt cooler on her skin.

Austin pulled into the parking lot behind the suites building and turned off the engine. Facing her, he said, "Thanks for being such a good sport about my late call. I really had fun."

"Me too."

He leaned toward her for a quick kiss.

As their lips met, Darcy's body jolted with pleasure. *Not only can this guy dance, he's great kisser,* Darcy thought dreamily, reveling in his embrace.

They pulled apart. "See you soon."

He started to get out of the car, but Darcy waved him back. "Thanks, but I can walk myself to the door." She needed a moment alone before going inside.

She stepped out of the car, gave him a little wave, and made her way to the door of her suite, thinking some girl would be very lucky to land Austin. He was turning out to be a very cool friend.

Inside, she found Regan and Sheena sitting on the couch chatting. They looked up at her with eager expressions.

"How'd it go?" Regan asked.

"It was fun," said Darcy. "He's a nice guy. Sure you won't change your mind about him, Regan? You met him first."

Regan shook her head. "I want someone whose kiss makes me tingle."

Darcy thought back to her kiss with Austin. Did a jolt of pleasure equal a tingle?

CHAPTER ELEVEN

SHEENA

Sheena was painting furniture with Regan and Darcy when her cell phone rang. *Tony*. She quickly picked up the call.

"Hi, honey! What's up?"

"Are you sitting down?"

A thread of worry wove through her. "Why?"

"Mom and Dad sold the house with the condition that we're all out within thirty days."

"Oh my Gawd! How are we going to do that?" Sheena slid her back down a wall and sat on the floor.

"What do you say we get rid of the furniture and have an estate sale along with Mom and Dad's stuff? I'm not attached to any of it. Are you?"

Sheena didn't have to think about it for long. "Okay. It will be fun to start all over again. We'll need a different style of furniture here when we're able to move from the hotel into a house of our own."

Living at the hotel, first in the house and then in the suite with hand-me-down furniture in less-than-perfect condition had given her a whole new perspective.

"Okay, I need you to make a list of the things you left at home that you still want," said Tony. "The kids and I will pack them up carefully and ship them with Mom and Dad's things. The timing of this is quite a shock."

"How are your parents taking it?"

"Surprisingly well. They'd already made the final

arrangements to buy the house they liked in Florida, so they don't feel homeless."

"Are you sure this is what you want, Tony? Are you going to be comfortable selling your business and moving here?"

"Yeah. Besides, John and Dave and John's friend Mark are thrilled with the idea of taking over from me. I couldn't go back on my word to them."

"And the kids?"

He laughed. "They're excited about having a swimming pool and going to the beach."

"They understand we'll be living here at the hotel temporarily until the end of the year, right?"

"Yes, though we need to know about school districts so they can get settled in the proper schools."

"I've already talked to several people about it, and the school district closest to the hotel is an excellent one. We'll be able to work something out, I'm sure."

"Well then, Mrs. Morelli, looks like we're about to become permanent residents of Florida. Who knew so many things would change in a matter of months?"

"Not me," said Sheena, still surprised by how it all had happened. "Please give your parents my congratulations. And, Tony, thanks for everything. I love you so much. And tell the kids I can't wait to see them, that I love them too. Just think. We'll be a real family again."

Sheena hung up the phone and let out a long, relieved sigh, her mind awhirl.

"What's going on?" asked Darcy.

"You okay?" Regan added.

Sheena nodded and grinned. "We're moving to Florida for sure. Paul and Rosa sold the house, and Tony is selling his business. That's the good news. The bad news is that we have to be out of the house in thirty days."

"Bad news? It's great!" said Regan.

"Thirty days? Wow!" Darcy held out her hand.

Sheena took it and jumped to her feet.

Regan and Darcy each grabbed one of her hands, pulled her into a circle and led her in a crazy dance.

When they slowed, Regan said to Sheena, "I'm very happy this is happening. Remember how scared you were to tell Tony about moving to Florida? Now the whole family will be with us."

Sheena pulled them to a stop. "You sure you don't mind having them here at the hotel? Teenagers aren't the easiest to live with."

Regan's expression grew serious. "I love them, and they need to be here with you."

"I love them too. We almost lost them in the fire. Remember?" Darcy quickly added.

Sheena gave each sister a hug. The bond between them was growing stronger each day.

After dinner, Sheena sat in her suite preparing a list of things she wanted from the house in Somerville. It wouldn't be much. The gold coin was tucked away in a zippered pocket in her purse where it would stay hidden, and she'd brought her few pieces of good jewelry to Florida—gold hoop earrings, a string of pearls, pearl earrings, a few silver charms strung on a necklace and a couple of silver bracelets. The rest could be sold or given away if Meaghan didn't want them.

As she mentally went through her closet and drawers, reviewing her clothing, Sheena realized how dowdy some of them seemed after living a carefree life in a tropical setting. She added only a few favorite items to the list of things she wanted and decided she didn't need the rest. Her kitchen was a different story. She wasn't ready to give up any of the items she'd lovingly acquired for cooking and serving meals. She'd have it all brought to Florida.

Sheena reviewed the furniture in the house, saving a couple of the lamps and a few decorative pieces. All personal pictures she'd keep. The rest of the household items, she decided, could be sold or given away.

She typed up the list for Tony, feeling as if a huge weight had been lifted from her shoulders. *Sometimes, holding onto things only weighed you down*, she thought, as excitement flowed through her.

She called Tony and went over the list of items she wanted. "How are the kids doing? Do they want to take a lot of stuff with them? Are we going to need to rent a storage unit?"

"Whoa! One question at a time. The kids are making their lists now. Michael, typical guy, doesn't want to take much from his room. Just some books and trophies. Meaghan, on the other hand, is a pack rat. I'll keep encouraging her to make her list shorter, but right now, she wants it all."

"That's fine with me," said Sheena.

"We won't have to rent a storage space. Mom and Dad said they'd store our stuff in their garage until we're ready for it. You can relax, Sheena. I've got things under control here."

"Thanks, honey," said Sheena, surprised by how Tony had stepped up to do the job that usually landed on her shoulders. She couldn't help chafing at her lack of control over the situation, but she'd do nothing to jeopardize the terms of Uncle Gavin's will by leaving the property. His will stated she and her sisters were to be there for the entire year.

"We're all pretty excited," Tony continued. "I'll be down there next week to finish up working with Brian on the guest bathrooms. I won't be able to stay long, but it'll be a good excuse to see you."

"Can't wait," said Sheena. They talked for a couple more minutes, and then Sheena hung up. Initially, she'd been anxious to do the challenge and be away from her family for a while. They'd treated her like a maid, demanding her to do various things for them like the entitled people they thought they were. With all the changes in their lives, she was ready to admit she sometimes missed being needed. Not that she'd confess that to any member of her family. Especially her sisters.

In the middle of the next week, Sheena was as eager as Darcy to meet the new man in Regan's life. Regan had told them all about Mo's family and how they'd welcomed her. But each time Sheena or Darcy asked for specifics about him, Regan had clamped her mouth shut. "You'll see," was the only comment she allowed herself to make.

Now, the three of them were waiting outside of Gracie's to greet him.

An old, white Nissan 300 ZX pulled into the parking lot.

Regan waved and waited for Mo to get out of the car.

Wearing gold-rimmed aviator sunglasses, a purple button-down shirt and khaki pants, the dark-skinned, thin young man who emerged from the car gave a wide grin to Regan and embraced her.

Sheena and Darcy exchanged shocked expressions.

"He's gay?" said Darcy softly. "No wonder Regan didn't want to talk too much about him."

"He's cute!" whispered Sheena as Regan and Mo walked toward them.

"Here he is! My guy!" said Regan with a twinkle in her eye.

Mo laughed. "Hi. I'm Moses Greene. Regan's a great woman, and talented, too."

"We've heard you're really good at your job," said Darcy, grinning at him. "Hi, I'm Darcy."

Sheena shook his outstretched hand. "I'm Sheena. We're pleased you're going to help us."

"Let's go in and have breakfast and then we can show Mo around," Regan suggested.

Sheena led the others into the restaurant, excited to begin work with Mo. His daring style was exactly what they needed.

CHAPTER TWELVE

REGAN

Regan smiled at Mo as they followed Sheena inside the restaurant. She'd purposely held back information about him, wanting to see how her sisters would react to him and his colorful style. Now, she was pleased she had because it was evident that they approved of him.

They took seats at a table for four in their favorite corner where they could observe others in the restaurant and yet have privacy.

"The food here is really good," said Regan. "Order anything you want."

After they all placed orders with Maggie, Regan turned to her sisters. "Mo has a great eye for putting things together. He's the one who found the pull-out couches for us. I'm hoping he can help with the selection of bedspreads and draperies or other window treatments."

"I like what Regan has described about her vision for the rooms," said Mo. "I have in mind something light and breezy yet practical. Sound good?"

"Oh yes," said Sheena.

"We're advertising the hotel as a 'quiet treasure'—something good for families and others. We don't want to pretend to be something we're not," said Darcy.

"What you see today is just the beginning of what we hope to make of this property," said Sheena. "But, yes, we want to keep it simple and tasteful."

Mo and Regan exchanged pleased glances.

"It's pretty much what we already talked about," Regan said to him.

He turned to her sisters. "How is it, working together? I'm an only child and can't imagine working with any of my cousins." He laughed. "They'd boss me around for sure."

Regan and Darcy glanced at each other but remained silent.

"I really liked Mo's cousins. They were all friendly toward me, which made my meeting them very nice." Regan smiled at Mo and turned to face her sisters. "And Mo's goddaughter, Mercy, is a little doll. And the food the family put together? To die for. Something you should do a review on, Darcy."

Darcy's face fell. "I'm not sure I'm doing reviews on anything. I still haven't heard from Nick."

Regan quickly explained Darcy's potential job to Mo.

"If you do start writing restaurant reviews, I've got several small places out of the mainstream for you to look at," said Mo.

Their food arrived, and the conversation came to a standstill as they all dug into their meals.

Regan was happy to see Mo's expression of delight as he bit into his omelet. He glanced at her and winked. "Delicious."

She loved the fact that in such a short time they'd become good friends. Earlier that week, Regan had met with Mo again to discuss patio furniture. And later, when his dinner break came, she'd joined him for a meal at a little café down the street from the store. Talking to him about colors and textures and other design qualities, she felt as smart as he thought she was.

As soon as everyone had finished their meals, Regan jumped to her feet. "Let's go. I can't wait to show Mo what I've done with the rooms."

They left the restaurant and stood outside the entrance while Regan described the layout and explained that the suites in the smaller building would have to be decorated at a later time.

As they headed across the lawn toward the Egret Building, Regan took Mo's elbow and led him over to the pool. "I think the furniture we picked out will be nice here."

Mo nodded. "The neutral colors will work well. And the furniture is top quality, so it should last."

Sheena and Darcy joined them.

"Eventually, I'd like to build a hut with a palm thatch roof next to the pool. Nothing too big or too loud, just a nice place for people to have drinks and maybe a small snack from Gracie's," said Sheena.

Regan turned to her with surprise. "When were we going to talk about that?"

Sheena's grin was a bit sheepish. "At the end of our challenge. But I can dream, can't I?"

Regan's brief irritation disappeared. They each had ideas of how they wanted to see the hotel completed, but they'd have to work together to make it better than it currently was.

They walked over to the Egret Building. "We haven't put a complete room together, obviously," Regan told Mo. "But after you help us select soft goods, we'll be able to photograph a room for publicity and then, hopefully, open up for business."

"Sounds good. Now, let's see what we're working with."

Taking a deep, worried breath, Regan led the others inside and over to one of the rooms they wanted to photograph.

As Mo stepped inside the room, Regan studied his face. It remained expressionless, and then a wide smile broke across it. "Sweetie, I love what you've done to the furniture."

Mo went over to the dresser and trailed his fingers across

the surface of it. "Some of the furniture makers have begun producing this shabby-chic style, but yours is even better because of the genuine brush strokes."

He studied the headboard attached to the wall. "Nice. When are the mattresses and box springs coming?"

Regan turned to Sheena.

"I got notice yesterday that, though delivery has been delayed, everything should arrive within two weeks," Sheena said.

"Okay, then, you'd better place an order for bedspreads right away. They can take some time," said Mo. "From the fabric samples of our less expensive selection, Regan and I have chosen something we think you two will like."

Regan stepped to his side and drew a piece of fabric out of the briefcase Mo had brought.

She held it up against the headboard. "What do you think?"

Sheena and Darcy looked at each other and then came closer to feel the material.

"I like it," said Darcy. "But is it going to be too much blue?" The fabric was a dark blue with waves of lighter blue and white in it.

"No, I don't think so," said Sheena. "I like it against the lighter-colored furniture. It makes it interesting."

"The pattern represents water," said Regan. "But I agree with you. We need a pop of color. I was thinking of ..."

"Sunsets," said Mo at the same time as Regan.

They laughed together.

"We have the sand and sea represented, so Mo and I agreed to stick to the beach theme by adding decorative pillows in the reds and oranges of sunsets."

Sheena clapped her hands. "I love it!"

Mo gave her a look of satisfaction. "For the windows, I suggest keeping a very neutral color, something in the same color wheel as the carpet, but darker. That way, even if wall colors change, you'll have a balanced look to the room."

"Good idea," said Darcy. "Very practical. What kind of window treatments do you want to put on the sliding glass doors?"

"Want to tell them?" Mo looked at Regan.

"Sure." She pulled out a sheaf of papers from the briefcase Mo had set on top of the bureau. "We'd like to see a drape on the sliding doors that extends from one side to the other, across the entire window—heavy ones that will block the sun and hold up to the humidity, heat, and sunlight. We feel they're suitable for this kind of location. And like Mo said, they'll be done in a deeper yet compatible color with the carpet."

A worried look crossed Sheena's face. "Are they expensive? And how long will it take to have them made?" The way things were going, and how many delays there could be in putting everything together, she was worried they wouldn't be able to open over Labor Day like they were planning.

Mo shared a look with Regan and cleared his throat. "When you see the price of them, you'll know they're not cheap. But we thought the cost was worth it for now and the future. And I'll try to keep on top of them to make sure they deliver the items on time."

"Great. Come up with an estimate for the rooms, add at least five thousand dollars, and then we'll see if we can do it," said Sheena with a grim expression.

Mo knelt and ran his fingers over the carpet. "It's good that this has a woven pattern to it. That and this deeper sand color will help with its appearance as guests use it. One of the things we advise our clients is to choose materials that will hold up. Some guests don't care if they trash a room."

The looks of horror on her sisters' faces matched Regan's

indignant feelings. After doing all this work to make things nice, she prayed their guests would show some respect. She'd heard plenty of stories about rooms being trashed. "We got the carpet at a bargain, but it's good. One of the Disney properties ordered too much of it."

Mo stood. "Then it's got to be good."

"Let's show Mo a room in the suites building," said Regan. "When the time comes, I want him to help us."

"You and Regan have done a great job together," said Darcy.

"Yes," said Sheena. She held out her hand. "Thanks, Mo. Welcome to the Sullivan Sisters team!"

As he shook hands with Sheena, the look of pleasure that crossed Mo's face filled Regan's heart with tenderness.

CHAPTER THIRTEEN

DARCY

Darcy left the meeting with Mo feeling down. Regan had found a new, great friend and was in her element helping with the decoration of the rooms. And Sheena was excited about her family moving to Florida while she, Darcy, was dealing with the kind of uncertainty that was tearing a hole in her gut.

She entered the office and sank down into her desk chair wondering if she should try to call Nick Howard one more time. Why, in God's name, hadn't she heard from him? Graham had indicated he'd talked with him. Why hadn't his uncle called her?

She opened her computer to check emails and, at the sight of Nick Howard's name, let out a small cry of delight. She clicked on the email and read: "Dee, I'm sorry I haven't been in touch. Read through the restaurant review. I want you to go back to the restaurant and do another one. You need to mention the chef, the location, and a description of the place, along with the description of the food. Let's meet sometime next week to discuss. NH"

Darcy let out a sigh of relief. He'd addressed her as Dee, the name he'd given her as a restaurant reviewer for the newspaper.

She quickly replied to his email: "Thanks for getting back to me. Will do the review and email it to you within a day or two. Dee Summers."

Typing the name, Dee Summers, brought unexpected moisture to her eyes. If she could pull this off, it would be the beginning of her dreams of becoming a new person, perhaps even a novelist one day.

She picked up the phone to call Graham Howard and set it down again. Restaurant reviewers visited restaurants *incognito*. Graham knew her as Darcy Sullivan. That's how it would be.

When Darcy joined Sheena and Regan for lunch at Gracie's, she bubbled with enthusiasm. "I heard from Nick, and I'll be going back to The Terrace for lunch tomorrow. Anyone want to join me?"

"I will," said Regan.

"Okay, but don't give me away. I'll be doing a review ... undercover."

Sheena laughed and placed a hand on Darcy's arm. "You sound like a spy."

Darcy straightened, unable to stop feeling indignant. "In some ways, I am a spy. It's important work."

"I'm glad you're doing this. I can see how excited you are," said Regan, the peacemaker.

Darcy relaxed, growing excited by the prospect. "It's a step in the right direction for me."

"Yes," said Sheena. "It's a good way to start a new career."

Sometimes Darcy appreciated having her sisters around. This was one of those times.

The next morning, just before noon, Darcy headed into St. Petersburg with Regan.

"No matter what happens with the hotel, I've decided to stay in Florida," said Regan. "I love this lifestyle of being able to hit the beach, go swimming in the pool, and enjoy the outdoors at all times of the year."

"It's nice," said Darcy, "but I want to travel too."

"Austin's parents own a travel service. Maybe you could set up something with them," said Regan.

"Yeah, I've already talked to him about it."

"He's a nice guy," said Regan. "Wish he was my type."

"Yeah, I know. He's not like the guys I usually like to date," said Darcy.

Darcy drove down to the Vinoy to show Regan the hotel and then found a parking place near The Terrace restaurant.

"The restaurant looks nice," said Regan, as they approached the patio.

"It is," Darcy said, taking a closer look at it in order to be able to describe it in her report.

Even though it was warm and humid, they opted to sit outside on the patio. As before, only a few tables were occupied.

As soon as Darcy and Regan took their seats, a young man approached them. "Good afternoon. Welcome to The Terrace." He handed them each a menu.

"May I get you anything in addition to water?" he said, greeting them pleasantly.

Darcy blinked in surprise at the change in service. "Thanks. I'd like a Diet Coke with a squeeze of lemon. Regan?"

"Water is fine with me. With a wedge of lime, please."

"Coming right up," the waiter murmured before hurrying away.

"I thought you said the service was terrible," whispered Regan.

"It used to be. I wonder how Graham got it squared away so quickly."

The waiter reappeared with their drinks. "Are you ready to order? Chef has done a nice job with the pasta special. And the

Cuban sandwich is a favorite. It's posted right on the front of the menu."

"I'm going to try the Asian Salad," said Darcy, eager to see if the quality of the food was consistent.

"I'll have the Mussels and *Pomme Frites*," said Regan, laughing when Darcy rolled her eyes.

"What?" said Regan, after the waiter left. "I can't splurge every once in a while?"

"No, that's not it. I need to check out several dishes, and that is one that a lot of people wouldn't order. But enjoy it."

Regan studied her. "You're serious about this, aren't you? I thought it was only something fun, but I can tell it's more than that to you."

"Someday, you may go into a bookstore and see a big, fat novel with my name on it," said Darcy. "That's my dream."

"I could never write a novel," said Regan, "but I hope it happens for you."

They chatted for a few minutes more, and then the waiter appeared with their food.

"Nice service," said Darcy, smiling at him .

"Yeah, well we aren't too busy," said the waiter. "Hopefully that will change as word spreads that the service has improved."

Regan took a few bites of the mussels and then forked a few of the french fries into her mouth. "Mmm, good."

Darcy munched happily on a piece of the crispy chicken topping on her salad. "Mine too." For the third time eating at the restaurant, the food was prepared well and worth a very nice review.

They were finishing their meal when Graham appeared. He smiled at Darcy. "You came back? How was everything?"

"Very good," said Darcy. "Graham, this is my sister, Regan."

Darcy watched his eyes turn round with pleasure as he studied her sister. For once, Darcy didn't care that Regan, as she usually did, stole attention away from her. This was a business luncheon, nothing more.

"You're working at the Salty Key Inn with Darcy?" Graham asked Regan.

"Yes, my sister Sheena, Darcy, and I are hoping to open the hotel sometime soon. You'll have to come check it out."

"That's where Gracie's restaurant is, right?" said Graham, addressing Darcy.

Darcy nodded. "Great food, like here."

"And the service here?"

"A whole lot better. Very nice, in fact."

A smile spread across Graham's rugged features. His green eyes sparkled. "It cost me my girlfriend, but I'm starting to get customers coming back. So, thank you, Darcy."

A couple walked onto the patio and took seats at a nearby table.

Graham lifted his baseball cap in a small salute to them and said, "I'd better get back to work. Hope to see you again."

"He's the chef?" asked Regan.

"And the owner. Cute, huh?"

"Very cute," Regan said, staring at his retreating figure.

"Wait here," said Darcy. "I'm going to go inside and look around."

As she walked inside, Darcy heard a commotion in the kitchen. "Dammit, Joe, you let the meat get too well done."

She recognized Graham's voice and thought of a couple of temperamental chefs she'd seen on television. *Maybe all good chefs were a little that way*, she mused.

Only two of the inside tables were occupied.

After checking the décor and the cleanliness of the ladies' room, Darcy made her way back to their table, satisfied by all she'd seen. The place was clean, cute, and appealing. She could hardly wait to write about it.

Outside, the waiter approached their table and handed Darcy the bill. "How was everything?"

"Delicious," Darcy said enthusiastically. "How long have you worked here?"

"Just a week. I'm actually a friend of Graham's and a graduate of the hotel school at Cornell. He asked me to lend a hand in training new staff. He's interviewing for positions now if you're interested."

Darcy laughed. "No, thanks. I've already got a job."

He handed her a business card. "I'm starting my own consulting business. Give me a call if you change your mind."

"Thanks." Darcy tucked the card unread into her purse.

They paid their bill and left.

"What did you think?" Regan asked her on the walk back to the car. "My food was delicious, and the service was excellent."

"I thought so too."

As they drove back to the hotel, a new idea came to Darcy. She turned to Regan. "I like the notion of a hotel school graduate consulting with Graham. Before we open the hotel, we might want to talk to someone like him."

"Good plan. Let's see what Sheena thinks."

Darcy and Regan laughed together. They loved Sheena but sometimes got tired of her role of big sister.

Regan's expression turned serious. "I never knew we both felt abandoned by Sheena when she left us to get married. And, until now, I didn't realize by getting pregnant at an early age, Sheena was very disappointed that she lost out on the college experience she always wanted. Funny, you can be sisters and still not know each other."

"This experience here in Florida has been good for all of

us," Darcy agreed. "Do you think Uncle Gavin knew we needed something like his challenge to pull us together?"

"Maybe," said Regan. "If like Sheena said, he and Mom communicated on a regular basis, then Mom probably told him something like that. She wanted us all to be close."

Back at the hotel, Darcy sat at her computer, typing up her new review of The Terrace restaurant, putting to use all the words she kept stored in her head and hardly ever used. She finished, took a quick look at it, and sent it off to Nick Howard, eager to prove how fast she could be.

Sheena walked in and sat down. "How'd lunch go?"

"Much better. The food was great as usual, and the service was excellent." At the surprised look on Sheena's face, Darcy laughed. "A Cornell hotel grad is helping Graham hire and train new wait staff. As a matter of fact, Regan and I were thinking we might want to hire him to take a look at the hotel before it opens. What do you think?" She handed Sheena his card.

"Kenneth Cochran? Hospitality Answers? I love it. We can talk about it later. Right now, I need to talk to you and Regan. I did some looking around on the internet and have found something I want you both to see."

Regan joined them, and together the three of them selected furniture that would work on the guest room patios until they could afford something more expensive.

"Well, that about does it. Until the guest-room furniture, drapes, and soft goods come, we're pretty much set," said Regan.

"No," said Darcy. "We all need to work on our advertising campaign. We need to print up cards with our logo and the information on the introductory specials we're offering. We can start with a mailing and then give them out in the restaurant and other places."

"And we need to get a reservations number," Sheena reminded them. "Darcy, we still haven't been trained on the front-office system you installed. Sally Neal is going to work as a housekeeper, but Regan, you will have to be in charge of getting the guest rooms ready. "We'll all have to help clean rooms until we hire staff, including a head housekeeper."

Darcy and Regan exchanged resigned looks. There was a still lot of work to be done before they could open to guests, and it appeared Sheena would be in charge.

CHAPTER FOURTEEN

DARCY

Darcy was working in the office when she got a call from Austin Blakely. At the sound of his voice, she couldn't help the thrill that ran through her. They'd been texting back and forth about the logo, but Darcy thought maybe that was only an excuse for both of them to be in touch. She looked forward to each one.

"Hey, Austin! What's up?"

"Just wanted you to know I have the sign for the hotel done. It's large and weighs about eighty pounds. You'll need someone with a truck to pick it up. I don't think it will fit in the hotel van and it definitely doesn't fit in my car."

"Sheena's husband, Tony, is driving his truck down to Florida this weekend. Is it okay if he picks it up sometime next week?"

"Sure. But I'd like to be there when you install the sign. It'll take some work to sink signposts in concrete and get them ready for the sign installation and then mount it."

Darcy was happy at the thought of seeing him again. "Maybe we'll have a party to celebrate that. Let me talk to my sisters, and we'll get back in touch with you. When are you going to be in town?"

"Actually, I'm coming there this weekend," said Austin. There was an unmistakable sadness in his voice.

"Oh, dear. Is your grandmother worse?"

"Afraid so."

"Oh, Austin, I'm so sorry. I know how much you love her."

"I guess this is to be expected, but it still hurts."

Darcy heard him draw in a deep breath and then he said, "I'll call you when I get into town, and we can figure out where the sign should be placed. Maybe you can go ahead and get your workmen to prepare the posts. I'll email you some dimensions."

"Good idea. I'm really sorry about your grandmother, Austin. Is there anything I can do for you? For her?"

"Thanks, but there's not much to be done at this point but to be there for her. Talk to you later."

Darcy ended the call and sat a moment, thinking of Austin. His devotion to his grandmother made her realize she should have been more present when her mother was dying of cancer. It was Sheena who'd been there every day as her mother's time neared the end.

Pulling herself away from those thoughts, Darcy went to work on the website for the hotel. If the sign Austin made was anything like the other stunning signs he'd made, she wanted to feature it on the homepage of the website.

She was still working on the website when she heard a ping on her phone warning her that she had a message. When she saw that it was from Nick, her pulse sprinted.

She read: "Dee, got your latest restaurant review. Let's talk about your writing. I'll come to the hotel tomorrow. Please let me know when you're free. N.H."

She swallowed hard. From his curt message, he must not have liked the review. Blinking away tears of disappointment, she took several deep breaths. *The hell with working for him! She'd find another newspaper to hire her, work hard, and be better than he'd ever thought she could be.*

Try as she might, Darcy couldn't concentrate on her work. She marched across the lawn to the suites building. Inside her room, she stripped off her clothes and put on her bathing suit. A brisk walk along the beach was what she needed.

She'd just finished putting on suntan lotion when Regan appeared.

"What are you doing?" Regan asked. "Going swimming?"

"No, I'm going to take a walk on the beach, and if I don't feel better about things, I'm going next door to The Keyhole and having a drink or two or three."

"Whoa! What happened? Why are you talking like this?"

Darcy sighed. "You know the review I just sent Nick? He wants to meet with me tomorrow." Her stomach knotted. "I bet he didn't like it."

Frowning, Regan shook her head. "Did he indicate that?"

"Not exactly. He wants to talk to me about my writing. Oh God! I've probably made a fool of myself."

"Darcy, if you want to get into the newspaper business, you have to develop a thick skin. I can't write, but you can. Look at the stuff you came up with for our advertising campaign. I'll walk down to the beach with you. Then, we'll decide about The Keyhole for drinks."

Sheena knocked and entered the suite, wearing a bathing suit and a floppy sunhat. "Want to take a break and go for a walk on the beach?" She looked at Darcy. "Guess you already thought of that."

"Darcy is upset about her latest restaurant review," said Regan. "Give me a minute to change. This calls for a beachy, sister pow-wow."

After Regan left to change, Sheena studied Darcy. "What's going on?"

Darcy shrugged, hating to admit to Sheena that, apparently, she wasn't much of a success at writing reviews. "I don't think Nick liked my review. He wants to talk to me about it."

Sheena placed a hand on Darcy's shoulder and gave her a steady look. "Darcy, you're a good writer. Believe in yourself."

Unexpected tears filled Darcy's eyes. Too emotional to voice her thoughts, she simply nodded.

Darcy followed her sisters across Gulf Boulevard to the beach, feeling like a failure. They knew she was upset, but she didn't think they realized how insecure she was about herself. She'd always tried to hide her feelings from them by teasing or joking. She hated the feeling of being the uninteresting one, the unpretty one compared to them. She wanted to show the world she was her own person, worthy of praise for being who she'd always wanted to be.

They made their way down the boardwalk to the beach. Flipping off her sandals, Darcy buried her feet in the sand, still warm from the late afternoon sun. The crowd on the beach was dispersing, no doubt heading back to their homes or hotel rooms for showers and dinner. Darcy let out a sigh of contentment. It was her favorite time of day at the beach.

She walked down to the water's edge and dipped a toe into the frothy edges of the waves meeting the shore. The water temperature on this day in June was nice—not too cold, not too hot. By comparison to the icy waters off the New England coast, it was just about perfect.

A sandpiper hurried by, quickly followed by a flock of others. Darcy had grown to love the bird life at the shore. Even the raucous cries of seagulls and terns as they swirled in the air above her was music to her ears.

She watched a trio of pelicans fly by in formation like the acrobatic fliers they were. She'd always been fascinated by their long beaks and the large throat pouch they used to catch prey. She'd read that the pouch was also used to drain water from the scooped-up contents before swallowing.

Sheena came up beside Darcy and gave her a quick hug. "Feeling better?"

Darcy turned to her and gave her a weak smile. "A little."

"C'mon. Let's go on a walk. Nobody can beat down one of the Sullivan sisters."

As the three of them strolled side by side along the water's edge, Darcy eyed her sisters. Regan's self-confidence had grown so much in the last few months she seemed like a different person. And Sheena had become much more relaxed away from her family and the responsibilities they'd constantly dumped on her. Uncle Gavin had thought they'd needed life lessons. Maybe, the three of them had already learned a few.

When Darcy returned to the boardwalk with her sisters, she felt a lot better. There was something about walking along the sand, getting her feet wet in the water, and the sounds of nature that healed her in a way that nothing else could.

"Shall we go get a drink at The Key Hole?" she asked, ready for a cool drink and some nibbles.

"Sounds good to me," said Regan. "How about you, Sheena?"

Sheena paused and then grinned. "Why not? Holly still owes Darcy for all her computer work there. Right?"

"Right." Darcy looked at Regan and chuckled. Sheena was in charge of handling the finances for their project and counted every penny.

They each put on their sandals, donned their beach cover-ups, and headed to the bar. Holly Harwood, the owner of the bar, and Gavin had enjoyed a long relationship—mostly platonic. He'd bought the bar for Holly to ensure she'd have a source of income and something to keep her busy. He'd also given her son, Brian, a responsible role in helping Darcy and her sisters with the project whenever they asked for help. As they entered the bar, Darcy noticed Regan glancing around the bar before sitting down at a table opposite her in a booth.

Sheena waved to Holly behind the bar and slid onto the bench next to Regan.

A cute, young waitress approached the booth. "What can I get you, ladies?"

Darcy waited for her sisters to order and then said, "Make mine a Texas margarita, and please bring us a menu."

"Guess this will be my last spontaneous outing for a while," said Sheena. "Tony and the kids will be here before I know it."

Darcy's brow furrowed with consternation. "Why say that? Your kids are old enough to be on their own. You should feel comfortable doing things for yourself. I thought that was one of the reasons you wanted to be here."

"I agree," said Regan. "We're not going to let you go back to being 'Supermom' too quickly. Michael and Meaghan really grew up during their spring break here when they had to do a lot of things for themselves."

Sheena's expression brightened. "You're right. That's what I was ready to do. Old habits die hard. How'd you two get so smart?"

"Not from you," teased Darcy as their drinks came, and the three of them laughed.

Darcy had just taken a sip of her margarita when Brian Harwood walked through the door.

Tall, tanned, and buff, he moved toward them. His warm brown eyes, sun-streaked light-brown hair, and delicious grin added to a package that was already close to perfect. "Good evening, ladies. Taking a break?"

"A much-needed one," said Sheena. "Care to join us?"

"No, thanks." He continued to focus on Sheena, for which Darcy was glad. She'd made an embarrassing move on Brian to prove that she was still attractive after being dumped by Sean, and she still regretted it. Regan, she noticed, was doing her best to ignore him, but Darcy could tell she was very aware of him.

Later, when they'd eaten a variety of appetizers and had their fill of drinks, the three of them left the bar and walked next door to the Salty Key Inn.

Stepping onto the property the three of them now owned, Darcy felt a new sense of homecoming.

The next afternoon, Darcy sat outside Gracie's waiting for Nick Howard to arrive. Her heart raced in nervous beats and then faltered with dread. She knew how brutal some newspaper reporters could be. Maybe Nick was here to taunt her about her lack of ability. He didn't appear to be that kind of person, but one never knew when dealing with someone who went undercover to report news, even if it was only a review of a restaurant.

When at last she saw the Santa Claus figure heading her way, she waved her hand. Her throat was too dry to utter a greeting.

"Hi, there, Dee!" he called to her.

She began to relax. She loved that he'd given her a pseudonym under which she could write reports.

"Hello, Nick. Would you like to go into Gracie's for a bite to eat?"

He shook his head. "Better not. We need to talk."

Darcy's stomach did a sickening somersault. "Okay, we can go into my office."

She led him past the entrance to the restaurant, the fenced-in area containing trash cans, and into a side door that led into the downstairs hallway and the office beyond the restaurant.

Taking a deep breath, Darcy ushered Nick into her office and closed the door behind them.

Her hands cold, she indicated a chair for him and sat behind her desk, glad for the tiny bit of distance between them.

"You wanted to speak to me about my writing?"

Nick studied her for a moment. "Are you serious about wanting to work for the paper, and more to the point, about writing a novel?"

Darcy stiffened. "Yes. Why?"

"Because I'm willing to help you if you listen, really listen, to what I have to say and heed my advice."

"Okaaay," she said, wondering exactly what he meant.

"You have good instincts, a sharp eye for things, and a natural ear for words. But if you're going to work for me and ever succeed in the publishing business, you have to care enough about the end result to make it the best it can be." Nick withdrew a piece of paper from the notepad he was carrying and handed it to her.

Darcy stared at the printout of the review she'd sent him. There was red ink everywhere. "What is this?"

"It," said Nick with a satisfied smile, "is a corrected copy of what you sent me. Now take a good look at it."

Darcy's temper flared. "This is bullshit!"

"Precisely," said Nick. "I don't ever want you to give me copy like this without first editing it—once, twice, maybe three times or more to get it right."

Darcy's cheeks flamed with mortification as she studied the misspelled words, the lack of commas, and the number of sentence fragments. Her mind spun. *Is this what professional writers go through? This pickiness? This humiliation?*

"If you think I'm harsh, wait until you try to break into the book publishing business. At least I'll help you by showing you what you can do to improve. Agents and editors won't be that kind. They probably wouldn't even respond to something so poorly written." Though his words were hurtful, Nick's expression was full of understanding. "Your review was spot on. Now, make it right, because, Dee, I'm handing over my weekly column to you, starting in two weeks. Want it?"

Darcy felt her sagging spirits jolt to attention. "Really? Are you serious? Do you think I can do it, even with this?" She rattled the sheet of paper in front of him.

He nodded. "Yes, I do. But I'm going to give you a crash course on writing and editing. You've got all the stuff inside you to make this work, Darcy. Your descriptions, the way you use the senses, everything is naturally there. Let's see what else is inside you."

She felt a frown forming on her face. "Why are you doing this for me, Nick?"

He let out a long sigh and stared out the window. When he turned back to her, a sadness drooped his features. "I just found out that the Big C has revisited me. And this time it's not good at all."

The blood left Darcy's cheeks. "Oh my Gawd! Are you talking about cancer?"

"I'm going to fight it, of course, but I won't be able to carry on my usual duties. I want to work with you on taking over my newspaper column, too. In return for my coaching, you'll continue the column that's important to me."

Darcy sat back in her chair, shocked by all he'd told her. At one time, she'd thought of Nick as St. Nick. If this idea went forward, it would be one of the biggest gifts she'd ever received. But then, she didn't want the hurt that came with it.

CHAPTER FIFTEEN

SHEENA

Sheena sat in the kitchen of her suite nibbling on tuna salad and making a list of groceries she needed to buy for her family. After leaving them behind in Boston while she and her sisters worked together to meet the challenge Gavin had given them, Sheena had found a sense of freedom she hadn't ever allowed herself. She loved being a wife and mother, but she'd become lost in those roles. Now, she was enjoying being Sheena Sullivan Morelli, who just happened to also be a wife and mother, as well as one of the owners of a hotel.

With her being away, Michael, at seventeen, and Meaghan, at almost fifteen, were learning to do more things for themselves and to be more grateful for all they had. Her heart warmed. Though her life was about to change with their arrival, she could hardly wait to see them. Michael would have a final year of high school in Florida, and then he'd be off to college. Meaghan would, she hoped, make better, nicer friends in her new school.

Sheena's cell rang. *Meaghan.*

"Hi, sweetheart," Sheena said. "What's going on?"

"Mom, I decided not to go to the End-of-School Dance. Now, Lauren and her friends are calling me a snob."

"And how do you feel about that?" Sheena said quietly, feeling sick inside that Meaghan was being picked on—once more.

"I know if I end up going, they'll just make fun of me there.

And, anyway, I'll be leaving for Florida and won't have to put up with them anymore."

"Sounds to me like you've made a good decision." Sheena couldn't hide her relief. Lauren and her two friends bullied many of the girls in Meaghan's class, and though it hurt, Sheena was hopeful that Meaghan understood how wrong that was.

"Mom? I can't wait to get to see all of you at the hotel. Gracie told me she was counting on me to help in the restaurant."

Sheena was pleased by the note of pride in her daughter's voice. Meaghan had been unhappy with the idea of bussing tables when she'd been forced to come to Florida after being suspended from school for a bullying episode of her own. But working with Gracie and Clyde and the others, Meaghan had seemed to flourish, especially when she'd learned to deal with Clyde's special needs and become much more accepting of others. "Well, I'm counting down the minutes myself until you're here. Only a few more days. How is Grandma Rosa?"

"She's busy but really happy about moving to Florida. The estate sale was a blast. We sold almost everything here and on Grandma's side too. The moving van comes tomorrow. Then, we're all staying at a hotel downtown. That's another reason I didn't want to go to the dance."

"Sounds like everything is right on schedule. See you soon, baby girl."

"'Bye, Mom. Love you," said Meaghan before clicking off the call.

Sheena sat for a while, thinking of the difficulties of being a teenager. Through all the social media, horrible things were being said and done to others. Communication had been turned from a good thing to something painful to many people.

Her cell rang again. *Tony.*

"Hi, darling," she said. "I just talked to Meaghan. Sounds like things are on schedule."

"Pretty much. Michael and I will be delayed for a couple of days. After the movers come, I'm staying to make sure the cleaning crew takes care of everything. Mom and Dad are anxious to leave for Florida, so I told them I'd do it. Hold on, Michael wants to ask you something."

"Mom? Randy Jessup wants to come to Florida with me for the summer. Can he? He said he'd work, too."

"Randall Jessup? I didn't know you and he were such good friends."

"While you've been gone, we've been playing baseball together, and he and I have become real buddies. He's a good guy."

"What about his family? They have a summer home on Nantucket. I would think he'd want to stay there."

Michael snorted. "With his father and his stepmother and their two bratty kids? Not likely. And his mother has a new boyfriend who hates Randy. He's desperate, Mom. We've gotta help him."

"You'd have to share a room with him, and, Mike, he'd have to work as hard as anyone else. Let me talk it over with your father, and we'll get back to you."

"Today. Okay?"

"I'll try," said Sheena. "Everything else okay? Are you set to pick up the Explorer from the car transport service when you fly down here?"

"Yeah. Before shipping it, Dad even put new tires on it."

"Good. Can't wait to see you!"

"Me too, Mom. Here's Dad."

"What do you think about Randy living with us this summer?" Sheena asked Tony, still surprised by the request.

"I'm shocked he'd even consider it. Our living quarters aren't the best. And does he understand that summer here is hot and humid and that even so, he'll be required to work outside?"

"Yeah, I've told him all that, but it's apparently not a good situation for Randy at home. And when I talked to his parents and explained the situation, including that Randy would have to work like the rest of us, neither one objected or even seemed to care that much. Pretty sad, actually, because he's a nice kid."

A long sigh escaped Sheena. "At the first sign of trouble, he'll have to leave. We plan to open the hotel Labor Day Weekend, and we'll be too busy this summer to deal with problems. Agreed?"

"Agreed." There was a pause, and then Sheena heard Tony chuckle. "Mike is giving us the thumbs up. He knows what a softie you are, but I'll sit Randy down and talk to him about our rules. I promise."

"Okay. I can't imagine how that boy must feel about being unwanted. Let me know how you do with him and all the final arrangements. Thanks, hon. It's been great that the kids have stepped up to help you while I've been down here."

"Yeah, it's been a strange few months. I haven't liked it much, but soon we'll all be together. Gotta go," said Tony.

Sheena ignored the slight edge to Tony's voice. "Can't wait to see you! Love you."

"Love you too," said Tony.

Coming to Florida with her sisters had changed the way her family functioned. As freeing as it was for her, it had been difficult for them to get along without her. But it had done each one in the family some good. She wondered how adding another person to the group would change that dynamic.

Punching in the number for her mother-in-law, Sheena decided to ask her about it.

Rosa picked up the call. "Hi, Sheena!" she chirped.

"How are you holding up with all you have to do for the move?"

Rosa laughed. "As good as can be expected. You should have seen all the stuff we got rid of. After forty years of living in this place, we had a lot of things to handle. Michael and his friend Randy were great about hauling stuff around."

"Really? You've met Randy?"

"Yes. He seems like a nice boy. Why?"

"He's going to be living with us for the summer."

"Ahhh, Tony mentioned that. I think it will do Randy good. His people might have money, but they seem to be running short on love."

At the thought of a child going through that, a rush of tenderness swept through Sheena. Her own children had always known they were loved.

They discussed details of the estate sale, and then Rosa said, "I'm so excited about starting over again. Paul has agreed to get all new furniture, but I need to find someone to help me decorate the new house."

"I know the perfect person. Regan has done a fabulous job with the hotel's guest rooms, and she's made friends with an interior decorator who works on hotels. The two of them would be great."

Rosa let out a little squeal of delight that caught Sheena off guard. "Oh, that would be wonderful! Regan will know what kind of things I'm used to and what I might like. Please let Regan know I'd love to hire her."

Chuckling softly, Sheena said. "Will do." Life, as she often thought, was full of twists and turns.

CHAPTER SIXTEEN

REGAN

Her pulse racing with excitement, Regan lifted her cell to call Mo.

As she waited for him to answer, she shifted her weight back and forth on her feet—a kind of nervous tap dance.

"Hi, sweetie! What's up?" Mo said.

"I've got some exciting news to share with you," said Regan.

"Me too," said Mo. "Want to meet at Sammy's for lunch? My treat. I can be there in ten minutes."

"Great! I'll be just a few minutes later. See you then!"

Regan ran next door to Sheena's suite. "I need the van. I'm going to meet Mo for lunch and give him the good news about decorating Rosa's house."

"Nice. Keys are on the counter where we always keep them. Have fun!"

Regan grabbed the keys and hurried out to the van. As soon as Austin came up with a more detailed logo, they were going to have it painted onto its doors. Right now, the plain silver van seemed like a golden chariot that would carry her to the start of a whole new life. That's if Mo would agree to work with her on Rosa's home.

She pulled into Sammy's parking lot, relieved to find an empty space. Next to St. Pete Beach, the bar and grill, known for its excellent seafood, enjoyed a brisk business for both lunch and dinner. As she climbed out of the van, she saw Mo's white car parked at the edge of the lot and hurried inside the restaurant. Regan paused and searched for Mo. Sammy's kept to a traditional beach décor with fishing nets, sand dollars, and other beachy accents. The atmosphere, though, was more sophisticated than most others. Turquoise-linen tablecloths covered the tables and were accented by the pink-rimmed water glasses at each place. In the middle of the table, a single sprig of bright-pink bougainvillea nestled in a white bud vase.

When she saw Mo, Regan smiled, waved, and hurried toward the table.

Seeing her, he stood, waiting for her to approach. He was wearing a pale-yellow Hawaiian shirt with large pink and red tropical flowers printed on it.

"You look fabulous," she said, accepting a kiss on the cheek from him.

"You too." He gave her outfit a careful look. "That navy shirt with the white jeans looks good on you."

Pleased, Regan gave him a quick hug. "You always make me feel so good." She slid onto the chair he held out for her. "Wait until I tell you my news."

He sat down opposite her. "Before you start, I want you to know I've quit my job at the store. I'm doing something entirely new."

"Whaaat? Are you quitting the decorating business?" Her stomach churned at the idea of losing an opportunity for them to work together.

"Here." He handed her a light-gray, business card. *Interiors by Moses Greene* in bold brown letters ran across the front of the card. An address and phone number appeared below. On the back of the card, she read: *Classy interior decorating for smart people.*

"Well? What do you think?" Mo's expression was uncertain.

"I love it!" she said, smiling. "You're so talented. When did this happen?"

"Last weekend. I've been working on a deal for months. Blackie Gatto, a financial advisor, helped me arrange the deal—he and his partner, a lawyer."

"Blackie Gatto? He's helping us," said Regan. "Sheena works with him and thinks he's great. He worked with my uncle for years."

"He's very good. He made sure I have a good deal. I'm working with Lowell's Furniture to be able to offer my clients discounts. Lowell's is the nicest furniture store around, and Blackie helped them understand it could be a win-win situation for both of us."

"Where's your office?" Regan asked him.

His smile was sheepish. "For the moment, it's my apartment. One of the two bedrooms holds all the fabric samples and books, etc. It's taken me weeks to set it up." He reached over and grasped her hand. "I'm glad I could help you with the hotel. Blackie told me not to say anything to anyone else until it was all settled. But if you have any trouble with delivery of anything, let me know, and I'll take care of it."

Feeling a little lost, Regan said, "I'm happy for you, Mo. I really am."

"Thanks. Enough about me. What's your news?"

"My news?" She felt her lips curve. "I may have your first client. Sheena's in-laws are moving to Florida, and Rosa wanted me to help her decorate the house from top to bottom."

Mo gave her a steady look. "My client? Why don't we do it together, Regan? It's something we've talked about for the future. Let's start now."

"You? Me? Together? Us?"

He laughed. "After I met you and worked on the hotel with

you, I was surer than ever I was doing the right thing. Someday, I hope to offer you a real job with me. We've clicked from the beginning, haven't we?"

Warmth flooded Regan. She nodded. "I've never had a friend like you before, someone I can be totally free with. Know what I mean?"

"Yeah. If you believe in multiple lifetimes, I'm sure we've known each other before."

Regan laughed. The idea was foreign to her, but she liked knowing he felt the same way about her as she did about him.

CHAPTER SEVENTEEN

DARCY

Darcy sat in her office and went over the small article she'd written about The Terrace one more time. After her meeting with Nick, she'd purchased an editing app and was finding it very useful in discovering, among other things, where commas did and did not go. She'd been saddened and exhilarated by the idea that due to Nick's struggle with cancer he was going to guide her through a crash course in writing and editing. The only thing he'd asked in return was a commitment from her to follow through on all his suggestions and directions. To keep in touch, they'd agreed to meet weekly.

In the meantime, things at the hotel were heating up. The delivery of the bedspreads had been delayed one more time, but when they arrived as now expected, they'd add one more finishing touch to the rooms. Training Regan and Sheena on the property management system would soon begin. Though they were opening with only twenty rooms, it was important for all of them to know how to use it.

Darcy emailed the review to Nick and sat back in her chair. She hoped he liked it this time. He'd turned it back three times. The last time she'd received it all marked up, she'd sat alone in her office and cried with frustration. But this, he'd warned her, was only the beginning of becoming a professional writer. If she wanted it, she'd look at his corrections and his suggestions and learn from each mistake.

The jarring ring of her phone brought Darcy back to the moment. She checked caller ID. *Austin.* She smiled and picked up the call. "Hi!"

"Hi, Darcy. Just wanted you to know I'm at my grandparents, and I've brought the final file with the smaller logo for your stationery, business cards, and other promotional materials."

"Great," she said.

"What's up with you?"

"I'm trying to write an article for the paper, but it isn't easy. I have so much to learn and sometimes I'm plain scared about doing something like this."

"Darcy, you don't strike me as the kind of person who easily gives up. Believe in yourself. You're better than you think you are."

At his words and the kind way he'd said them, warmth filled Darcy's body. Austin was such a good guy.

"Thanks," she said. "You're right. I can't give up just because it's hard."

"Life is hard sometimes," Austin said. "Just keep at it, Darcy."

"Austin, would you mind if I came there to pick up the work you have for us? I need to talk to you about something personal."

"Sure, come ahead," he said. "It will be good to see you." He gave her the address and then said, "See you soon. Thanks."

As she pulled up to the modest house, Darcy wondered if she'd made a mistake in inviting herself there. But she'd felt a deep need to talk to Austin about how he dealt with a grandmother who was dying. She was devastated to think that

Nick might not survive the cancer that had begun a couple of years ago and was now rapidly spreading throughout his body.

Darcy parked the van and got out.

Austin came outside to greet her. "What's going on? You sounded upset on the phone."

Seeing him, hearing his concern, all the angst about dealing with Nick surfaced. She stood a moment and held her face in her hands, drawing deep breaths to keep from breaking down.

Austin rushed to her side and put an arm around her. "What's the matter? Are you okay?"

Darcy lifted her head. "I'll be fine. I just needed to talk to you. You always make me feel better. A friend of mine, a new one, is fighting cancer and it's obvious he's not going to make it."

Austin smoothed his palm against her back in comforting strokes. "I'm sorry. It's never good news. Want to talk about it? We can sit on the front porch. No one will bother us there."

He led Darcy to one of two folding chairs on the front porch and then sat in a chair next to hers.

"Okay, why don't you tell me about him," Austin said, wrapping his hand around hers.

Darcy sighed. "Okay. My friend is a wonderful, older guy who's helping me with my writing. I'm doing some secret work for him."

At Austin's cocked eyebrows, Darcy wagged a finger at him. "I trust you, but you can't tell anyone else. My working name is Dee Summers, and I'm starting to do restaurant reviews for him for the *West Coast News*. I met him when he came to do an article on the hotel. Now he wants me to take over a weekly column for him. It's writing about different people in the area, sort of like a getting-to-know-you thing."

"That sounds interesting."

"Yes, but it's happening only because he's ill. I feel terrible about it, yet, I'm glad for the opportunity. You know?"

He gave her hand a squeeze. "I think what you're suffering from is what one might call 'survivor's guilt.' Don't worry about it. It's not at all unusual."

"But I want him to survive. I really do. Even if it means I have to find another way to learn to write so I can write a novel one day."

"I'm sure you do want him to survive, but it's out of our hands. The best thing you can do for him is to do a good job. Agreed?"

Darcy slowly nodded, feeling the knot in her stomach begin to ease.

"We hate it when something bad happens to people we love or even like," said Austin, sounding like the medical professional he was.

"How do you manage with your grandmother? It's clear that you love her."

"Yes, I do. I give her as much of a normal existence as I can by filling her in on what I'm doing, just like I used to. And whenever she's been up for it, we do familiar things. Even though he's turning his column over to you, I can't imagine your friend suddenly wants you to treat him as if he can't write anymore. He's going to continue to help you, right?"

Darcy nodded again.

"Then let him give you all the help he can. Don't take that away from him. Understand?"

"I don't know him all that well, but I respect him like crazy."

"Okay, then, you've got a plan. Want to come in and meet my grandparents?" He grinned. "They're very curious about you. It's not often a girl asks if she can come over."

"Oh, but ..."

He raised a hand to stop her. "It's all right. We don't have to pretend it's more than friendship."

She felt confused by the disappointment that swirled through her.

As they walked into the kitchen, a small, gray-haired woman looked up at them from her place at the kitchen table and gave her a sweet smile.

"You're a new friend of Austin's?"

"Yes." Darcy went over to her and took hold of her hand. "I'm Darcy Sullivan. Austin has been doing a lot of artwork for my sisters and me for our hotel."

"Oh, yes," said Austin's grandfather, standing at the stove, stirring a pot of something. "Aren't you one of the young women who bought the kayaks and got the wooden carving in our garage sale."

"That was my sister, Regan. But we all love Austin's wooden carvings."

"How about having some lunch with us?" his grandfather said. "It's nothing fancy, just some of Margery's favorite soup."

"Homemade chicken noodle. Always tastes good," Margery said. "And Bill makes it just right." She gazed at him lovingly.

He chuckled. "Anything for my girl."

Darcy and Austin exchanged amused glances. "It's a real love nest around her," he said, and they all laughed.

Austin went to the cupboard and pulled out four bowls and a plate for crackers.

While his grandfather ladled out the soup, Austin poured four glasses of ice water.

Darcy took a seat opposite Margery, and paused, wondering what to say.

"Tell me about the hotel," Margery said, her voice weak.

Darcy realized the effort Margery was making to be

sociable, and her heart went out to her. Briefly, she told them about Gavin leaving the hotel to her and her sisters and how they had to figure out how to get it ready to open.

"Lots to learn," said Bill, sitting down at the table. "After I got back from 'Nam, I worked at a few hotels until I saved enough money to open my own business."

"Grandpa owned and ran a restaurant supply store," Austin explained.

"Really? Perhaps you can help me learn all the lingo for the various items in restaurants," said Darcy.

A pleased smile spread across Bill's face. "Well now, I can do that."

"She has a secret job," said Austin, giving her a teasing wink. "Something she might not be comfortable enough to share with you."

Darcy laughed. "Okay, I'll tell you two, but you have to do a better job of keeping it a secret than it appears Austin will."

Amid the laughter that broke out, Darcy said, "I'm going undercover and writing restaurant reviews. It's a lot of fun."

"Any advice you need, I can give you," Bill reiterated. He glanced at Margery, lost his smile, and got to his feet. "Time for Margery to rest."

Bill took his wife's arm, and they left the kitchen.

Darcy noticed the sadness that crossed Austin's face. She reached out and rested her hand on his arm, wanting to help ease his pain.

"Thanks," said Austin, emitting a long sigh. "Let me clean up the kitchen, and then maybe we could go for a walk."

"Okay, sounds good. I'll help clear the table."

While Austin quickly rinsed the dishes, Darcy wondered if this is what a happy, peaceful home was like. Growing up, the Sullivan household had never had this easy, relaxed atmosphere.

"C'mon, let's go!" said Austin, putting the last of the dishes in the dishwasher and wiping his hands on his shorts.

Outside, they walked down the street to a pond that sat in the middle of the neighborhood. As Darcy and Austin found seats on a park bench in the shade, a couple of Muscovy ducks waddled by, quacking noisily, before splashing into the water and swimming away.

"Pesky things, but fun to watch," Austin commented. "My grandparents used to bring me down here to feed them."

"Your grandparents are so nice," Darcy commented. "You're lucky to have them. I was never close to my grandparents. All but one died when I was very young, and the one who survived moved out of state."

"Too bad," said Austin. "Mine have been great to me." He sat back against the slats of the bench and draped an arm over the back of it. "I've decided to stay at school this summer. I can take two courses and then I'll be able to start my internship in the fall."

"Nice," said Darcy. "And you're going to set up practice here?" She gazed into his startling blue eyes, intrigued by the intelligence and kindness she saw there.

"Yes, I have two offers to consider. I guess as the population grows here, more and more people are needing dentists."

Darcy's cell phone pinged with an incoming call, startling her.

She checked caller ID, looked at the time, and let out a gasp. She clicked on the call. "Sheena, I'm sorry. I didn't realize how late it is. I'll come right home." Darcy jumped to her feet. "I'm sorry, but I have to get back to the hotel. Sheena needs the van to pick up her family from the airport."

Austin easily kept pace with her as she hurried back to his grandparents' home and stopped beside the van.

"Here's the flash drive for the logo," said Austin, handing it to her.

"Oh, I almost forgot it," said Darcy, staring into his eyes as she accepted it from him. "Thanks so much for your help. And please thank your grandparents again for lunch."

Austin studied her a moment and then, his gaze glued on hers, he drew her into his arms. Darcy leaned against his broad chest, realizing she'd wanted this all along. His arms were strong, comforting. She sighed with pleasure. It felt so good to be held like this. She felt treasured.

Austin lifted her chin and then lowered his lips to hers. His lips were soft, yet demanding. A surprised tremor moved through her as her body tightened with sexual tension and then loosened in hot waves as his kiss extended. Giving in to the pulsing beat inside her, Darcy whimpered softly and opened her lips to his tongue.

His arms tightened around her, and when he finally stepped away, she felt ... empty.

Austin's look of wonder matched what she was feeling. They stared at each other for a few moments, then, almost sadly, Austin said, "Guess you'd better go."

Though her body continued to pulse with desire, she climbed into the van, still shaken by the chemistry that had exploded between them.

As she drove away, Darcy raised her hand to say goodbye to Austin and then brushed her fingers across her lips, wondering what had just happened to her, to him, to them.

CHAPTER EIGHTEEN

SHEENA

Sheena drove to the airport with mixed feelings. She was, of course, anxious to see her daughter and to greet her in-laws. But she worried that with their arrival, she might be forced into her old pattern of constantly trying to meet their demands.

She parked the car in the short-term lot and went into the baggage claim area to wait.

Moments later, at the sight of Meaghan, Rosa, and Paul heading her way, her heart filled with joy. They were her family, and she loved them.

"Mom! Mom! We're here!" cried Meaghan, running ahead of her grandparents.

Sheena swept Meaghan into her arms and hung on tight.

As Rosa and Paul approached, Sheena released Meaghan and greeted each in-law with a hug. "Welcome to Florida. This time, for good."

Rosa beamed at her. "I can hardly believe it! Who would've thought a few months ago that Paul and I would pull up roots and come live in Florida? Not me." She smiled at Paul and turned back to Sheena. "But we're both happy to do this. Paul can't wait to get out on the golf course."

"It'll have to be early in the morning, though," Paul complained. "I've been keeping my eye on the hot, summer weather." Though he spoke gruffly, Sheena knew by the excitement in his face how pleased he was with the move.

"Let's hurry and get our luggage. I want to get to the hotel and go swimming," said Meaghan.

They walked over to the rotating, baggage conveyor belt and stood with the crowd. Sheena turned to Rosa. "Sure you don't want to stay at the hotel? We could temporarily fix up something for you."

Rosa shook her head. "Thanks. We're staying at the motel right near the entrance to our development, so when the moving van comes, we'll be able to go back and forth from the house to the motel. Most of our things are small, household items, but it will still take us a while to unpack. As for the furniture, I've told Regan what we need, and she's got a number of things for us to look at. Though she and Moses Greene are working together on furnishing the house, it will be a couple of days at the very least before we'll be able to move into it."

Sheena smiled. "I think you're in for a surprise. Regan and Mo make a great team."

They gathered their luggage, and then Sheena led them to the van.

"Oh," gushed Rosa. "You've got a large logo painted on the van. It looks great!"

"Yes, I think so too. Darcy and Austin worked on the design for the van. He's come up with another one to be used on all the stationery, business cards, and other media. Tony is picking up the large, carved, wooden sign Austin made for the hotel. After he gets here with it, we'll hold a little ceremony to mount it."

"When do you officially open?" Paul asked, sliding suitcases into the rear compartment of the van.

"We're planning to open over Labor Day. We're awaiting delivery of the bedspreads for the guest rooms, but they've been back-ordered. And the drapes for those rooms won't be done for several weeks. But we're slowly making progress. The furniture has already arrived, and the wi-fi was just upgraded for the reception office. After we get the guest rooms set up, we can add a few final touches. We're still trying to decide what we can do to make the pool nicer."

After they all buckled in, Sheena made her way through the traffic exiting the airport.

"Mom? Do I really get to stay in the suite with Darcy and Regan?" asked Meaghan sitting beside her.

"Yes, as long as things go well." She spoke to Rosa and Paul. "Randy and Michael will share the second bedroom in the suite Tony and I share. Hopefully, after the end of the year, we'll be settled in a new house." Sheena kept an upbeat tone to her voice, but buying a house was still very much up in the air. The sale of the plumbing business had yet to be completed, and until that was done, she and Tony couldn't move forward.

"Meaghan, sweetie, you can come stay with us anytime you want," said Rosa from the back seat of the van.

In the rearview mirror, Sheena shot Rosa a smile of gratitude. "It will seem strange not to have you living next door to us. I'm glad you decided to come to Florida and especially happy you chose to live in a neighborhood not too far away from the hotel."

After living in a duplex for years with her in-laws, they'd formed a special attachment. Yet, Sheena and Tony had no desire to live too close to his parents again. With Michael going away to college in a year's time and Meaghan following him in a few years, she and Tony intended to enjoy not only their freedom but a privacy they'd never had.

After Sheena dropped her in-laws off at their motel, she turned to Meaghan in the passenger's seat and gave her hand a squeeze. "Good to see you, honey. I think living here is going to be nice for you."

Meaghan smiled. "I hope so. I never want to see Lauren and her friends again."

"Oh?"

"Yeah, they told everyone at the dance that I was too fat to get into any dress." Meaghan's eyes filled. "Dad said to ignore them, but it really hurt."

Sheena hid the anger she felt. "You do realize you're not fat, right?"

"I'm not skinny."

"You're perfect," said Sheena with feeling. "A beautiful, young girl." With Tony's darker coloring and the fine Sullivan features, auburn hair and hazel eyes, Meaghan was lovely-looking. A fact Sheena hoped Meaghan would one day realize.

Sheena pulled into the hotel and drove to the parking lot behind the suites building.

She helped Meaghan with her suitcase. Most of her clothes and other belongings were in the moving van with Rosa's and Paul's things.

"Wow! It's hot!" said Meaghan. "After I change my clothes, can I go to the pool?"

"Sure," said Sheena. "I may join you. First, I want to see how Regan and Mo are decorating the reception area."

Meaghan frowned, looking confused. "Who's Mo?"

Sheena couldn't help the smile that spread across her face. She and her sisters had fallen in love with the sweet guy who'd befriended Regan. "He's the man helping us decorate the hotel. He and Regan quickly have become good friends. She's hoping to work with him one day, after our year of Gavin's challenge is over."

"But who's going to run the hotel?" asked Meaghan.

"Though I want to remain a part of the operation, we'll have to hire a manager, someone who understands the business better than the three of us."

"Oh," said Meaghan, giving Sheena a worried look. "But I thought you said the hotel could one day become Michael's and mine."

Sheena wrapped an arm around Meaghan. "At some point, my share of the hotel, one-third, might be given to you and Michael. In fact, you might want to go to the hotel school at Cornell or to a hotel program at another university to study the business."

The distress on Meaghan's face melted away, quickly replaced by a look of determination. It wouldn't surprise Sheena a bit to see Meaghan take over the entire hotel one day. She was just that kind of kid.

Sheena hoped Meaghan would find nice friends in Florida to accept her for who she was.

A few days later, Michael called Sheena from the airport to tell her that he and Randy had landed in Tampa on time and were going to pick up the Explorer in Clearwater and would soon be at the hotel. Relief swept over her. Michael had wanted to drive the car himself from Boston to Florida, but both she and Tony had decided the best way to handle it was to have the car shipped and make Michael responsible for getting it to the hotel.

Standing outside to wait for his arrival, Sheena used the time to check the landscaping. The first chore for Michael and Randy would be to work on that project. It would be hot work, but she and her sisters could save a lot of money by having the boys do it under the training and supervision of Brian Harwood or one of his men.

Brian had become an important part of their lives—helping her and her sisters at the hotel, hiring Tony, and coming to the rescue every time something went wrong. She didn't know what they'd do without him. But after his advances were rejected by Regan, and Darcy had made a fool of herself over him, he'd kept his distance, declaring he wanted nothing more to do with the Sullivan sisters. She, the old married woman, was the one with whom he preferred to do business.

Sheena heard the beep of a car horn and turned to see Michael pull up to the curb and get out of the car. Pride filled her at the sight of him. Tall and athletic, Michael looked a lot like his father, with strong features, dark hair, and brown eyes that sparkled with intelligence and humor.

She rushed into his arms. "Hi there, stranger!"

He hugged her, patting her back in a regular rhythm she found endearing. When they broke apart, Sheena faced Randy.

Randall Jessup III was the child of R.J. Jessup and his first wife, Sharon. Sheena had heard from several sources that the breakup between his parents had been particularly hard on Randy, an only child. From a poor background, his mother had always had difficulty dealing with the wealthy Jessup family. After the divorce, she'd changed from a quiet, submissive wife to someone who was, well ... wild. She'd moved in with a boyfriend in Somerville, and though she hadn't stayed with him, she'd stayed in Somerville so Randy could continue school there.

Randy was shorter than Michael but well-built with a muscular, stocky body. Blond-streaked hair hung over his eyes, making it difficult to see their blue color. A nice-looking boy, his hunched shoulders and the way his gaze quickly left her indicated his insecurity.

Sheena's heart went out to him. She stepped forward and gave him a quick squeeze. "So, you're going to be under my control this summer?" she teased.

He grinned and shrugged. “Guess so.”

She placed a hand on his shoulder. “Don’t worry. As long as you obey our family rules, it should be easy.”

“Mom!” Michael protested. “You make it sound as if we’re in kindergarten. Randy and I are going on eighteen. You don’t have to treat us like babies.”

“I don’t expect to have to do that,” Sheena said calmly but with a warning note to her voice.

Michael made a face. “C’mon, Randy. Let’s get our stuff inside and then we can go to the pool or the beach.”

Sheena remained quiet as she helped them carry their things into the suite. Tonight, she’d lay down the rules. If Randy didn’t like them, he could leave. And if Michael gave her any trouble, he’d have to discuss it with Tony. She loved having her children around, but she needed to be able to concentrate on doing her duties here at the hotel without worrying about them. The hotel was entering a crucial phase.

CHAPTER NINETEEN

REGAN

Regan stepped back and took a critical look at the small reception office. She'd wanted it to look classy but casual, fitting the style of the hotel.

"What do you think?" said Mo.

Regan studied the sea-green carpet—dark enough to hide footprints and light enough that it wouldn't show the sand that people were likely to drag inside. The walls were a soft gray-green that appeared soothing in the heat of the day and offset the carpet nicely. The light oak counter and the framed, bright, tropical, floral prints in reds, oranges, and yellows added a needed welcoming touch to the room. The two light-brown, Naugahyde chairs would accommodate wet bathing suits if necessary and matched the countertop.

"I think we've done it," said Regan, giving Mo a high-five. The small office was the initial exposure guests had to the hotel, and it was important that it looked nice.

"Now Darcy can finish setting up the front-office system here," Regan said. "Sheena is going to organize the rest of the office. She's good at stuff like that."

"It's a good team," said Mo. He checked his watch. "I'd better go. I'm meeting a friend of Grandma's. She's looking for a new couch."

"Are we all set to meet Sheena's in-laws tomorrow?"

"Yes. I've kept the whole day open. See you then."

Regan walked him to the door and stepped outside with

him. "Thanks again." She gave Mo a quick kiss on the cheek and looked up in time to see Brian Harwood heading their way.

"Nice," murmured Mo, as Brian came up to them.

"Hello, Regan," said Brian. "I'm here to check out the storage room. Sheena wanted shelves added to it."

Regan drew a deep breath and told herself to ignore the fluttering inside her. Still, she needed to be polite. "Brian, I want you to meet Moses Greene. He's opened his own interior decorating business and is helping me with the hotel décor."

Brian shook Mo's hand. "Nice to meet you. Aren't you helping Sheena's in-laws too?"

"Actually, both Regan and I are doing that," said Mo, smiling at Regan. "She's very talented."

Brian bobbed his head. "Right." He left them and went inside.

Mo studied Regan. "Wow! You two are on fire one minute and frozen the next. What's that all about?"

"Every woman around him falls at his feet, and he loves it. Even my niece, Meaghan, is breathless each time she's around him. He'd be nothing but trouble for me."

"I can see why. Be careful, sweetie."

Regan watched Mo cross the lawn toward the parking lot, thankful for his concern. He'd had no problem in understanding how Brian could hurt her.

When she couldn't avoid going inside any longer, Regan entered the reception office.

She was angry at herself for her reaction to Brian. Damn him! He wasn't that good-looking, that wonderful, was he? And why had he sounded so unimpressed by Mo's compliment of her work?

She heard pounding in the storage closet and couldn't resist taking a look.

Brian had a couple of nails sticking out of his mouth as he hammered a board into place. When he noticed her, he turned his back to her to lift another shelf.

"I just want to make sure you're doing a good job for us," Regan announced. She was well aware of how childish she was acting, but she couldn't seem to help herself. Brian messed with her emotions.

He finished pounding a board in place and turned to her, a roguish grin on his face. "I do a good job at everything I do." He took a step toward her.

She intended to back up. She really did. But as his arms went around her, God help her, she leaned into him.

"Regan?" he said, his voice husky. "When are you going to let go of that silly idea of yours and stop fighting what's happening between us?"

Heart pounding, she looked up at him. His brown gaze reached deep inside, demanding too much of her. But when he placed his lips on hers, she couldn't hide a happy sigh that escaped her.

When they finally pulled apart, he smiled at her. "See? That wasn't so bad, was it?"

She shook her head, too stunned by the effect of his kiss to say a word.

"Let's just move forward, shall we?" He studied her, waiting for a response.

"Okay," said Regan. "We'll see what happens, but I can't promise to be more than friends."

Brian laughed. "That's a start. I'll be patient, though I'm warning you my patience won't last forever."

"Anybody here?" Sheena's voice sent Regan spinning away from Brian. She stepped into the hallway to greet her.

"The added shelves are going to be nice. What do you think of the room?" More anxious than she wanted, Regan waited for a response from Sheena.

Sheena gave her a quizzical look.

"Well? What do you think?" said Regan.

"The room is perfect—practical, but very attractive."

Regan glanced at Brian to see if he'd heard Sheena's compliment to her, but he was busy lifting another piece of shelving.

"As soon as you're done here, will you let me know?" Sheena said to Brian. "I want to get things organized here before Darcy puts us through our training session."

Brian stepped out of the closet. "Sure thing. What do you hear from Tony?"

"He's on his way. He's driving his truck and bringing all of his tools."

"Good," said Brian. "There's work waiting for him. We all need to sit down and discuss final plans for rebuilding the house. I want his input on the plumbing and electricity."

"Sounds good." Sheena turned to Regan. "C'mon, I'll treat you to a cup of coffee at Gracie's. The kids are all here, and I already feel the need for a jolt of caffeine."

Regan laughed and followed her sister out of the registration office. But her mind remained on Brian's kiss. She couldn't deny her attraction to him, but she knew a lasting relationship needed more than that. And she still wasn't sure of him. Or herself.

CHAPTER TWENTY

DARCY

Darcy fought to control her impatience as she went over the necessary protocol in registering a guest for the hotel one more time. Neither Sheena nor Regan was used to the front-office system she and Chip Carson had set up, and trying to teach them was a chore. She looked up from behind the registration desk as Chip entered the building. Blond and buff, he was the type of guy she'd always been attracted to.

"How're things going?" Chip asked.

"Maybe you can explain things better than I," Darcy said diplomatically. "It seems to be confusing. As you talk, I'll make notes and then type up a 'cheat sheet' for us."

Darcy stood by as Chip went over the procedure, detailing each step. Writing furiously, she noted each one. She'd been finding herself less and less interested in computer stuff now that she'd begun working on restaurant reviews. Nick had sent her a restaurant review he did recently and asked her to change it up a bit. She'd rearranged some sentences, added a few words and, hands ice-cold had sent it in. It came back to her with one small correction and a happy face that didn't do justice to the smile on her own.

"Any questions?" Chip asked, bringing Darcy back to the moment.

"I think I've got it," said Sheena.

"Me too," Regan said, giving Darcy a roguish grin. "Better type up that cheat sheet, though."

Darcy laughed and lifted the notepad. "Got it here. As the other rooms come online, we'll follow the same procedure."

Sheena checked her watch. "Gotta go. I've got a hungry family to feed, and I want to make sure everyone is on board with the family rules."

"Good luck," said Regan. She and Darcy exchanged doubtful looks. During spring break, Michael had been a challenge to all of them with his swings in moods and his laziness. And now that he had a friend with him, they suspected there'd be even more trouble.

"Want to go out this evening?" Chip said to Darcy. "It's getting late, and I need a little fun."

Darcy narrowed her eyes at him. "What about your girlfriend, Mel? Are you broken up for good or is it just a little tiff between the two of you like last time? I don't want any more scenes like that and have you leaving me abandoned and feeling like a fool."

"*Ex*-girlfriend," Chip amended. "This time, it's for real. I promise."

Darcy turned to Regan standing by. "Want to join us?"

Regan shook her head. "Mo and I are working on Rosa and Paul's house. I'm meeting with them again tonight."

"Okay, see you later, Darcy," said Chip. "I'll pick you up at seven."

After he left, Regan gave Darcy a questioning look. "I thought you told me you weren't interested in him."

"I'm not. At least I don't think I am. Actually, I'm not interested in getting serious with anyone right now." Darcy was not about to tell her sisters about the special moments she'd shared with Austin. They were flukes, she'd decided. Besides, she'd already told her sisters that as soon as the year was up, she was going to take off and do some traveling while starting the novel she'd always wanted to write.

###

Though she wasn't interested in Chip as a boyfriend, Darcy fussed over her appearance. The last time she'd been on a date with him, a friend of his ex-girlfriend had made cruel fun of her appearance.

She slipped on a solid blue, cotton sundress. Sleeveless, V-neck, and above the knee, it was daring without being obvious. She hooked a silver chain holding a flower pendant around her neck and slid silver hoops into her earlobes. Stepping in front of the mirror, she studied herself. She wished she didn't have red hair, but others had told her that those rebellious curls and her sexy shape fit her personality.

When Chip appeared at the door to her suite, Darcy was ready for an evening of fun.

"You look great. Ready to go?" Chip led her to his Jeep and waited for her to climb in, before going around the back of the car and sliding into the driver's seat.

Chip turned to her. "Okay if we go to the Pink Dolphin? I hear they've got a new band."

Darcy smiled agreeably. "Okay with me."

They headed down the beach to the bar where Chip had once taken her for what had turned into a dismal evening.

Chip reached over and took hold of her hand. "I've wanted a second chance. I like you, Darcy."

"That's good because we'll be working together at the hotel for quite a while."

He frowned. "That's not what I meant."

She chuckled. "I know."

He let go of her hand to maneuver the Jeep around a pothole.

Darcy looked out at the scenery, content to let the wind tousle her hair. The heat and humidity of the tropical air had given her curls an additional strength she found hard to battle. Better to just let it go, she'd finally decided.

They arrived at the Pink Dolphin to find the parking lot full. Chip drove on and was able to find a spot alongside the road.

"Guess that band is as good as everyone says," said Chip. He hopped out of the car and waited for her to join him. "I told my old roommate we'd meet him here. Hope you don't mind."

"Fine, as long as he doesn't have that creep Kevin with him. I still think he's the one who drugged Regan."

A worried look crossed Chip's face. "Haven't seen him since. I can't think of anyone else who would do that kind of thing. Not in my crowd."

As they neared the bar, excitement filled Darcy. It would feel good to be among people her age intent on having a good time. Sometimes, she felt as if her responsibilities at the hotel were like a heavy chain around her neck.

They entered the crowd gathered around the main bar. As Darcy waited for Chip to search for his friend, she looked around. Her gaze stopped in surprise when she saw Austin with his arm draped across the shoulders of a girl with long blonde hair. Shocked, disappointment coursed through her. She quickly turned her back, unwilling to face him.

Chip came up to her and took her elbow. "C'mon! Bill and Jenna snared a table outside."

Wooden decks were layered in three tiers outside the building. Chip led her to the middle one off to the side.

Bill Schmidt gave her a casual wave. "Hi, Darcy. This is Jenna Lynch." He turned to the dark-haired girl next to him. "Jenna, Darcy Sullivan."

As Darcy sat in a chair next to her, she and Jenna exchanged smiles.

Chip waved a waitress over to the table and faced Darcy. "Margarita, right?"

Darcy smiled back and nodded.

"How long have you known Chip?" Jenna asked her.

"Just a few months. He's helping my sisters and me with computer systems for our hotel."

"Ah yes, I've heard about you. Didn't one of you get drugged at Bill's party?"

"My sister Regan. We think it was that creep Kevin."

"Is your sister okay? And it's really true? You own a hotel?"

"At the moment, it owns us," said Darcy. "But if we get it renovated, opened up, and meet a couple of other challenges, it will be ours."

Their drinks came.

Darcy took a sip and looked out over the crowd. As before, several couples were dancing on the sand. She searched through them for a glimpse of Austin but didn't see him or anyone else she knew.

She turned back to Jenna. "Tell me about yourself. What do you do?"

"A friend and I own a boutique together," Jenna said. "You ought to come see me sometime."

Darcy eyed the floral skirt and coordinated top Jenna was wearing. They looked great on her. "I'd like that. I'll bring my sisters too. We've been so busy working on the hotel we haven't gone shopping for nice clothes in a long time."

"Good. I'll take nice care of you," Jenna said, raising her glass to her.

Darcy suddenly realized there would be life for her after meeting the challenge—a life that didn't include office work, greeting guests, painting furniture, and other chores. Feeling freer than she had for a while, Darcy quickly said yes to another margarita.

Later, when the band let loose with a good dance number, Darcy tugged on Chip's hand. "C'mon! Want to dance?"

He jumped to his feet.

On the sand, Darcy kicked off her sandals and began to dance. Feeling the music flow through her veins, Darcy closed her eyes and let loose. Her steps matched the beat of the music as she twirled and twisted. It felt so good to be free like this, she laughed out loud. When she opened her eyes, she realized a crowd had formed in a circle around Chip and her. She laughed even harder as someone started clapping to the beat of the music and others joined in. Normally she wouldn't like this kind of attention, but she didn't know these people, and for once, she didn't care what they thought of her.

When the music ended, Chip threw his arms around her, and they hugged, breathing hard, laughing together. Looking over Chip's shoulder, Darcy's gaze landed on Austin. She quickly sobered. The girl with the long, blonde hair was still at his side.

Darcy started toward him, but Austin turned around and walked away.

For the rest of the evening, Darcy told herself to enjoy the company, the place, the music, but she couldn't forget the look of dismay on Austin's face.

"Ready to go?" Chip asked.

Darcy rose. "It'll be another busy day at the hotel." She didn't mention she had a meeting with Nick Howard first thing in the morning.

As he drove Darcy back to the hotel, Chip turned to her with a smile. "The band was good, huh? And, Darcy, you're a great dancer." A leer replaced his smile. "You got all the right moves."

Darcy grinned but remained quiet. She stared out at the palm trees lining the road. As much as she liked Chip, she didn't want to become romantically involved with him.

At the hotel, Chip slid the Jeep into a parking space behind the suites building and turned off the engine. He reached for her. "I had a great time. Do you want to go inside together?"

Darcy searched for kind words. "Chip, I'm not interested in anything more serious than hanging out and having a good time."

A look of hurt and disappointment crossed Chip's face.

"I'm sorry." She leaned forward and gave him a kiss on the cheek. "Thanks for a fun evening."

She climbed out of the car, gave him a little wave, and went inside.

Regan greeted her in the living room. "How'd it go?"

"Good, but I'm not interested in Chip beyond being a friend." Remembering Austin walking away with another girl, she fought emotion.

Regan frowned. "Are you all right?"

"Just tired, I guess," Darcy lied.

After a restless night, Darcy awoke to the sound of raindrops hitting the building with tropical fierceness. In the few months she'd been in Florida, she'd learned that even showers had a way of making their presence known in a driving force that slapped surfaces with a resounding smack.

Thinking of her date with Chip, Darcy was glad she'd been upfront with him. She didn't want to date in the same way she had after Sean Roberts dumped her for coming from the wrong part of Boston. Those dates had been an act of revenge, a way for her to try to prove that she was not the loser he and his family thought she was. Now that she'd broken out of that sorry state, Darcy wanted quality, not quantity.

Her thoughts naturally drifted to Austin. She'd been so surprised and then hurt to see him with another girl. But then, why would she think he wouldn't date anyone else? He was a great guy, and they had no real relationship going on between them except for a couple of wonderful kisses. Sighing at the way life could become so complicated, Darcy rose to face the day. She was to meet Nick at Gracie's for an early breakfast, and she didn't want to be late.

After dressing for her breakfast meeting, Darcy hurried toward the restaurant. Austin had suggested she keep talk of cancer out of conversations with Nick, but the big C-word weighed heavily on her mind. And when she saw Nick get out of his car and head to the entrance of the restaurant, he looked so fragile it was all she could think of. In a matter of weeks, his robust appearance had diminished. Now, his shoulders rounded slightly, and his step was slower.

Darcy rushed to greet him. "Hi, Nick! Good to see you!"

He smiled. "Hi, Dee!"

Pleased by the professional name he'd given her, she led him inside and over to her favorite corner table. The restaurant was just beginning to stir with activity. Darcy caught Lynn's eye, and then sat back with satisfaction when Lynn quickly brought cups of coffee and menus to them.

"Gracie's breakfasts are just as good as her lunches," she reminded Nick, still trying to hide her dismay at his appearance.

He looked up at Lynn. "Don't even have to think about it. I'll try those pineapple pancakes."

"They're good," Darcy assured him before ordering her usual—a poached egg on English muffin with cheese.

"I got the short article you worked on for me," Nick said without preamble. "I like what you did with it. You've got a real knack for storytelling. In addition to the restaurant reviews, I want you to begin to do a whole series of articles—stories, more or less—on ordinary people you know or meet. Think you can do that?"

Darcy nodded enthusiastically. "You bet I can. I've bought a couple of editing apps for my computer. I'm getting better about renegade commas."

Nick laughed. "Editing is a never-ending process. I don't care how many times you look at something; there are always mistakes. But if I can teach you something about writing and the editing process, I'm happy to do it. We never had kids of our own, and I hate to think of leaving this earth without teaching someone a little bit about what I learned along the way." He shook his head. "So many newspapers today have typos, misspelled words, and bad grammar in them. I remember when the *Wall Street Journal* was known for its excellent editing. All the papers strived to be like that."

"I know I still have a lot to learn," said Darcy with a ringing sincerity to her voice, "but I'm willing to listen to whatever you say."

Nick gave her a nod of approval. "Listening is the mark of a good writer. There are stories everywhere if you simply tune into them. That's why I want you to concentrate on taking over my column. *Talk Around Town* can go in many directions. If you start with pieces about people, you've got something interesting."

Their meal came. But even as she ate, Darcy listened to everything that Nick said between bites, well aware of the gift he was giving her.

Toward the end of the meal, she realized Nick was becoming tired. She dabbed her mouth with a napkin. "Nick, thank you so much for meeting with me. I'll send you an article as soon as I can. Right now, I'm supposed to meet Regan."

Nick gave her a grateful look and got to his feet. "Send me what you can when you can. I'll call you to set up another meeting."

Darcy rose and went over to him. "Thanks, again." She gave him a quick hug, and in the process realized that the broad, thick figure of St. Nick not that long ago was now wishful thinking. Beneath his clothes, he was becoming bone thin.

Darcy walked Nick out to his car and stood watching him drive away. She wasn't sure what kind of cancer he was fighting, but it was obvious in the short time she'd known him that he was losing the battle.

Sad, she headed to the workshop to see how Regan was doing with an inventory of the tools and equipment there.

As she neared the shop, she heard voices and paused, wondering who her sister was talking to. When she realized that the male voice belonged to Rocky, she cautiously approached the entrance to the workshop. Rocky Gatto scared her with his pirate-like looks and the way his dark eyes seemed to see inside her to where she tried to hide her insecurities.

"Hi, Darcy," said Regan with a cheerful grin. "Rocky is helping me sort through things here. Most of these tools are necessary. Some might not be needed, but we'll still keep most of them."

Darcy was amused by the changes in Regan. Right now, she sounded more like Sheena than the baby sister she used to know.

Rocky stood by, watching her carefully.

Darcy forced herself to smile at him. "Hi, Rocky."

"Hello." His dark eyes swept over her from top to bottom and back to her face. His approval surprised Darcy. Usually Rocky dismissed her with a derisive look.

Darcy searched for something to say. "Gracie said you were an engineer."

"Yes, I did that job on several boats, including tugs, but let's just say I know a lot of stuff about stuff and leave it at that," he said gruffly.

Darcy couldn't stop wondering about the story behind him and pressed on. "You've mentioned meetings in Ybor City. What is that all about?"

Rocky studied her and then spoke. "A number of mutual-aid societies were founded in Ybor City in the early nineteen hundreds. Some continue to this day. I belong to one of them as a way to keep tied to my Cuban heritage."

"Interesting," said Darcy. "It's just a social thing?"

Pain flashed in Rocky's eyes and quickly disappeared. He didn't answer; simply shook his head.

She wanted to ask him more questions but understood "keep away" signs when she saw them. Someday, she vowed, she'd go into Ybor City and see it for herself. Then, maybe she'd have a better idea of what Rocky was doing there.

"'Bye, thanks," Darcy said, ready to leave.

Rocky stopped her. "I saw you talking to Nick Howard. I know him from way back. Is he a friend of yours?"

Darcy nodded, unable to hide the sting of tears. "Yes, I'm doing some work for him."

Rocky's gaze settled on her and then as if making a decision, he said, "Someday I'll take you to Ybor City with me."

Darcy blinked in surprise. Twice now, Rocky had reached out to her. What was that all about?

CHAPTER TWENTY-ONE

SHEENA

As she hurried to her suite following the training session, Sheena could hardly wait for Tony to arrive. With two teenage boys and Meaghan under her wing, she was feeling a little vulnerable. Seventeen-year-old boys who thought they were adults weren't the easiest to handle, and Meaghan, about to turn fifteen, was ... well ... a teenage girl.

Sheena set the meal before them—spaghetti and meatballs for the boys, salad for Meaghan.

Joining them, Sheena sat at the table and helped herself to the salad. "You boys are going to work under Brian or one of his men. I understand he's going ahead with the idea of cleaning up the waterfront area and fixing the dock."

"Yeah, and I'm going to run the sports rental business for both our hotel and the bar next door," Michael said proudly.

Sheena studied Randy. "You're okay with all of this? No one in the family will be spending days simply lounging around. Not with the amount of work that needs to be done."

Randy nodded. "I didn't want to spend the summer with either of my parents. They didn't want me anyway." His matter-of-fact way of stating it indicated this was nothing new.

Sheena filled with sympathy. How, she wondered, could parents do that to their children? Giving him an encouraging smile, she said, "While you're here, you'll be part of our family."

He simply shrugged.

"Mom, we're going to a beach party tonight," said Michael. "The kids I met during spring break have invited us."

"What part of the beach? And how many kids are you talking about? Do you know them well?"

"Mom!" Michael protested. "They're good kids, and the party is just down the beach. Don't worry so much."

"Fine," she said, "as long as you're home by midnight and there's no alcohol or drugs."

After everyone had finished eating, the boys got up and went into the bedroom they were sharing.

Meaghan let out a sigh. "What am I going to do? I haven't made any new friends yet."

"I've been looking into some youth programs at the high school for you. There are some cool afternoon activities."

"Mom, that's so lame!"

"We can talk about it later. In the meantime, how about movie bingeing with me?

A devilish grin lit Meaghan's face. "Can I choose?"

"As long as it's not X-rated stuff," Sheena teased. She laughed when Meaghan made a face and said, "Yuck!"

Meaghan had just fallen asleep on the couch next to Sheena when a knock came at the door. Thinking Tony might have miraculously made better time than he'd thought, Sheena hurried to answer it.Grinning, she opened it. "Hello!"

A policeman stared at her.

Sheena staggered back, her heart pounding so hard she thought she might faint. "Officer? Is everything all right?" she managed to squeak out.

It was then she noticed Michael and Randy sitting on the grass beside the sidewalk.

"These two kids yours?" the officer said.

"Yes ... no ..." Sheena began, cleared her throat, and then said, "Yes." Her gaze swung to the boys. Michael looked ill, and Randy had gone from a sitting position to sprawling face down in the grass.

"Oh my Gawd!" Sheena said. "What happened?"

"I would say too much booze and probably some drugs. We busted up a party on the beach that got out of hand. It was obvious these two could never drive anywhere themselves, so I offered to take them home. I got Michael to confess he was underage. Thought you could probably do a better job of handling punishment than the courts. Next time, though, neither they nor you will have that opportunity." The policeman's gaze drilled into her.

Sheena suppressed a shiver. "Don't worry," she said with a barely controlled anger. "There will be no second chances from me. I'm sorry this happened, officer, and I appreciate your help."

He bobbed his head. "I appreciate your concern. Some parents would laugh it off. I'm glad you're not one of them." He glanced at the boys. "Need help getting them inside?"

Sheena shook her head. "No, sir. For the moment, they can stay right where they are. A couple of buckets of cold water ought to get their attention."

"Here are the keys to the car. It's still at the beach, but I made sure it was locked." He tipped his cap to her and walked back to his patrol car.

Trembling, Sheena watched him turn around in the parking lot and leave. She started to walk over to Michael and found her legs wobbly. Anger strengthened them.

Michael stared up at her with glassy eyes. "Sorry, Mom."

"Do you think you can manage to get inside by yourself?" She helped him to his feet. "Go right into the bedroom."

Regan drove up in the van and got out. "What's going on?" She glanced at Randy sprawled on the grass.

"Couple of drunk and probably drugged boys," Sheena said grimly. "Help me get Randy inside."

The two of them managed to get Randy to his feet and half-dragged, half-carried him inside to the bedroom.

Michael was passed out on one of the beds fully clothed.

Mumbling to himself, Randy allowed them to help him atop the other bed.

Standing back and staring at the two boys, Sheena let out a long sigh.

Regan studied her. "From the looks of it, tomorrow is going to be a really bad day for the two of them."

"In so many ways," Sheena said grimly.

The next morning, Sheena waited until Meaghan had left for work at Gracie's and she'd had a second cup of coffee before going into the boys' room.

"Time to get up, boys!" she announced loudly.

Michael stirred. "Go away. I don't feel so great."

"You get up right now. Hear me?" said Sheena, tugging on his arm until he was half off the bed. "Go take a shower and meet me in the kitchen. And you'd better make sure Randy is with you. Understand?"

Michael's eyes widened. "What's the matter? Why are you so mad?"

Sheena held a shriek of frustration inside. "Are you seriously asking me such a stupid question? After the stunt you pulled last night, just do what I say." She gave him a look fierce enough to fell a lion. "Understand me?"

To his credit, Michael stumbled to his feet and headed into the bathroom.

Sheena hesitated and then went over to Randy. "Time to get up," she said loudly, shaking his shoulder.

He glanced up at her. "Get the fuck away from me."

Thinning her lips, she poked his shoulder again. "Randy, listen to me. I want you up and out of this bed now. You, Michael, and I have a lot to talk about."

"No fucking way," Randy snarled.

"Yes," Sheena said. "And you can stop with the f-bombs. And if you don't cooperate with me now, you can start packing your bags."

He stared up at her bleary-eyed. "Huh?"

Trying to control her anger, she glared at him. "I mean what I say, Randy."

He sat up. "God, I knew it. Staying here was never going to work. I'm not taking this shit from anyone."

"You'd better start packing because you're right. I'm not taking this shit from you. Get dressed and meet me in the kitchen."

"Where's Michael?" he mumbled.

"Taking a shower and dressing for the work day."

"Whaaat?"

Sheena turned on her heel and left. Discovering a policeman at the door of her hotel suite had scared her to pieces. No way did she want that to happen again.

Sometime later, the two boys stumbled into the kitchen looking ragged.

Sheena waved them to a seat at the kitchen table. "Time to talk. Randy, are you staying or leaving?"

"Staying," he murmured, not looking at her.

"Then you better adjust your attitude. There are certain things we don't tolerate in this house. Do you two have any idea how humiliating it was to have a policeman deliver you to the door? If it wasn't for his kindness, you might very well be in jail. And what if you'd tried to drive the car in that condition, Michael? The two of you might be dead."

Michael seemed shaken, Randy uncertain.

"You've lost car privileges for the next two weeks, Michael, and both of you are grounded," Sheena said. "Good thing you're working right on the property and don't need the car to continue your jobs. Do both of you understand the gravity of the situation?" Sheena looked from Michael to Randy.

"Yeah," murmured Michael.

"How about you, Randy?" Sheena said, willing to toss him out of the house if it came to that.

He gave her a challenging look. "I can leave right now, you know."

"Okay, if that's what you want, go pack your things, and we'll call your parents. I'd like you to stay and be part of our family, but we have rules as well as fun. And like you and Michael have planned, being here allows you a chance to play on the summer baseball team. The choice is yours, Randy. Make it a good one."

"Aw, Mom ..." protested Michael.

Sheena swung her gaze to him. "If Randy is going to be a part of our family, he's going to be treated like one. Believe me; no coach is going to permit bad behavior from either one of you and, if necessary, I won't hesitate to let the coach know about your problem. Got it?"

Michael bobbed his head and turned to Randy. "What are you going to do?"

Randy shuffled his feet and then looked up at Sheena. "Okay if I stay?"

"As long as you follow the rules. You may get away with bad behavior with your parents, but I'm not like them."

"I know."

As Sheena left the room to go into her bedroom, she heard

Randy say, “Your mom’s a hardass, but she’s cool.”

She smiled. *Good for Randy*.

CHAPTER TWENTY-TWO

REGAN

A couple of days later, Regan clutched her hands nervously as she stood beside Mo outside Rosa and Paul's house. They'd placed furniture, hung paintings, and displayed decorative pieces throughout the space in what she considered a perfect blend of color and shapes.

Mo patted her back. "No worries, sweetie. They'll love it."

"I hope so. This is my first time at doing a job with you, and I want it to be perfect."

He squeezed her hand. "I understand, but don't let them see how uncertain you are. You're naturally good at this, Regan."

Paul, Rosa, and Sheena strode up the front walk toward them. "Let's see what the two of you have done," said Rosa. "Can't wait to move in. Five days in a motel are enough for me."

With a flourish, Regan opened the front door of the house. "Please come into your beautiful new home."

Regan and Mo followed the others inside and listened for comments.

"Lovely," gushed Rosa. She clapped her hands and turned to Paul with a smile. "I can't believe it's ours!" She hugged him hard and then turned to Regan and Mo. "I couldn't have dreamed anything better."

Regan let out a sigh of relief. While the reds and oranges requested by Rosa would not be her color choices, she and Mo had worked hard to come up with color combinations that were pleasing, contemporary, and yet a little bit old-fashioned like Rosa and Paul had requested.

Sheena gave her a hug. "Perfect for them," she whispered. "Can't wait until you and Mo can do a house for me."

Regan grinned, pleased and worried at the same time. It was one thing to work for an understanding, appreciative family. It would be another thing entirely to work for strangers like Mo wanted her to do in the future.

After the group had toured the house, Mo spoke to Rosa. "As long as you're satisfied with the results, we'll get together for a final review of everything tomorrow. What time would you like to meet?"

"Tomorrow afternoon," said Rosa. "That will give me time to get the last of our things settled. And please have several business cards ready. I'm sure I'll be able to hand some out for you."

Regan's heart warmed at Rosa's generosity. Rosa wasn't her mother-in-law, but Rosa felt like family to her.

Mo signaled her, and they left the house together. "Thanks so much. We did a good job together. You've certainly earned a percentage of my fee."

Regan shook her head. "No, consider it the fee for learning about the business from you."

"You've earned it, Regan. I'll take care of it," he said, giving her a broad grin. "In the meantime, have fun tonight with Chip. Juan and I are going into Tampa." He wiggled his eyebrows. "Dinner and dancing."

Regan laughed. She'd met Juan Cardoza and thought he was as cute as Mo.

Waiting for Chip Carson to pick her up for a date, Regan

paced back and forth across the carpet in her bedroom. She'd been attracted to Chip from their first meeting, during which he'd ignored her. While Brian Harwood persisted in wanting a relationship, Chip had always acted as if he couldn't care less. This intrigued her because guys usually made a play for her. She didn't know whether to be flattered by his behavior or worried.

Regan turned at the sound of a knock on her bedroom door. At the last minute, Darcy had agreed to go with them as the date of a friend of Chip's who was unexpectedly in town. Seeing Darcy now, dressed in her favorite green sundress, her hair a halo of red curls, Regan felt a surge of love for her sister.

"You ready?" said Darcy. "They should be here any minute."

Regan twirled around for her. "What do you think?"

Darcy gave her an "are-you-kidding-me?" look. "You even have to ask? You're beautiful, as always."

Though Regan smiled, her nervousness returned at the thought of keeping the conversation going with Chip. He was all about computers, and a lot of that talk confused her. Her lack of knowledge had turned off guys before, ruining several dates.

The door buzzer sounded. Regan swallowed hard and followed Darcy through the suite to answer it. Darcy opened the door. Chip—the picture of surfer-boy with his muscular body and sun-streaked hair—smiled at them. "Wow! You two look great!" His gaze rested on Regan. "Really great."

"I guess you're Drew Chaplin," said Darcy, holding out her hand.

"Oh, yes!" Chip said, dragging his gaze away from Regan. "Drew, this is Darcy, and that is Regan."

"Hi." Drew grinned and shook Darcy's hand before turning to Regan.

Tall and thin, Drew's hazel eyes sparkled with intelligence behind his black-framed eyeglasses. His strawberry-blond hair, regular features, and wide smile were pleasing. Regan glanced from him to Darcy. Seeing Darcy's smile, the tension that had gripped Regan eased. It was going to be a fun evening.

"Thought we'd go up to Clearwater to a place that's supposed to be real special."

"Tamales?" said Darcy.

"That's a hot spot for sure, but we're going upscale for the two of you." Chip's voice was full of pride. "Gills is a nice seafood place for dinner."

He held out his arm, and Regan took it.

Gills, as reflected by its name, was a restaurant whose décor was devoted to fish. A large aquarium greeted guests by the front door, and in a back room where they were seated, another aquarium sat against a black wall. Strategically placed lighting exposed jellyfish whose transparent bodies moved in the blackness rhythmically as if orchestrated by the soft music playing in the room.

Awestruck, Regan stood and stared at the beauty of it, impressed by how something so simple, so natural, could make such a strong statement.

"Nice, huh?" said Chip.

Regan nodded, wishing Mo could see it.

They were seated at a small, white-clothed table in the corner of the room. Their water glasses were efficiently filled by one server, and then a waiter approached with menus.

"Good evening," he said, as he handed out the menus. "May I get you something to drink?"

"White wine okay with everyone?" Chip asked. At their

nods, he ordered a bottle of pinot grigio, and then they all perused the menu. Regan smiled at the interest Darcy was showing in all the details of both décor and service. Little did the guys realize that a restaurant review of the place would, no doubt, show up in the *West Coast News*.

Regan studied Chip, who, at the moment, was talking baseball with Drew. Out of the office, he seemed more relaxed, more worldly. Chip noticed her looking at him and gave her a smile.

"Do you know what you're going to order?" he asked, picking up his menu again.

"Not yet. There's so much to choose from."

He laughed. "Order anything you want. I'm working for a very wealthy client."

Regan joined in the laughter of the others.

"Yeah, but we're the nicest. Right?" teased Darcy.

Settling his gaze on Regan, Chip nodded.

Later, as Regan took bites of the crab-stuffed snapper she'd ordered, she listened as Chip told of how he'd once played a gag on one of his college professors. Instead of being amused by the cartoon he'd drawn, the man had been furious and had kicked him out of the course.

"Thus, my art career ended, and I decided I'd better stick to computer stuff," Chip said.

"A good thing you did," said Regan. "We've needed your help." At a discreet cough from Darcy, she quickly added, "Of course, Darcy is able to do a lot of the work too."

Chip grinned. "Yes, she's good." He raised his glass of white wine. "Here's to the Sullivan sisters!"

Laughing, Regan lifted her wine glass and clicked it against Darcy's.

Drew's cell rang. He glanced at it and picked it up. "Hey, Austin! How are you? Yeah, I'm back in town for a few days.

Any way we can hook up?"

Regan and Darcy exchanged glances. "Is Austin in town to help put up the sign for the hotel?"

"I don't know," said Darcy. "Sheena didn't mention it."

"All right," Drew said on his cell. "I'll meet up with you and Jasmine tomorrow. See you then." He clicked off the call and gave them an apologetic look. "Sorry. Just catching up with a buddy of mine."

"No problem," said Regan. "By any chance was that Austin Blakely?"

Drew looked surprised. "Yeah, how do you know him?"

Regan explained their use of Austin's wood carvings. "He's a really nice guy," she ended, suddenly aware of the frown on Darcy's face.

Light conversation continued as they finished their meals.

When the waiter asked if anyone wanted dessert, everyone but Darcy shook their heads.

"If you don't mind, I'd like a look at the dessert menu," said Darcy.

"Gonna order one?" teased Chip.

"Yep," said Darcy. "I want to taste as much as I can. So far, the food has been delicious."

Regan knew exactly why Darcy wanted to try a dessert but kept her mouth closed. Dee Summers was doing her job.

CHAPTER TWENTY-THREE

DARCY

Darcy tasted the *Crème Brulee* and let out a sigh of satisfaction, glad for an excuse to try to keep her mind off the conversation Drew had had with Austin. He'd said he'd meet up with Austin *and Jasmine*. No doubt Jasmine was the attractive blonde Darcy had seen with Austin at the Pink Dolphin. Darcy took a last bite of dessert and dabbed at her mouth with her napkin, scolding herself for turning a couple of sweet moments with Austin into something that apparently wasn't as magical for him.

"Ready to go?" Regan asked her. The guys were already on their feet.

Darcy put down the menu and rose. "Sorry. I was studying it and didn't realize you were ready to leave."

As she walked out of the restaurant beside Drew, Darcy reminded herself that Austin had a life of his own that didn't include her. Now, even though it hurt, she decided to try and forget him and enjoy Drew, who seemed like a nice guy.

"There's a cool bar down the street. Let's walk there and have an after-dinner drink," said Drew. "It's great to be here and away from work."

The four of them headed down the sidewalk.

"So, you do computer work," said Drew, making conversation. "What hobbies do you have?"

"I'm a writer," Darcy said and then caught her breath. It sounded so real, so professional. And yet, with her lack of experience, was it like lying?

"Really? Sounds interesting. What do you write?"

Darcy felt her cheeks grow hot. "Actually, I want to write a novel. Right now, I'm just working on some short articles for a newspaper."

"Sounds interesting. It's not my thing. I'm like Chip—into computers, numbers, and such."

"Numbers are easier to work with," Darcy admitted. "But after my year at the hotel is up, I want to travel and have time to write my book."

"You're not going to stay in Florida?"

Darcy shook her head. "I don't think so. It depends on what work the hotel will continue to need from me."

"Isn't the hotel business exciting?"

"I don't know," said Darcy, chuckling. "We haven't even opened yet."

Drew stopped walking and looked down at her. "Know what, Darcy? I like you. You tell it like it is."

She smiled up at him.

The rest of the evening was fun—drinking, dancing, and good conversation. Her first impression of Drew's likeability proved to be the real thing. He was a nice guy who didn't take himself too seriously. She liked him a lot.

While Regan and Chip were dancing, Drew offered Darcy his hand. "Let's walk out onto the dock and get some fresh air."

Darcy took his hand and slid off her bar stool. "Sounds good. It's hot in here."

When they stepped outside, warm, humid air caressed her. Darcy breathed in the smells of the inlet—salt water, engine fuel from the motorboats tied up to the dock or sitting in nearby boat slips, and the occasional whiffs of smoke from cigarettes.

"Beautiful night," commented Drew, leading her out onto the commercial dock the bar operated. The glow from the walkway lights edging the dock every few feet shone on the worn, wooden slats and spilled out onto the water below.

Darcy stopped and gazed down at the shadows she saw flitting about. "Good fishing," she commented.

"Do you like to fish?" Drew asked her.

"I don't know. I've never tried," she said.

He tugged her to him. "There are a lot of things I'd like to teach you," he murmured, and then lowered his lips to hers.

Darcy adjusted her thinking, deleting Austin's broad, solid body from her mind, accepting Drew's tall, thin shape in its place.

When they pulled apart, Drew smiled. "Nice."

"Yes," Darcy agreed.

Happy now with the contact they'd made, they easily moved together to go back inside.

As they entered the bar and joined Regan and Chip, Regan glanced up at her and shot Darcy a questioning look.

"We just went outside for some fresh air," Darcy explained.

"Want to dance?" Drew asked her.

"Sure." Darcy followed him out to the dance floor set up in the middle of the bar. They no sooner had reached it when the DJ put on a different song—a slow one.

"Even better," said Drew, drawing Darcy into his arms.

They moved well together, Darcy thought, trying to chase mental images of Austin away as she settled into Drew's embrace.

That night, after saying goodbye to their dates, Darcy and Regan sat on the couch, talking softly.

"Drew seemed like a good guy," Regan commented.

"Yes," said Darcy, forcing a positive tone to her voice. "He really is."

Regan narrowed her eyes at her. "What are you not telling me?"

"Nothing," said Darcy, lying through her teeth. "How about you and Chip? It looked like you were having a good time."

"We did." A smile spread across Regan's face. "Oh, Darcy, he's as great as I thought he might be. And not once did he make fun of me for not understanding what he was trying to explain. You know I don't understand computers too well. And then when we were dancing, he whispered the sweetest words to me. Who knew he was such a romantic?"

"Chip? A romantic? Wonders never cease." Darcy reached over, took hold of Regan's hand, and squeezed it. "I'm happy for you. I really am."

"I'd better get to bed," said Regan, getting to her feet. "Another early day tomorrow."

"See you in the morning," said Darcy, making no effort to get up. She knew it would be a long time before sleep would come to her. She had too many things to sort out in her mind.

The next morning, after she'd checked the website for activity, Darcy did a few updates and then wrote down notes on the visit to Gills. She decided to go ahead and write a practice restaurant review for Nick to critique.

Florida was full of good restaurants—many of them very casual. Gills was set apart by décor, service, and the upscale menu. Her thoughts flew to Drew. He worked for a company in Atlanta, Georgia, and had a nice position in their IT department. Still, both he and Chip had spent a lot of money on the evening. She'd have to write the review in such a way that people would understand that, though Gills was relatively expensive, it was a special place.

Sheena walked into the office and took a seat opposite her. "How'd your date go? Regan is bubbling over with excitement."

"Drew is a nice guy, and we got along well. He lives and works in Atlanta, though, so I'm not sure if anything will come of it. How are you? Tony arrives today. Right?"

Sheena's smile lit her hazel eyes. "Yes. He's taken care of business up north and is finally on his way. That's another reason I needed to talk to you. Meaghan will move in with you and Regan. So, we'll have to work out sleeping arrangements for when you and Regan are out. Even so, it's much better than having the boys bunk in with you, because I need to keep an eye on them."

"But the suites can connect, right?" said Darcy. "You ought to be able to stay in your suite and be available to her. And she is going to be fifteen sometime soon, right?"

Sheena raised a hand in protest. "I know you think I'm babying her, but I want her to feel safe and secure."

"Okay, we'll work it out," said Darcy. "How are the boys doing with their curfew?"

Sheena let out a long sigh. "It isn't easy being the big, bad mom. But it's really important for me to make a point, and the point is they could've been in big trouble if the policeman hadn't helped them."

"Michael isn't happy about it, I'm sure. What about Randy?"

"I think he's surprised by my reaction. I get the strong feeling his mother is so busy partying herself, that she doesn't care what he's doing. Pretty sad, if you ask me."

Darcy nodded in agreement. "Guess it's a good thing you're naturally bossy, huh?" she teased.

Sheena laughed. "Guess it's a good thing I had you to

practice on, huh?"

Feeling closer to Sheena than she had in years, Darcy smiled. "Want to take a look at the new pictures on the website?"

Sheena pulled her chair over next to Darcy's, and they pored through the photos on-line, discussing marketing ideas. They'd already started promoting the idea of special discounts for reservations made during the early renovation period.

Darcy's cell rang. She picked it up. *Drew*.

"Hey there," Drew said. "I was wondering if you would join me for a double-date with my friend, Austin? It should be another fun evening."

Trying to hide the spurt of pain that stabbed her, Darcy managed to say, "No thanks, I've got plans. But thanks for thinking of me." No way could she meet Austin under those circumstances.

"Well, maybe another time," said Drew. "I had fun with you last night."

"Yes, me too," Darcy said. "It was ... nice."

Darcy clicked off the call and turned to find Sheena's steady stare on her.

"What was that all about?" asked Sheena. "What plans do you have tonight?"

"I don't know yet," Darcy replied, determined not to get into any such discussion with her older, sometimes bossy, sometimes nosy sister.

CHAPTER TWENTY-FOUR

SHEENA

Excited, Sheena ended her call with Tony. In just a few minutes, he'd be at the hotel. God! She'd missed him, needed him!

She went into the bathroom, ran a brush through her hair, and went outside to wait for her husband.

When his silver truck pulled into the parking lot, her heartbeat sped up. There was something to be said about the old cliché, "Absence makes the heart grow fonder." From behind the windshield, Tony's grin was electrifying. He jumped out of the truck, rushed over to her, and swept her up in his arms.

Laughing, she hugged him to her, loving the feel of his strong, solid body next to her. It felt so right to have him with her again. She lifted her face.

Tony's lips met hers in a hungry kiss that told her how much he'd missed her.

When they pulled apart, Sheena caressed his cheek. "Glad to have you home."

"Me too." He looked at the suites building. "Guess this is it for now. The sale of the business isn't going through for a while."

"Troubles?" Sheena asked.

"The financing has been an issue. It'll all work out, I'm sure, but it will take time."

Sheena's excitement ebbed. She hoped he was right. Tony

was sometimes overly optimistic about things, and they were counting on the sale of the business to make the move to a house.

Tony lifted her chin. “Hey, don’t be such a worrywart. It’ll be fine, and at least we’re together as a family again. Now, come and look at the sign I picked up at Austin’s workshop. I talked to him on the phone. He’s here in town, so I’ve invited him to come to our ceremony when we put it up.”

“Nice,” said Sheena. “We’ll have a small celebration at Gracie’s. I’ll talk to her about it.”

Tony looked around. “Where are the kids?”

“Working,” said Sheena.

Tony grinned. “Hey, maybe we could ...”

She cut him off. “Sorry. Things are a lot different with Randy and the kids here. Remember, the boys are in the second bedroom in our suite, and Meaghan comes and goes from our suite to my sisters’ unit. No privacy.”

“We’ll see,” said Tony, giving her behind a loving pat. “Now, let’s get my gear inside.”

They’d just carried Tony’s luggage and a few other items inside the suite when Michael and Randy appeared.

Tony looked up with surprise. “Thought you guys were working.”

“Aw, Dad, it’s so hot, we had to take a break,” said Michael. “Right, Randy?”

Randy’s cheeks were flushed as he nodded his agreement.

“Did you check in with Brian on this break of yours?” Tony asked.

“Naw, his men are used to working outside. We’re not,” said Michael.

Tony glared at him. “You’d better get back on the job right now. You’ll get used to the heat in time.”

Michael faced his father with a scowl. “What is this? Some

kind of prison?"

"I could be at the beach on Nantucket," said Randy, turning to Sheena and giving her a look that told her he was testing her earlier conversation with him.

"I hope you'll stay—as a member of our family," Sheena said quietly. "Before you came here, Tony talked to your parents about you working for us as well as playing baseball. It's all part of being here. But if you want to go ahead and call either one of your parents, we'll certainly abide by your decision to leave. We'll even take you to the airport. Unlike what Michael says, this is not a prison."

Sheena watched a variety of emotions cross Randy's face—from defiant, to doubt, to resolution.

"No, I'll stay. But like Michael says, it's hot out there," Randy said quietly.

"True," said Sheena. "That's why Brian has you do your outside work in the mornings and why teams play baseball in the evenings, not the afternoons."

"Both you boys signed up for the special summer baseball program at the high school?" asked Tony.

Michael and Randy bobbed their heads together.

"Okay, it's settled then," said Sheena. "As promised, you boys will work part-time for Brian doing whatever he asks of you. That still gives you time for relaxation and baseball. But it also means there will be no slacking off work for Brian. Understand?"

Michael and Randy looked at each other and then nodded.

"Grab a couple of bottles of water on your way out," Tony said.

Once the boys were gone, Tony turned to her. "You've had to put up with this attitude?"

"Yes, this is a hard age for boys. They want their freedom, but it's not time yet. And we're a strict family." She raised a finger. "But, mark my words, Randy is happy with the idea of family and structure. He proved it just now."

Tony gave her a thoughtful look. "At his age, I think I'd rather be on Nantucket."

"With a family that doesn't want you?"

"No, not like that, I wouldn't." He shook his head. "Too bad. Well, let's see what we can do for him. When they come in for lunch, I'll have them help me move the sign."

Later, after she had helped Tony settle his things, Sheena went over to the reception office. Regan and Darcy were there, going over the different package options Darcy had recently put up on the website.

Regan glanced at her and broke into a grin. "The patio furniture we ordered is being delivered next week."

"Any word on the window treatments or the bedspreads?" Sheena asked.

Regan shook her head. "No word yet. It's so frustrating!"

"How's the clearing project by the dock going?" said Darcy. "I want to make that a nice area as soon as possible and post a picture on the web."

"Tony and I just had a little pep talk with Michael and Randy. I know it's tough work, but it needs to be done. And Tony is going to speak to Brian about keeping them busy. At their age, Tony was working on his plumber's apprenticeship."

"Nice to have him back, huh?" Regan said.

Sheena laughed. "Very nice. I need his support. I don't know which is more difficult—teenage boys or teenage girls."

CHAPTER TWENTY-FIVE

DARCY

Hurry!" Sheena said into Darcy's cell phone. "Tony is ready to mount the sign for the hotel."

Darcy shut down her computer and left the office. Sheena had told her that after the sign was put up, they were going to celebrate at Gracie's. She was ready. It had been a long day of reworking the advertising campaign they'd set up. Among other things, she'd had to design and order new brochures. And then she'd done a first draft of the restaurant review for Gills. She knew she would have to edit it before she dared to send it to Nick.

As she dashed to the hotel's front entrance, she was surprised by the crowd gathered around the sign. It wasn't until she got closer that she realized one of the people standing there was Austin Blakely. She came to an abrupt stop.

"C'mon, Darcy," Regan called to her. "We're waiting for you."

Darcy reluctantly made her way to the edge of the crowd and stood behind Rocky, hoping Austin hadn't noticed her.

"Here we go!" Tony announced. He held one end of the sign, Austin the other.

Brian stood by with a hammer to pound big bolts through the four holes in the sign and through the two pressure-treated posts that had been sunk in concrete several days ago.

"Gorgeous!" said Regan. Standing in front of the sign, she

let out a little cheer.

Sheena stood at her side. “Nice job, Austin.”

“Very professional,” said Gracie. “My patrons will like it.”

“Pretty. Pretty,” repeated Clyde with excitement. Of all the people in Gavin’s group, Clyde, with his disabilities, touched her most.

Darcy, not wanting to be noticed, said nothing.

“Okay, guys, let’s tighten those hex nuts,” said Tony, stepping aside as Michael and Randy finished off the installation. They, Brian, Tony, and Austin stood back and beamed at the round of applause the crowd gave them as Regan took pictures.

“Okay, everybody, time for a celebration! Gracie’s is open for our private party,” said Sheena.

Gavin’s people led the way. While Regan stayed back to talk to Austin, Darcy decided to make a run for the suites building.

“Hey, Darcy!” called Regan. “Come say hi to Austin.”

Stifling a wish to choke her sister, Darcy sighed and turned to them. “Hi, Austin!”

His smile was friendly as his gaze settled on her. “Hi. I heard you had a great time with Drew.”

“Yes, it was ... nice.”

“Sorry you couldn’t join us tonight,” said Austin. He checked his watch. “As a matter of fact, I have to go.”

“’Bye,” Darcy said, fighting a sinking feeling in her stomach. Seeing him again, she recalled every thrilling second of their embraces, the way his arms had felt around her, and the acceptance of her that she craved. She turned and made a dash for the building.

“Wait!” called Regan.

But Darcy wasn’t waiting for anyone. She needed time alone to pull herself together. She didn’t want anyone else to know that once more she’d fallen for a guy who realized she wasn't good enough for him. Sean had appeared to think she was fine until suddenly she wasn't. Now Austin seemed to be doing the same thing.

The next morning, Darcy sat in the office looking over the restaurant review she'd written. It wasn't too bad. Still, she went through it one more time to check the punctuation and to see if there was a better choice of words. Satisfied at last, she emailed it off to Nick.

She was in the midst of PR work for the hotel when she got an email from him. "Good stuff, Dee. It'll go in next week's paper."

Darcy clapped her hands. "I did it!"

"Did what?" said Sheena, coming into the office.

"My review for Gills will be in the paper next week. My first real newspaper article done on my own." She grinned. "I should say Dee Summers's first article. Nick wants me to do some interviews with local people. I was thinking of asking Holly Harwood if I could write an article about her."

"It might be good PR for the Key Hole," said Sheena.

"I think so too." Darcy rose. "Hold on; I'll be right back. I'm going to ask her now."

The sound of Sheena's laughter followed Darcy as she raced out the door.

Darcy sat in her office, stunned. Holly had told her, "Not everyone wants their story told, Darcy. Choose wisely. There are many silent heroes and heroines around. Seek them out."

Her thoughts flew to Gavin's people. After he'd rescued Meaghan, Sam had made it clear he wanted no part of publicity. She'd have to gently probe the others to see if they'd agree to be interviewed.

Glumly, she went back to work on projects for the hotel. She was deep into a new promotional campaign—something for the holidays—when she heard a knock on the door, and Rocky walked into the office.

"Hi! Can I help you?" she asked him, surprised by his visit.

"You said you wanted to see Ybor City. I'm leaving in ten minutes. Be ready." He turned and left the room.

Surprise erupted into laughter. She picked up her purse, tucked a notebook and pen into it, and called Sheena to tell her that she was leaving.

After greeting her, Rocky got into his truck and stared ahead without speaking. When she tried to talk to him about the various advertising programs she was setting up for the hotel, he glanced at her occasionally but said nothing. Everything about him spoke of tension as they made the awkward, thirty-five-minute drive to Ybor City.

She was staring out the passenger-side window when Rocky announced. "We're here. Take a good look around." He pulled up to the curb in front of a red-brick building with a wrought iron balcony. "I'll meet you back here in an hour."

"Okay, thanks." She got out of the truck and watched him take off down the street. From behind her, she heard a noise and turned as a yellow streetcar trimmed in red headed her way. She walked down the street to a small park and sat down on a bench. To her amusement, a rooster strutted by in search of food. With its narrow streets—some of them still made of brick—red brick buildings, and charming balconies, Ybor City was unlike anything she'd seen. She walked into the commercial district, lured on by the smell of coffee roasting. Restaurants lined the street, along with little shops offering cigars and tourist-type gifts. She picked up a couple of brochures that told of the city's history and decided to find a place to read them. At a small, outdoor café, she ordered coffee and leafed through the information. Now that she was a member of the press, so to speak, she wanted to learn what she could about the place.

Ybor City, she read, was founded in 1886 by Vicente Martinez-Ybor when he moved his cigar factory from Key West to Tampa. For over a century, Ybor City was known as Tampa's Latin Quarter.

Darcy took a sip of the strong, hot coffee and read about some of the social clubs that had been formed. Rocky had mentioned them to her. After reading about the cigar industry and the way Ybor City had thrived, and failed, and then revived into what some now called the "Greenwich Village of Tampa," she became fascinated with the various groups of ethnic people who'd always been part of the city.

Deep in thought, she set down her cup of coffee. Her sisters thought she was impetuous. If she was going to interview people for articles, she'd have to learn how to talk to them, draw them out. Holly had told her to search for heroes and heroines. She glanced around at the number of tourists laughing and talking as they walked along the sidewalk. Down the street, a shopkeeper lounged in the doorway to his store, waving cigars in his hand to attract attention.

She paid for her coffee and stood, wondering where to begin when a voice called to her.

"Darcy! Over here!"

She looked up to find Rocky waving to her from his truck. She hurried across the street to talk to him.

"Get in," he said.

She rounded the truck and climbed into the passenger seat. "Where are we going?"

A deep sigh escaped him. "After talking it over with a couple of friends, I've decided to show you why I come to Ybor

City so often."

Rocky drove away from the commercial area to a quiet street at the edge of the city. He pulled up to a small red-brick house that, though old in design, looked well-tended.

Rocky turned off the engine. "I've made a commitment to keep an eye on things here. Come on in."

Curiosity had always been a driving force with her. Darcy opened the truck door and got out.

Rocky waited for her to reach him, and they walked up the front sidewalk together.

He rang the doorbell and stepped back.

A short, gray-haired woman opened the door. "Back again, Rocky?"

"Yes, I want Gavin's niece, Darcy Sullivan, to meet Duncan."

"Oh!" The woman brought a hand to her chest. "We haven't had time to prepare him for visitors. But, come in."

"Darcy, I want you to meet Elena Garcia, an angel in disguise."

The woman's smile lit her face even as she shook her head in denial. "No angel."

Rocky held the door for Darcy, and she walked into a hallway. The familiar smell of her favorite cleaning spray met her nose. A small living room sat on the left. The room on the opposite side of the hallway was set up with a hospital bed.

Darcy shot Rocky a nervous glance.

"This way," he said, indicating the room on the right.

She stepped into the room and drew in a sharp breath. Sitting in a chair facing her was a person unlike any she'd ever seen.

Rocky stepped up behind her and put an arm on her elbow for support. "This is Gavin's son, Duncan," he said quietly, with an uncharacteristic tenderness to his voice.

The young man who faced her had no arms and gave her a blank stare. Saliva dribbled from his open mouth. A light blanket was wrapped around him, but Darcy noticed that short appendages appeared in place of normal legs.

"My God!" she whispered, and then covered her mouth. When Duncan did not acknowledge the soft cry she couldn't hold back, she let out the breath she'd been holding.

"He's thirty and quite a medical miracle for living this many years. Gavin always insisted that Duncan be kept comfortable in a home-like setting for as long as he lives. That's why he bought this house and hired good people to take care of him. I promised Gavin I would visit regularly."

As they talked, Duncan's gaze seemed to focus on her before sliding away. Darcy's body reacted with an unintentional tremor.

Taking a deep breath, Darcy moved forward. Kneeling on the floor in front of him, she said, "Hello, Duncan. I'm your cousin, Darcy."

Though Duncan's brown-eyed gaze settled on her momentarily, he showed no other reaction.

She rose on unsteady legs and faced Rocky, unable to hold back the sting of tears. "He's always been this way?"

"Yeah. Though his mother abandoned him, Gavin never would."

Elena joined them. "Why don't you come sit down in the living room?"

Darcy nodded numbly.

Rocky took her elbow again, and Darcy allowed him to lead her away on legs gone weak. The shock of meeting Duncan and realizing he was part of the family who'd never known about him continued to churn her stomach. She found a seat in a chair and drew in a couple of shaky breaths.

"I'll be right back," Elena said as Rocky took a seat on the small couch.

Elena returned, carrying a tray of drinks, which she set down on the coffee table in front of the couch. “Thought you might like a little refreshment. Everyone likes my limeade.”

Darcy gratefully accepted a glass of the iced drink from Elena and waited until they all had a glass in hand before taking a sip.

The cool liquid felt good as it slid down her throat. She hadn’t realized how dry it had become. Glancing across the hallway to the room that held Duncan, she felt her eyes fill. Life was so damn unfair! The head that held the blank face was topped by auburn hair the color of Sheena’s. What might a child of Gavin’s have done with his life if given a normal chance at it?

Darcy studied Elena. Though her face was lined with age and care, bright, dark eyes studied her with understanding. She wondered what kind of woman lived with someone like Duncan, overseeing him.

“How long has Duncan been with you?” Darcy asked her.

“Going on twenty-two years now,” the woman answered. “My mother had the care of him before me.” She sighed. “My fiancé died in Vietnam, and I’ve never married. Gavin made sure my mother was provided for and then made sure I had a way to support myself.”

“Do you have someone help you?” Darcy asked. She couldn’t imagine Elena lifting Duncan.

She smiled. “My nephew, Rafe. He works at the General Hospital during the day but helps me in the evenings. Sometimes my sister drops by. You could say Duncan is part of our family.”

Darcy exchanged glances with Rocky and then turned to Elena. “Rocky was right. You are an angel.” Again, tears stung her eyes, but she blinked them away.

Rocky rose. "We'd better go. I'll see you next week, Elena. Anything more than the usual that I should bring?"

Elena got to her feet. "No, sweet boy, but thanks for asking."

At the term, "sweet boy," Darcy blinked in surprise. She'd never considered Rocky sweet. Now, she looked at him with fresh insight.

"Thank you, Elena," Darcy said, then impulsively leaned over and kissed her wrinkled, tan cheek.

In the hallway, Darcy stopped and looked in on Duncan once more. "'Bye, Duncan," she called as if he could react to her. Still, he was a member of her family and would, she decided, be treated like one.

After Darcy and Rocky were situated in the truck and on their way back to the hotel, Rocky turned to her. "I'm glad you know. I wasn't sure how you'd react, but you did just fine." His lips curved for a moment and then went back to their usual somber position.

Feeling as if she'd been given a wonderful gift with his smile, Darcy gazed out the window, watching the scenery go by, wondering what her sisters would think of Duncan. Gavin might not have been welcome in her father's home, but she was proud to be a relative of his.

CHAPTER TWENTY-SIX

SHEENA

Sheena put the finishing touches on the lasagna that Tony loved so much. She'd made two big batches. The boys had settled down to working outside in the mornings and doing occasional special projects in the afternoon. By dinnertime, they were both ravenous. Tonight, her two sisters and Tony's parents were going to join them at the rented table and folding chairs that formed an impromptu dining room in the suite. She couldn't wait until she and Tony were able to have a real home of their own. She'd just cleaned greens for a salad when Meaghan and the boys came in from the swimming pool. "We're having company for dinner so get dressed for it."

Shoving and pushing against each other, the boys headed into their bedroom.

"I'm going next door," said Meaghan. "I'll change there."

When Rosa and Paul arrived with Tony, Sheena rushed over to greet them.

"Glad you could come," said Sheena. "Are you finally settled in your house?"

Rosa smiled. "We unpacked the last box today."

"I'm never moving again," complained Paul. "You'll have to take me out of there in a wooden box."

Rosa sat down in a chair. "Who knew it would be this hard? Paul's right. This is it for me."

Regan, Darcy, and Meaghan came into the room a few minutes later.

"Great," said Sheena. "Everybody's here."

"I've invited Mo. Hope you don't mind," said Regan. "Afterward, we're going to work on ideas for another client of his."

"Not a problem. We've got plenty of food. Maybe you'll take care of fixing the garlic bread."

"Sure," said Regan. "That's easy."

Sheena turned to Darcy. "You're awfully quiet. Everything okay?"

"Yes, but after everyone sits down, there's something I have to tell all of you. Got some wine?"

Sheena held up a bottle of pinot noir. "I bought a couple of bottles of a very nice wine to celebrate our being together."

"Here, I'll pour," said Tony.

Sheena handed him some plastic wine glasses. "Our kitchenware is still packed up. This is what we have for now."

"Fine with me," said Tony. He poured each adult a glass and handed them out.

The group, sitting in cheap folding chairs, relaxed together. For Sheena, the setting, the group couldn't be better. Meaghan and the boys were playing games on their phones, and the adults were chatting easily together.

"Where did you go today?" Regan asked Darcy. "I saw you get in the truck with Rocky."

"That's what I wanted to talk to you about," Darcy said, setting down her wine glass. "Rocky knew I wanted to see Ybor City, so he offered to take me there. And then he showed me the reason he often goes there. It's Gavin's son, Duncan."

"He has a son?" A thought tickled Sheena's mind. If she was Gavin's daughter, Duncan would be her brother.

"Where is he? What does he look like?" said Regan.

"Why haven't we met him?" said Sheena.

Darcy drew a deep breath. "Because he's unable to care for

himself or interact with people."

Sheena was surprised by the tears that sprang to Darcy's eyes. "He's outlived expectations. He's severely mentally disabled and without arms and normal legs." Tears rolled down Darcy's cheeks. "I've never seen anything like it."

Michael and Meaghan joined them.

"He's like Clyde?" Meaghan said.

"No," said Darcy. "Duncan is abnormally formed and unable even to respond."

Sheena felt cold, so cold. "Where is he living? Can we see him?"

"After Duncan was born, his mother took off. Gavin bought a house in Ybor City and had a family there look after him. Elena Garcia is his caretaker now. She took the job over when her mother could no longer do it. It's become a family affair, with her nephew helping her out. Gavin made sure they all would be taken care of, and Rocky promised Gavin he would visit on a regular basis." Darcy stopped talking and lifted her glass of wine to her lips with a shaking hand.

"Is there anything we can do to help out?" Sheena asked.

Darcy lifted her shoulders and let them drop. "You can talk to Rocky, but I don't know what it would be."

"I'd like to see him," said Regan. "After all, he's family."

A knock at the door stopped conversation.

Regan jumped up. "That must be Mo. I'll get it."

Sheena turned to Tony as they stood. "You haven't been introduced to Mo yet. He and Regan are working together on a few decorating projects. They did your parents' house."

Regan approached them with Mo in tow. "Tony, this is Mo. He's the best interior designer ever and a dear friend of mine."

Tony held out his hand and, with a sweep of his arm, indicated the suite. "I guess you'd call this the "before" of any project."

Mo laughed as he shook Tony's hand. "Regan's told me all about it. When it's time to redo the suites, I hope I can help." He turned to Regan with a smile. "But, Regan here, might not need me."

Sheena smiled at the easy camaraderie between the two of them. Tonight, Mo's purple shirt matched the floral print of Regan's new sundress.

"Come sit and have some wine with us," Sheena said. "Dinner will be ready soon."

Rosa patted the empty chair next to her. "Have a seat by me, Moses. I want to ask you some questions about the patio furniture I want to order."

He smiled good-naturedly and lowered himself into the chair beside her.

"I'd better check on things in the kitchen," said Sheena.

"I'll help," said Darcy, getting to her feet.

"Me too," Regan said, hurrying to join them.

In the kitchen, the three of them formed a group.

"What do you think about Gavin having a son like that?" Regan said. "I wonder why no one ever mentioned it?"

"I imagine it's not something easily shared," said Sheena, realizing how difficult a situation it must have been for Gavin. She wondered if he'd shared that news with her mother and couldn't help wondering again exactly what their relationship was.

"Hard to believe Rocky making the trip to Ybor City to check on him," said Regan.

"I used to be afraid of him, but I'm not now," said Darcy. "Not after seeing him there in the house with Duncan."

"Does he look anything like us?" Regan asked Darcy.

"From what I could tell, he has Sheena's hair. That's all."

Sheena tucked away that piece of information to think about later when she was alone.

CHAPTER TWENTY-SEVEN

REGAN

"Well, what did you think?" Regan asked Mo. "Are they as easy to get along with as your family?"

Mo laughed. "Easier. At least nobody asked me about any girlfriends like my grandmother does." He turned serious. "I'm thinking about asking Juan to marry me. We've been together two years, and I really love him."

"Is that what he wants?"

Mo gave her an uncertain look. "I'm not sure."

Regan couldn't stop a frown from forming. "Why don't you wait until you're more certain that he's at the same place, commitment-wise? I think you should be sure of his feelings before you ask."

Mo remained silent for a moment. "Yeah, guess you're right. I just love the idea of setting up housekeeping with him. Guess after fixing up everyone else's homes, I want one of my own. Ready to work on another project?"

Regan grinned. "Yes. I love working with you."

"Me, too, sweetie!"

Long after Regan had climbed into bed, she lay there staring at the ceiling, thinking of relationships. She hoped Juan wouldn't break Mo's heart. Mo was such a kind, open soul, and Juan didn't seem that serious. Her thoughts settled on Chip. She'd enjoyed being with him. The kiss they'd shared had been so sweet, so nice. Darcy sometimes made "nice" sound unappealing, but Regan liked the calm, comforting feeling she had with Chip. Better yet, he treated her with respect. The next time he called, she'd definitely go out with him.

She rolled over and, hugging her pillow, thought of the surprising news of a cousin they'd never heard of. Uncle Gavin had been a man of mystery. Even now, they were discovering more and more about him. At the end of the year, if they met his challenge, what else would they discover about their uncle?

CHAPTER TWENTY-EIGHT

DARCY

Darcy tossed and turned, trying to get comfortable in her bed. But images of Duncan kept flashing in her mind. It was obvious that he'd been well cared for, but it was a life no one would wish on another. Rocky's dedication to him, as well as Elena's and her family's, had been a surprise. Even now she could see the kindness in Rocky's eyes when he was talking to Elena and hear the tenderness in his voice when he'd talked to Darcy about Gavin's loyalty to the son who'd never be able to speak, or play, or do anything else.

Darcy wasn't sure when she fell asleep, but when she woke, it was with a determination to see people differently. Meeting Duncan, realizing how some people were forced to live, she knew how lucky she was. And even if some people in her past hadn't felt she was good enough for them, she'd push aside her hurt and face life with a gratefulness for those who loved her.

After dressing and eating a quick breakfast, she headed into the office, sat down at her computer, and began to type.

It was almost lunchtime when she'd finished editing what she'd typed. She sent it off to Nick. He'd either like it or not, but either way, her words had come from the heart.

Emotionally drained, Darcy left the office, crossed the street, and walked down to the beach. Fresh sea air, sunshine, and the cry of birds helped erase the tension in her shoulders and ease the ache inside her. She slipped off her sandals, delighting in the warmth on her feet, the feel of the grains of sand against her skin. The cries of seagulls caught her attention. Watching them spread their wings, she whimsically wished she could fly too.

She headed down the beach, sticking close to the water's edge where the sand was packed down. Her walk turned into a run, and soon her hair was flying behind her, a mass of springy red curls. But even as her feet pounded the sand in regular beats, she couldn't escape the memory of her cousin and the limitations he had.

Darcy stopped and caught her breath. Then she turned around and headed back to the hotel, walking slowly, kicking at the frothy edge of the water, letting the water wash over her toes.

At the hotel, she went into Gracie's for lunch.

Meaghan saw her and waved.

Darcy waved back and took a seat at the corner table that was more or less reserved for the family.

A few minutes later, Regan walked in.

Seeing her, Regan hurried over and sat opposite her. "The patio furniture for the first floor of the Egret Building is set up. It looks fabulous. Have you checked for any early reservations today?"

Darcy shook her head. "I will this afternoon. I think we need to go ahead and work on some ads to put in the local newspapers. I'll work up something, and we can talk it over later."

Lynn came over to the table with Darcy's order and turned to Regan. "Do you know what you want?"

"Thanks, Instead of my usual salad, how about a grouper sandwich and a glass of iced tea."

After Lynn left, Regan said, "I can't stop thinking about Duncan. I'm going to ask Rocky to take me into Ybor City the next time he goes."

"Now that we know about him, I'm sure Rocky will understand and be pleased to take you there."

"Funny, we used to think he was very scary, but he's just a quiet guy," said Regan.

"Yes, I know that now."

Regan's sandwich came, and as she began to eat, they sat in silence, each lost in her thoughts.

Darcy finished her egg salad sandwich and stood. "Hate to eat and run, but I've got to get back to the office."

"See you later," said Regan. "Maybe we can talk about the ads this afternoon."

Darcy waved goodbye and hurried into the office, anxious to see what, if any, Nick's response had been to her article.

She checked her computer. An email from Nick was there. It simply said: "Call me."

With fingers grown cold, Darcy punched in his number.

"Yes?" he answered.

"It's Darcy. You wanted me to call you?"

"Yes. I want you to read aloud the beginning of your article."

"Why?"

"Just do it, Darcy."

Darcy swallowed hard and began to read:

> "Angels Without Wings. Angels are usually described as having wings, but I've come to believe that, as someone once told me, we are surrounded by heroes and heroines who qualify as true angels. They are not people one would recognize or, perhaps, even notice in a crowd. They have no wings, no halos. How do I know this? Because I met one yesterday.
>
> This angel is an older woman whose job is to care

for someone who can never tell her thank you, hug her, or even smile at her. Yet she treats him with kindness and respect. I cried when I met him and saw the situation, but she remains strong.

Angels are around us—here in Florida and elsewhere.

How do I know this?

Because I met one."

"Should I stop?" Darcy asked.

She was met with silence, and then Nick said in a quivery voice, "I knew you had it in you to write something like this. I'm handing my column over to you today. We'll forget the restaurant reviews. You need to be doing this."

Darcy sank back in her chair, stunned by his reaction. "You liked it?"

"I loved it," Nick said simply. "Keep to that theme, Darcy. It's a good reminder to all of us to live a better life, to be thankful. Good job, Dee."

He hung up before she could tell him she was scared she could never write anything like it again.

Darcy sat with her sisters in the suite she shared with Regan. After she'd recovered from her surprising phone call with Nick, she'd set to work writing up ads for the newspaper. Now, she was sharing them with her sisters.

"They look really good," said Sheena. "How much will they cost, and how long will they run?"

"They'll run for five Sundays," Darcy said, handing Sheena a sheet of paper. "We'll do one-time ads in a couple of the smaller, weekly papers." She drew a deep breath, hoping her sisters would understand. "I've got some other ideas to discuss with you."

At their questioning looks, Darcy launched into her idea of devoting more than two rooms for the disabled and offering a permanent discount for wounded veterans. "I'd like to see us recognize those who face physical challenges."

Regan gave her a steady look. "Does this have something to do with meeting Duncan?"

"Absolutely. We owe it to Gavin to do something like this."

"What a lovely thought," said Sheena. "I'm impressed with you for thinking of this. It's a great idea."

"Good. Because I've drawn up a special ad for the website. I want you two to take a look at it."

Darcy opened her computer and went to their web page. An ad, showing the American flag, was simple but effective:

"We thank our wounded servicemen by offering them and their families special opportunities to stay with us. Please contact us for arrangements."

"I like it," said Regan. "Simple and direct."

"Me, too," said Sheena. "Maybe we can make better use of our gift of the hotel than we thought."

"And when the house is rebuilt, we can add special accommodations for the handicapped. Heaven knows, I don't want to live there," said Darcy.

"Tony and I don't either," Sheena added.

Regan shook her head. "I can't imagine living on the property with guests hounding you all the time. But if we don't want to live there ourselves, maybe we could rent it out for a lot of money."

"Or turn it into a restaurant," said Sheena. "Remember, Gavin had talked about doing that. In that particular location, it could be just the small, exclusive place he wanted."

Regan's face lit with excitement. "Can I show the plans to Mo? He has his degree in interior design. Maybe he can give us some input in making it into a small restaurant."

"Okay, it's not too late to make changes. The slab hasn't even been poured," said Sheena. "I'm going to call Blackie now. Maybe he can convince Archibald Wilson and his law firm in Boston that we have the right to change the plans for the house."

Darcy smiled at her sisters. A few months ago, this might never have happened. But now they were pulling together like a real team.

Michael stuck his head into the suite. "Mom? When's dinner? Randy and I have to eat before we go to baseball practice."

Sheena sighed and rose. "Guess I'd better go."

Darcy got to her feet and impulsively threw her arms around Sheena. "You're a good mom, Sheena."

Sheena's face brightened. "Thanks. Congratulations on your newspaper work. Can't wait to read your first column."

Darcy's stomach fluttered. The thought of doing a column every week scared the hell out of her.

CHAPTER TWENTY-NINE

SHEENA

"See you later, boys!" Sheena said, waving Michael and Randy off to their practice. "Good luck!"

She smiled as she watched the two of them head to the Explorer. Michael was laughing at something Randy was saying. Since the confrontation with him, Randy had become a real part of the family, making his bed in the morning, helping with projects around the hotel, and treating her with the respect she deserved.

Sheena wrapped her arm around Meaghan, who was standing beside her. "Shall we go for a walk on the beach before we fix dinner for you and Dad?"

Meaghan nodded. "Okay."

They headed out. As they walked across the hotel property, Sheena studied her daughter. Away from her cruel friends in Boston, Meaghan's normally sweet temperament had reasserted itself. Meaghan was growing fast, losing her childishness as she became a beautiful young woman. The day would come when she, like Michael, would be gone away to school. They crossed the street and walked down the boardwalk to the sand. Slipping off their sandals, they headed down to the water. As always, Sheena felt a sense of peace as the blue waves she faced moved in a regular pattern, flowing one after another to the shore and pulling back again.

"Mom?"

She turned to Meaghan. "Yes?"

"How am I going to make new friends when I'm working at the hotel?"

Sheena's heart squeezed. "Aw, honey, I'm sorry. I know how important it is to have friends. Let's call the school to see if they have any new summer programs going on, ones you're more interested in."

As they walked down the beach in step, Sheena realized Meaghan was almost as tall as she. Sheena couldn't help thinking of the day Meaghan would be a bride. She was so lost in thought that it took her a moment to realize Meaghan had stopped in front of a group of kids gathered together, sitting on their beach towels, listening to music.

"You new in the neighborhood?" Sheena heard one girl ask Meaghan.

"Yeah, I'll be a freshman at the local high school. Do you live around here?"

Sheena was both surprised and pleased by Meaghan's outgoing behavior. She gave her a little wave and walked on, turning back just once to make sure the conversation was going well.

Working in the restaurant had helped Meaghan's self-confidence, she realized, mentally crossing her fingers that Meaghan had found good new friends.

The solitude gave her time to think about her sisters and how they'd changed since coming to Florida. Her thoughts flew to Tony. He'd changed too, happy with his new situation. He'd begun his job with Brian and found himself surprisingly busy. It was a great way to work for state certification, and the steady income would be nice. During troubling times, owning a small business wasn't all that wonderful.

"Mom! Wait for me!"

Sheena stopped and turned around.

"I did it!" Meaghan's eyes shone with excitement as she

caught up to Sheena. "I talked to a couple of girls my age. And guess what? I'm going to meet up with them tomorrow afternoon here on the beach."

"Great," said Sheena, giving her a hug. "I'm so happy for you. Now, we'd better get back to the hotel. Dad will be hungry."

Meaghan all but skipped as they made their way past the empty space where her new friends had been and onto the boardwalk leading back to the road and the hotel.

Sheena was in a happy state of mind when she entered the suite. Her family was settling down into a normal routine.

When her cell rang, she picked it up and stared at the unfamiliar number. "Hello?"

"Is my son with you?" said an angry voice.

"Who is this?" Sheena asked, frowning.

"Sharon Jessup. I need to talk to Randall right away. He isn't picking up my calls. I need you to put him on your phone right now."

"I'm sorry. He's not here. He's at baseball practice."

"When he gets back, you have him call me." She hung up before Sheena could reply.

"Who was that?" Meaghan asked wide-eyed. "I could hear her screaming at you."

"Randy's mother. I'm not sure what it's all about, but he should call her."

"Randy says she's nothing but a bad word," said Meaghan. "She has a lot of boyfriends."

"Well, I think he'd better talk to her. She's upset about something."

Tony walked in the door. "Hey, there! What's for dinner? I'm starving! You won't believe all the work I got done today." He kissed Sheena and winked at Meaghan. "How are my girls?"

Meaghan smiled. "I made some friends today."

"Good for you."

"Tony, while I make dinner, we've got to talk," said Sheena. "It's about Randy's mother."

"Boring," said Meaghan. "I'm going to find Regan and see if she wants to go for a swim."

"Okay," said Sheena. "I'll let you know when dinner is ready."

Tony grabbed a beer from the refrigerator. "Want one?"

Sheena shook her head. "I'll have a glass of wine instead." She poured herself a glass from the bottle of the previous night.

"It was damn hot out there," Tony said, after taking a sip of his cold beer and letting out a sigh of contentment. "What's up with Randy's mother?"

"I'm not sure. She sounded drunk when she called, demanding that Randy get in touch with her. Believe me, I understand how frustrating it can be when your child doesn't answer the phone, but there was something off about this. I don't know much about her, but the kids don't speak well of her."

"She seemed okay when I talked to her," Tony said.

"What about his father?"

"When I discussed the situation with him, he sounded like a nice guy. A little stiff, maybe, but friendly."

"They're obviously not close. When Randy was talking about spending a lazy summer on Nantucket with his father, he didn't look happy about it."

"Well, we'll follow through and have Randy call his mother." He sidled up to Sheena. "In the meantime, how about a kiss for your hubby?"

Sheena laughed and pushed at him playfully. But when Tony put his arms around her and pulled her close, she nestled up against him and let out a happy sigh.

When the boys returned to the suite hot and sweaty, Sheena handed each a bottle of water. "Take a minute before you dash off for the pool. I got a call from your mother, Randy. She needs you to call her right away."

He let out a snort of disgust. "What does she want?"

"I don't know, but you'd better phone her. She sounded upset."

Randy stomped off to the bedroom and slammed the door behind him.

Sheena gave Michael a questioning look. "Why is he so upset?"

He shrugged. "Randy doesn't like her much anyway, but after hooking up with her latest boyfriend, he doesn't like her at all. They drink too much, and Randy thinks the guy is after what little money his mother has."

Michael reached into the cupboard and brought out a box of cookies. He'd just opened it when Randy stormed into the kitchen.

"Are you okay?" Sheena asked, observing the redness around Randy's eyes.

"My mother says I have to go home, that I can't stay here. My father is threatening not to pay for child support for the time I'm gone. She's furious with him and me. Says I screwed it up for her. I called my father and left a message, telling him what's going on. But he won't care. C'mon, Michael, let's get changed and go for a swim."

Sheena and Michael exchanged looks of concern, and then Michael followed Randy into the bedroom.

Later, after they left, Sheena went into the room she shared with Tony. He'd fallen asleep on top of the bed in front of the television. Sheena studied him. Months of worry about the business in Boston had added a couple of lines to his brow, but his face in slumber looked more peaceful than she'd seen it in months.

Tony's cell phone, sitting on the bedside table, chirped. She saw the name on Caller ID and picked it up.

"Hello, Mr. Jessup. How are you? This is Sheena Morelli. Tony is unable to answer the call."

"My son called me this evening and left a disturbing message. He said his mother wants him back in Boston, so I won't discontinue child support payments. That's absurd! He also says he wants to stay in Florida and continue working for you. What is this about working? I thought he was going to have a fun summer playing baseball."

"Yes, that too. But being part of our family means working together as well as having a good time. I'm sure you understand that."

"Frankly, I don't. I understand your husband has a plumbing business. Surely, you're not training my son to be a plumber."

Sheena held an angry retort inside and then let out a shaky breath. "He's working at the hotel my sisters and I own. And working as a plumber is a respectable job. Is there anything else you wish to say to us, or are you through?'

"Tell my son to call me. This whole arrangement has been unfortunate." He clicked off the call, leaving Sheena with a lot of things unsaid. Furious, she set down the phone, left the bedroom, and went outside to the patio to calm down.

Sitting there, she watched from a distance as Michael and Randy fooled around in the pool. Looking at them, she wondered what the future held for the boy whose parents didn't want him.

CHAPTER THIRTY

DARCY

Darcy walked into the small newspaper office with Nick, feeling as if she were entering an exciting, foreign land. Three people working at their desks looked so professional, so confident that her insides quivered with terror. It was one thing to think of herself as a newspaper woman, but that didn't mean a thing if her co-workers wouldn't accept her.

"Hey, Nick! How are you, man!" said a bespectacled young man, hurrying over to them. An older woman looked up from her computer and smiled. "Good to see you, Nick."

A man talking on the phone at the third desk waved at them and kept on talking.

"Darcy, this young man standing here with us is Jeremy McCarthy. He does our reporting on sports. Jeremy, Darcy Sullivan, known to readers as Dee Summers, is replacing me for my weekly column."

Friendly brown eyes behind horn-rimmed glasses studied her. Jeremy smiled and offered his hand. To Darcy, with his small, thin stature and thinning brown hair, Jeremy looked like the typical, bookish guy who'd worked on his high school paper and made it his career.

"Pleased to meet you," she said, shaking his hand. "Maybe you'll give me some pointers on how to meet constant deadlines."

"Deadlines?" said the other man in the office, rising from his desk to join them. "Pesky little things that grow over time."

Nick introduced her to Bruce Gilman. Black hair hung over a broad forehead and matched his trimmed mustache. A toothpick stuck out of his mouth, even as he exclaimed over her willingness to take on Nick's job.

The last person to join them was a woman Darcy guessed to be in her forties. With her bleached-blonde hair, painted, red lips, and multiple, bangle, bracelets jangling on her arm, Darcy wondered what her role was at the newspaper.

Nick grinned. "Looking good as ever, Lainey. I want you to meet Darcy Sullivan, writing as Dee Summers. Darcy, this is Lainey Edwards, our social events editor."

"What's going on here?" growled a voice behind them.

Darcy turned to see a stocky, gray-haired man walking toward them.

"Ah, here's our illustrious editor, Ed Richardson," said Nick. "Ed meet Darcy Sullivan."

"You're the angel girl, huh? Nick tells me you're eager to learn. If your other columns are as good as that one, you'll do. But none of us is irreplaceable. Right, folks?"

The others around her dutifully bobbed their heads.

"Okay, then, get back to work. We've got a paper to get out tonight."

Nick led Darcy over to a desk in the corner. "You'll share this desk with anyone who needs it because you'll do your work from home and simply hand it over. You okay with that?"

"Yes, that will be the easiest way to meet my deadlines," Darcy said. "I still have my work at the hotel. At least until we can hire a professional to run it."

"Okay, if you don't mind, I think I'd better get home."

"Not a problem," said Darcy, noticing how pale Nick's face had become. She took his arm. "I'll drop you off at your house right away."

He gave her a weak smile. “Sandy should be home by now. I want you to meet her.”

“Yes, I’d like to,” said Darcy. She’d wondered about Nick’s wife, the woman who’d once reminded him of his diet. Since that call on their first meeting, Sandy would have no reason to worry about Nick’s weight. He’d lost so much of it.

They got into the hotel van, and then Darcy drove to a quiet neighborhood where palm trees provided shade, and tropical flowers added color to the landscaping around the stucco, one-story homes. Darcy pulled into the driveway of a small, beige house.

“We’re here,” Darcy said softly, gently prodding him. He sat back in the passenger seat with his eyes closed. “Nick?”

His eyes flashed open. “Oh, here already? I’m sorry I fell asleep, but I’m so damn tired all the time. Not like me at all.”

Darcy got out of the van and went around it to help Nick out of his seat. Though she wanted to, she forbade herself from showing any sadness. Austin had told her it upset some patients, and Nick seemed the kind of person who didn’t want to be fussed over.

As they were making their way up the walk, the front door opened and a pleasant-faced woman came outside to greet them. Her brown hair was streaked with blond. Darcy noted her thin figure and agile step and realized she was quite a bit younger than Nick. As she approached, her gaze landed on Darcy and quickly turned to Nick.

“You okay, honey?” she said, taking his arm.

“Yeah, just so damn tired,” Nick said. “This here is Darcy Sullivan, the one I keep talking about.”

“Oh, yes. The angel writer. Hi, I’m Sandy Howard. I’m very glad to meet you. It’s wonderful that you can take over for Nick on the paper. It means a lot to him.”

“Believe me, it’s an honor for me to be able to do it,” said

Darcy. "I'm learning so much from him. We'll continue working on it together for a while."

"You can stop talking about me as if I'm not here. I'm not dead yet," grumbled Nick.

Darcy gasped. "I didn't mean..."

"It's okay," Sandy assured her. "Gallows humor has become a thing around here." Tears filled her green eyes, but she quickly blinked them away. "It's Nick's thing. Not mine."

After they'd ushered Nick inside, Darcy said, "Guess I'd better be going."

Sandy shook her head. "At least stay for a glass of iced tea or lemonade. It's hot, and you've been busy."

"Thanks," said Darcy, "I will." She was curious to learn from Sandy how best to handle her time with Nick. At the paper, no one had mentioned his illness. Is that how she was supposed to deal with it?

"I'm going to go on into the bedroom and lie down," said Nick. "Thank you for everything, Darcy. I think the gang at the paper liked you. That'll make things easier for you because it gets pretty tense sometimes when deadlines approach."

"Thank you for taking me there and introducing me, Nick. Sometime this week, I'll email you my next column."

He nodded and gave her a weak wave before disappearing down a hallway.

"Come into the kitchen. We can talk there," said Sandy.

Yellow walls and gray, granite countertops welcomed Darcy when she followed Sandy into the kitchen. A glass-topped table sat by a bay window that looked out over a screened-in lanai and pool.

"Lovely," said Darcy.

Sandy smiled. "Thanks. We recently renovated the kitchen and the two bathrooms. I'm pleased with the way they came out. Lemonade?"

"Yes, please." Darcy drew a breath, searching for the right words. "I'm very sorry about Nick. He seems like such a wonderful man. He's certainly been nice to me."

"This isn't the first time he's had cancer," Sandy said. "We thought he had it beat, but now it's come back with a vengeance." Tears filled her eyes once more. "My heart is broken at the thought of him leaving me. It's the second marriage for both of us, and I thought we'd have several years together."

"How did you two meet?" Darcy asked. At first glance, they seemed so different.

"At a Christmas party. Nick was, of course, playing Santa Claus. I'd brought my niece to the party, and when he asked who else wanted to talk to Santa Claus, I raised my hand." A smile crossed Sandy's face. "The things he whispered to me ... I still get giddy every time I think of it. We got married three months later."

"How long have you been married?" Darcy asked, tucking this information away for later use.

"Six years." Tears swam in her eyes. "We won't even have enough time together to get that seven-year itch everyone jokes about."

"What can I do to help you and Nick?" said Darcy, speaking around a knot of sympathy in her throat.

"Just keep on doing what you're doing. Writing and keeping Nick involved at every step. It pleases him no end that you're very excited about doing this. You are, in your own way, an angel, Darcy."

Darcy shook her head firmly. She knew very well she was no angel.

Darcy headed back to the hotel with fresh determination to

do a good job for the paper. She owed it to Nick; she owed it to herself. And she was a little scared of Ed Richardson. He'd made it clear he was not about to accept a bad column from her.

As she turned into the parking lot, she saw an unfamiliar car pulled up to the suites building. Curious, she got out of the van and turned in surprise as Meaghan raced down the sidewalk toward her.

"What's up?" Darcy asked.

"Randy's father is here, and he's yelling at Mom and Dad." Meaghan grabbed hold of her arm. "C'mon, you go talk to him."

"Where's Regan?"

"She left with Mo to pick out some extra tables for the pool. Hurry."

Alarmed by the hint of tears in Meaghan's eyes, Darcy followed her to Sheena's suite.

Meaghan rushed inside, leaving Darcy to stand awkwardly in the doorway as Sheena, Tony, and a tall, distinguished-looking man turned to face her.

"Hi, everyone," said Darcy. "Meaghan asked me to come say hello, but I can leave if this is a private matter."

Sheena waved her inside. "As you are part of the family, you might as well hear this. Randy's father, R.J. Jessup, is here to take Randy home. He says he had no idea that his son was working for us and in a place like this."

Darcy's temper flared inside, burning to burst out of her in a hot flash of words. But with her recent vow to allow people to have their say, she simply said, "Really?" But her tone brought a flush to R.J.'s cheeks.

"Randy told me he was here to play baseball, not to work," retorted Randy's father.

"Hold on," said Tony in a barely controlled voice. "When I

spoke to you, I explained that if we were to have Randy for the entire summer, he'd have to live as part of our family and follow our rules. One of them was to help on this project. You didn't have any problem with that then. Boys this age don't need to lie around all day."

R.J. shook his head. "Randall doesn't need to stay here. He should be with our people. I don't know what my ex was thinking, sending him down here. Where is he now?"

"He and Michael are down at the waterfront on the bay, helping to clear that area," said Sheena quietly.

"I'll go get him," said Meaghan, her voice high with worry.

"I'll go with her," Darcy said. She knew if she stayed to give Sheena support, she'd blow it by telling R.J. he was a total ass.

CHAPTER THIRTY-ONE

SHEENA

Sheena watched Darcy and Meaghan leave the suite and braced herself for more tirades from Randy's father. Tony stood beside her flexing his fingers. She knew he was itching for a reason to smash the guy's face in for his disrespect of them and their family.

She placed a warning hand on Tony's arm. "Why don't we sit down to wait for them? R.J., can I get you something to drink? I made fresh iced tea this morning, and the kids always like my lemonade."

"Just water," R.J. responded. He took one of the folding chairs they were using temporarily and sat, his shoulders straight and stiff.

"Tony?" Sheena prompted.

"Thanks, I'll have an iced tea," he said curtly.

Sheena used the time getting the drinks to draw in and release several deep breaths. She was well aware of their present circumstances, how unfinished the suites were, the state of the hotel. Still, that was no reason for R.J. Jessup, wealthy man that he was, to treat them in this manner. Though she kept an outwardly calm appearance, inside, she was ready to claw his face for his smug look as he gazed around the unfinished room.

At the sound of running feet outside the door, the three of them stood.

Michael and Randy rushed inside the room, stopped, and

faced them.

Randy scowled at his father. "What are *you* doing here?"

"I've come to take you home. You'll spend the rest of the summer on Nantucket with Ginger and me and our two girls."

"Fat chance of that happening," scoffed Randy. "Mom said I could be here. I have written permission to stay here, medical releases, everything I need."

"Well, she's changed her mind." R.J.'s face softened. "I know things haven't gone well between us in the past, but this is a chance to change that."

Randy shook his head. "No, Dad, I don't want to go. I'm a real family member here. They treat me like one of them, and I like it."

Standing beside him, Michael slung an arm over Randy's shoulder. "Mr. Jessup, please let Randy stay. We're having a great summer, and he's playing really good ball."

"Yeah, Dad, I'm playing shortstop, and I'm good at it," Randy said proudly.

"But you have to work here at this ... this ... motel," R.J. said.

Randy scowled at his father. "It's more than a motel. It's going to be beautiful when it's done. What you see is just the beginning. Don't you get that?"

"Mr. Jessup, R.J., you know nothing of the circumstances surrounding this property. I suggest you hold your judgment until it is complete," said Tony.

Sheena couldn't hold back any longer. "Perhaps you've never had to work for anything in your life, but starting out with a project like this can produce good things in many ways. Things like pride in workmanship, a sense of accomplishment, and helping others. I think your son is learning that." She gave R.J. a meaningful look. "He is welcome to leave if he chooses, but I sincerely hope he doesn't.

As he said, Randy has become part of our family, and we'd miss him terribly if he left."

At the flush of emotion that crossed Randy's face, his father closed the mouth he'd opened to speak. "That true, Randall? You like being here? You want to stay?"

"You know Ginger doesn't want me around. Neither does Mom. I'm happy here."

R.J. shook his head and looked at Sheena. "After all I've given him, you'd think he'd appreciate it."

"How about love and attention?" Sheena said quietly. "Why don't the two of you go out to the patio or down to the dock and have some time alone together."

"How about I give you a tour of the property?" said Randy. "You can see what it will be like one day."

R.J. nodded. "Okay, let's go."

After they left, Sheena sank into a chair, feeling emotionally drained. She'd had to deal with snobbery before, but R.J.'s dismissal of the Salty Key Inn really hurt. She and her sisters were working hard to make it attractive. And later, if they met the challenge, they'd be able to do much more with it. But, for now, it would have to be a work in progress.

When R.J. and Randy returned to the suite, Sheena sensed a new ease between them.

"I showed him how everything is going to be fixed up like we've talked about," said Randy with a note of pride.

"Yes, I must say your motel is ideally located. If you ever want to sell, I'd be interested, though, I confess, I'd tear it down and build a new high-rise, something that could bring in a lot of money."

"But that kind of building wouldn't fit into this neighborhood," said Sheena, appalled by the idea. "You'd never be able to get permission to do something like that."

"Ah, there are ways of getting around things," said R.J. with such confidence, Sheena bit back a nasty retort. People like that were ruining many coastlines—all for money.

"Any decision on Randy's staying here?" said Tony.

"Yes, I've told Randy he can stay here for the summer. He turns eighteen in the fall, and I want to be able to celebrate that with him."

Michael gave Randy a friendly push. "So, I still have to share my room with you? That stinks."

Randy laughed. "And I still have to listen to Meaghan whine."

"Oh, you're just as bad as my brother," Meaghan said, and then a wide smile creased her face. "Oh, wow! I guess you kind of are my brother."

"For the summer," warned Sheena.

"Well, I'd better go," said R.J. "I apologize for taking your time."

"We'll be certain to take good care of your son," said Tony, leading him to the door.

"Oh yes, thanks. I appreciate it," said R.J., holding out his hand.

To Sheena's relief, Tony shook it.

"If we need to get in touch with you for any reason, we have the business card you gave us," Sheena assured him.

"Good-bye, son," said R.J. He paused.

Sheena waited for them to embrace, but Randy simply gave his dad a little salute. So much for father-son affection. And that, thought Sheena, said it all.

After R. J. left, Meaghan said, "Can we go out to eat to celebrate tonight?"

Sheena studied the smiles on all three young faces, glanced at Tony, and relented. "Yes. And Randy can choose the place."

"As long as it's not too expensive," said Tony, shaking a playful finger at Randy.

Michael gave Randy a teasing little punch on the arm, and Meaghan sighed.

Tony and Sheena exchanged smiles. Things were back to normal.

CHAPTER THIRTY-TWO

REGAN

A few days later, Regan sat with her sisters in a booth at the Key Hole. It had been a while since the three of them had had quality time together, and she'd missed it. But spending most of her time with Mo was turning into a very good thing. She was learning a lot about interior decorating and meeting a lot of the people in the business.

Listening to Sheena repeat her conversation with R.J. Jessup, Regan felt heat rise to her cheeks. "What a jerk!"

"He truly is. I admit I was very pleased when Randy asked to stay with us. I think working and living with an ordinary family has helped him tremendously."

"It burns me up to know that if his father could buy the hotel, he'd get rid of it," said Darcy. "I was shocked when I first saw the Salty Key Inn, but I've come to like this funky part of the coast with its brightly painted buildings."

"Me too," said Regan. "Some of the places look modest from the outside but are beautiful inside."

"Sort of like people," said Darcy. "Guys, I've got to come up with a new column each week. How am I going to do that?"

"Have you talked to any more of Gavin's people? We know a little about Sam and Rocky. What about the others?" said Sheena, lifting her glass of red wine.

Darcy reviewed the staff in her mind. "What about Lynn Michaels? She said her husband and Gavin were best friends."

"See what her story is," said Regan. "We were told they all

were friends of Gavin's."

"Yes, but some people don't want details of their lives exposed," protested Darcy. "Holly told me that." She looked up as Holly, the owner of the bar, came over to their table.

"Well, it looks like a Sullivan sisters special evening. Have a drink on me."

"Why don't you join us?" said Sheena.

Holly shook her head. "Thanks, but I'd better keep an eye on the crowd. We have a bunch of young people, and I need to make sure they're old enough and sober enough to be here."

Regan had just taken a sip of wine when she noticed Brian come through the door.

He approached them. "Ah, the lovely Sullivan sisters. Are you here celebrating the rebuilding of the dock?"

Darcy grinned at him. "It looks great! Meaghan and I went kayaking yesterday afternoon and used the dock."

"How about you, Regan?" Brian asked.

Fighting against the tide of energy that flowed through her at his steady look, she shook her head. "I haven't had time to do anything like that. I'm working on some projects of my own."

Sheena smiled at him. "Seems both my sisters have a lot of talent that I didn't get."

"Ah, but, Sheena, you keep the project rolling along. That's a talent. Tony talks about all the help you gave him."

Sheena made a face. "Only when he let me. Now, it's different."

"Tony's a good man. I like having him on our team."

"Thanks," Sheena said, beaming.

Regan watched the interplay between them. Brian was a good man. But on a personal level, she was afraid of the way he made her feel. She knew danger when she felt it, and frankly, he scared her to death.

CHAPTER THIRTY-THREE

DARCY

One afternoon some days later, Darcy walked into Gracie's wondering how best to approach Lynn. Lunch service was over, and Lynn, Sally, and Maggie were sitting at a table, sipping cold drinks, and talking.

"Hi, Darcy!" said Maggie. "Want to join us?"

"Sure. Thanks."

Darcy made her way over to the table and took the fourth chair. "Good day?" she asked.

"Busy as ever," said Lynn. "We're building a good business here."

"But busy is exhausting," said Sally. "Guess I'll go up to my room. Good to see you, Darcy. You haven't had lunch here in a while."

"Who was that adorable guy you were with? The one that looked like Santa Claus," said Maggie.

"He's a friend of mine—someone who works for the *West Coast News*. I'm writing a weekly column for the paper."

Lynn's eyebrows lifted. "Really? That's wonderful."

"Yeah? When are you going to write a novel? It's something I've always wanted to do," said Sally, standing and pausing at the table.

Darcy tensed. Writing a short column for the newspaper was one thing. Writing a novel was quite another. "I ... I don't know."

"Well, I'm proud of you for doing the newspaper work,"

said Lynn.

"As a matter of fact, I wanted to talk to you about that," said Darcy, diving into the subject.

Maggie got to her feet. "Okay, I'll leave you two alone. See you later, Darcy."

She left the room with Sally.

"Yes, dear? What can I help you with?" said Lynn, giving her a quizzical look.

Darcy tried to settle her nerves by clearing her throat. "I'm wondering if you can give me some information about how you knew my uncle. You mentioned that he and your husband were close. Are you willing to share that story?"

"You aren't going to print it in the paper, are you?"

Darcy paused. "I don't plan to use real names, and I don't write under my own name. So, it's all pretty confidential stuff."

"Okay, let me get another glass of iced tea, and I'll tell you. It's sweet really."

Darcy withdrew a notepad and pen from her purse and sat, ready to take notes. Lynn returned to the table, saw the paper and pen, and shook her head. "No notetaking. I'm simply telling you a story."

Darcy quickly put them away. "Okay, I'm ready anytime you want to talk."

Lynn sat back and studied her a moment. "I'm telling you this because your uncle loved you and your sisters, and he was a good man."

"I take it you knew him from way back," Darcy said, prodding for information.

Her expression softened. "At least thirty-five years."

"You knew about Duncan then?"

Lynn's surprise was noticeable. "You know about him? How?"

"Rocky," Darcy said. "He took me there a week or so ago."

"Well, then, my Benny and Gavin met when Gavin was investigating diving for gold. They shared an interest in finding shipwrecks and became fast friends. Gavin was a lively guy, always laughing, always thinking of fun things to do. My Benny was kind of quiet and shy, and Gavin was good for him.

"One day a couple of years after they met, Gavin announced he had the money and the time to try his hand at searching for gold like he'd talked about. He'd invested some money in the stock market and had made a killing. Benny and I talked it over. Even though they'd be gone for a couple of months, I encouraged Benny to go with Gavin."

Lynn stopped talking and took a sip of her tea. "He was very excited. He took a leave of absence from his job at one of the hotels, packed his bag, and took off with my blessing."

"And did they find gold?"

"Not really. I think they each got something from somewhere, but there was nothing big. A gold coin, a trinket. But they didn't care. Gavin and Benny and Rocky became close and that, as it turned out, was worth a whole lot more to me than gold."

"Did you ever meet Gavin's girlfriend, Duncan's mother?"

A troubled expression filled Lynn's face, deepening the lines. "She was a pretty young thing, enamored of Gavin and his money. But I could see she was as shallow as a sidewalk puddle. I mentioned it to him once, but he became angry with me, and I never mentioned it again."

"And when the baby was born?"

Lynn's snort of disgust was telling. "She left the baby in the hospital and took off during the night. Turns out she had a boyfriend on the side, someone younger, of course. Gavin was told to let the baby die, but Gavin eventually took him out of the hospital and found a woman to take care of him."

Gazing into the empty room, Lynn dabbed at her eyes. "I knew Gavin had loved one other woman and lost her, but this time, a woman he thought he'd loved broke his heart by leaving their baby behind. He never thought of Duncan as horrible, you know. He just couldn't, not with Sullivan blood flowing through that body. It changed everything for a while."

"What happened?"

"Gavin became terribly depressed, drank way too much, became violent sometimes. My Benny was the only one who seemed to be able to reach him through that darkness. And then one day, Gavin announced he was back on track, he'd been in communication with your mother, and he was going to be all right."

"What? My mother? But we weren't allowed to mention his name in the family."

"Oh, but they kept in touch. That's how he knew so much about you girls. But it doesn't end there, Darcy."

"Okay, go on."

"Gavin remained good friends with us. And when Benny was dying of lung cancer, it was Gavin who came to sit by his bed to give me a break. It was Gavin who helped pay the medical bills that we couldn't afford. It was Gavin who made sure that afterward, I had a place to live and work." Lynn ignored the tears streaming down her face, reached over and squeezed Darcy's hand . "Sometimes the best things come from the unlikeliest of places. Understand?"

Darcy sniffed and blinked back tears of her own. "Yes, I think I do." She rose and gave Lynn a long, tender hug. "Thank you for sharing."

Lynn sighed. "Some stories are worth telling."

Darcy left Lynn and went directly to her office, her mind

bubbling with ideas. She sat in front of the computer and began typing. Sheena called on her cell, but Darcy didn't pick up the call. She wanted to get her words down. When she finally finished, Darcy looked at the words she'd written:

> Angels come in all sizes and shapes. Some are big and gruff, so disguised one would never guess that behind their brisk manner gentleness guides them.
>
> How do I know?
>
> Because someone told me a story to prove it.

Darcy skimmed the details of the article and the follow-up paragraph telling of the need to care for those who couldn't help themselves. After making a few changes, she laid down the article she'd written, her mind spinning. The one thing she couldn't reconcile was the relationship Gavin had had with her mother. Was her mother the woman he'd loved and lost?

She left the office and went to find Sheena.

Darcy told Sheena what Lynn had shared with her and then gave Sheena a long look. "Do you think Gavin and Mom were in love, that she was the one Gavin loved and lost?"

"I think maybe she was. Sad, isn't it?" said Sheena.

"Maybe that's why Dad never wanted Gavin's name mentioned," Darcy said. She felt her eyes widen. "Oh my Gawd! Do you think that's why Mom always had those headaches of hers? Some sort of lovesick thing?"

Sheena shook her head. "I happen to know that her doctors thought the headaches were associated with hormonal changes they couldn't control. If it had to do with Gavin, that would be awful. Simply awful."

Regan swung into the room. "What's awful?"

"Sit down," said Darcy, grimly. "I've learned something that will interest you."

Regan took a seat on the couch next to Sheena and reached out to touch her hand. "Are you all right?"

Sheena nodded. "Just worried about what Mom's life was really like. Hear what Darcy has to say. She'll give you the story."

Regan listened as Darcy filled her in, dabbing at her eyes with a tissue. "I used to get very mad at Mom for being sick all the time. But maybe it was more than a medical thing that gave her so many headaches."

"I wish I'd been more understanding," said Darcy.

"Well," Sheena sighed, "we don't know the whole story, but I told you about the letters they exchanged. I saw some that Gavin wrote Mom, but he destroyed the ones she wrote him. It's probably a good thing. We owe them that privacy."

"What about Dad?" Regan asked.

"We can't tell him," said Darcy. "That would hurt him."

"I think he's always known," said Sheena. "But I don't think he'd like the idea of our knowing it too. Maybe that's why the subject was never to be brought up."

Darcy studied her sisters. They were so much more precious to her than she'd once thought. Stories meant a lot of different things to people. She wanted to write about things that helped people. And maybe, just maybe, she'd write a novel that people loved.

CHAPTER THIRTY-FOUR

SHEENA

Sheena lay in bed thinking about the situation with Gavin and her mother. Was she, as she sometimes thought, Gavin's daughter? She supposed she could try for a DNA test, but with Gavin being her uncle she wasn't sure what help that would be with his genetics so close to her father's. Besides, she didn't want to do anything to disrupt her growing relationship with her sisters.

Tony rolled over and pulled her close. "Are you okay?"

"Just thinking about life and all the changes in the last few months," she said against his wide, muscular chest.

He cupped her cheek with his broad hand, toughened by all the work he'd been doing for Brian. "You've saved Randy from a dreadful summer. And, Sheena, you and your sisters are doing a good job with the hotel no matter what R.J. thinks."

"Thanks," she murmured, moving closer.

Tony's body suddenly indicated he was ready for more than a snuggle.

Sheena smiled. It felt wonderful to be wanted, to be needed. When Tony's lips met hers, she was ready to give him all the love she felt.

As he stroked her, Sheena couldn't help thinking of her parents and wondering if they had tender moments like this. Sure, they'd had sex; they'd produced children after all. But the tenderness she felt with Tony was more than a sexual act;

it was the ultimate demonstration of love.

All thoughts of others disappeared as their bodies began to move in rhythm. This is what she wanted. And, later, cuddled up against Tony, listening to his heartbeat gradually slow, she wondered what he'd say if she told him she might want another baby after she met Uncle Gavin's challenge.

As she cooked breakfast the next morning for the three men in the household, Sheena brushed aside thoughts of babies. Babies grew up to be teenagers—hungry, demanding, and sometimes a little gross with their jokes, their smelly sneakers, their burping.

Still, she bid Michael and Randy goodbye with an affectionate squeeze for each. She'd tentatively started doing that after she realized how little affection Randy received in his life. Now, to her satisfaction, Randy responded with a quick smile. Michael, like Meaghan, had always been open to hugs and hugged her back.

She went next door to the suite her sisters shared to make sure Meaghan was off to her morning shift at the restaurant.

Regan and Darcy were sitting at the kitchen table with mugs of coffee in their hands.

"Grab some coffee," Regan called to her. "I want to show the two of you something."

Sheena fixed herself a cup and took a seat at the table. "What's up?"

"I'll be right back." Regan went into her bedroom and returned, holding a whole sheaf of blueprints.

"I haven't been around much. This is the reason why. After Mo and I picked these up from the architect, like Blackie arranged, we've been working on this."

Regan laid the plans across the table. "We agreed we

wanted something that could be used as a restaurant in the future, so that's what we concentrated on." She gave Sheena a smile. "We even went to the restaurant that Blackie took you to for your ... 'business meeting.'"

Darcy laughed when Sheena groaned and said, "Not that again."

"Just teasing," said Regan. "But he and Gavin are right. We can do something like that restaurant here. The footprint of the building can easily be changed. Let me show you."

Sheena watched with growing excitement as Regan pointed out how each window would open to either a view of the water or a small garden. "We even talked to Kenneth Cochran at Hospitality Answers for advice." She turned to Darcy. "And when the time comes, I have a feeling we can get Graham Howard interested in being our chef. He's such a cutie."

"I thought you were interested in Chip," Darcy said to Regan.

A pretty pink color filled Regan's cheeks. "Oh, I am." She sat down and looked from Sheena to Darcy. "I think he's the one. Mo does too. But, Sheena, how do you know if a guy is the right one for you?"

"For one thing, he has to make you want him." Sheena let out a chuckle. "God! Tony makes me crazy. Last night, I was even thinking of having another baby. Tony makes me feel so feminine, so loved ..." Sheena stopped talking when she realized her sisters were gaping at her.

"Another baby? Are you serious?" Darcy shook her head. "We need you for the hotel, Sheena. We couldn't do it without your guidance and business sense."

"Yes," agreed Regan.

"How about you get a dog instead?" Darcy said, and the three of them laughed.

"Seriously," said Regan, "when it's true love, you know it like that?"

Sheena studied Regan. "Putting aside all practical issues, yes, I think it should be like that."

"Chip makes me feel like I'm smart," Regan said.

"You are smart, Regan," protested Darcy.

"Well, how about you? Have you found anyone to make you feel like that?" Regan said.

Darcy looked away and then shook her head. "Let's get back to hotel talk."

After reviewing the blueprints and asking more questions, Regan said. "We've been told by the insurance company to work fast to get the building closed in before guests come."

"Our advertising campaign is based on a Labor Day opening. Can we still do that?" Darcy asked.

"I don't see why not," said Sheena. "With the latest deliveries, we're getting closer to having things ready. I went ahead and hired a professional laundry to handle our sheets and towels for the rooms and the pool like we agreed. And I'll talk to Brian again about getting the building closed in, so we don't have any liability there. But I've thought that we need to have some people come in as guests to test our facilities and routines after we have all of our proper permits and the hotel opens. I can ask Rosa and Paul to come and test the facilities."

"I could ask Mo's cousin and her family to help too. Mo and I have been trying to get her to open her own cleaning business. She already cleans house for her grandmother and an aunt. She could build a wonderful business with snowbirds as well as year-round people."

"Would she consider doing the cleaning here at the hotel with a crew of her own? I've been looking into outsourcing the cleaning. It would save us time and effort."

Regan's face lit with excitement. "Really? I'll ask her. Her name is Bernice Richmond. She's small but full of energy and very business-like. It would be a wonderful way for her to start her business. She's already agreed to do Rosa's and Paul's house. We talked to them about it when we delivered the final chair."

"Wow, Regan! You and Mo make quite a team. I'm impressed by all you are doing," said Sheena.

"Me too," said Darcy. "It's great."

Regan smiled. "Once we meet the challenge, I'm planning on going into business with Mo. He's asked me, and I said yes."

"You can't do that," said Darcy. "We'll still need you here."

"You're saying this to me?" Regan snapped. "You're the one who's planning on traveling and seeing the world."

Sadness filled Darcy's eyes. "With my new responsibilities to Nick, I'm going to have to put that off for a while."

"There's no use arguing about who's going to stay and who's going to move on to other things," Sheena said. "As soon as we can, we'll need to hire a manager. It doesn't mean I plan on giving up my responsibilities here. I want to continue to make this hotel be all it can by overseeing the operation. But that's all in the future. Right now, the three of us have to continue to work together to get this hotel off the ground. Agreed?"

Regan and Darcy looked at each other and nodded.

Sheena breathed a sigh of relief. They'd come a long way, but she wouldn't relax until she and her sisters had met the challenge.

CHAPTER THIRTY-FIVE

DARCY

Feeling blue, Darcy headed into the office. Sheena and Tony were happily paired, but prospects for her own love life were at an all-time low.

At her desk, Darcy reviewed the wording on the website, making sure that customers visiting the property while it was undergoing renovation understood that the special coupon they'd get was in exchange for the inconveniences of renovation. She never wanted to be accused of false advertising.

When her cell phone rang, Darcy checked caller ID and hesitated. *Austin Blakely.*

Her heart pounded rebelliously in her chest as she picked up the call.

"Hello?"

"Hi, Darcy. It's Austin. I thought you might want to know that my grandmother died last night. The funeral is going to be on Friday. I think my grandfather would appreciate having you there. Though my grandparents only met you once, they both liked you, and they both appreciated the thank-you card you sent them."

"Oh, Austin. I'm so sorry for your loss. I liked them too. Such a sweet couple. What will your grandfather do without her?"

"I don't know. So, you'll come to the funeral?"

At the pain in Austin's voice, Darcy quickly responded, "Of

course. Thanks for letting me know." She hung up the phone saddened to learn of Margery Blakely's death. She wished Austin had told her he wanted her there because he needed her, but she understood that with his girlfriend there for him, Austin would have no reason to ask her.

Two days later, Darcy filed into a small community church with a group of mostly older people. The off-white, stucco exterior was matched by stark simplicity inside. White walls, a series of stained-glass windows, and a wooden altar offset a large, wooden cross mounted on the wall behind the altar. Wooden pews were made more comfortable by burgundy-colored cushions. A long, red carpet led people down the center aisle.

Unsure of herself and where she should sit, Darcy found a seat in the back of the church. Listening to the organ music, Darcy was reminded of angels. She couldn't help reflecting on how her life had changed since coming to Florida and, most recently, meeting Nick Howard.

A movement at the front of the church caught her eye.

Austin stepped through a side door and into the main room with his grandfather and the blonde she'd seen him with at the Pink Dolphin. They were followed by a middle-aged couple Darcy assumed were Austin's parents. Darcy moved restlessly in her seat. She'd thought she and Austin had shared a special moment with that lingering kiss and wondered how she could have been so mistaken. But then, of all the Sullivan sisters, she was, apparently, the clueless one when it came to men. Certainly, Sean and Brian had proved it to her.

The service was short but sweet, with gentle reminders of the kind of person Margery was and how she valued her family. When Austin spoke briefly, emphasizing his love for his grandmother and the way she'd always been a part of his life, tears sprang to Darcy's eyes at the anguish she heard in his voice. Why had she once thought he wasn't exciting enough for her? He was the nicest, sweetest guy she'd ever met.

At the end of the service, Austin and his grandfather headed up the aisle, followed by the blonde who Darcy assumed was Jasmine and the couple she thought might be Austin's parents.

When Darcy realized they'd lined up at the doorway to greet people, she swallowed hard. She had no desire to meet Jasmine or to come face to face with Austin.

The man next to her in the pew nudged her and Darcy stepped into the aisle, unable to avoid moving toward the door.

Bill Blakely's eyes lit up at the sight of her. "Thank you for coming, Darcy. Austin told me he'd called you."

Darcy gave him a gentle hug. "I'm very sorry for your loss. If there's anything I can do for you, please let me know."

He clasped her hands in his. "How about coming to see a lonely old man once in a while?"

"You got it." She turned to Austin. "I'm so sorry. I know how much you loved your grandmother."

"Yes. Darcy, I want you to meet ..."

Darcy cut him off. "You must be Jasmine," she said to the blonde standing at his side. "Nice to meet you. I'm sorry, but I have to run. I'm late ... for a meeting."

"Oh, but ..." Jasmine said.

Darcy forced a smile and gave a little wave as she escaped, slipping through the crowd gathered at the doorway.

She hurried to the van, got in and sat a moment telling herself to stop being such a jerk. It had been one damn kiss—one damn delicious kiss that had rocked her soul.

###

Darcy knocked on the front door of Nick Howard's house gently, so as not to disturb him. His wife, Sandy, was expecting her. After listening to Lynn Michaels talk about how Gavin had relieved her from taking care of her sick husband, Darcy decided to offer the same relief to Sandy.

When Sandy opened the door and saw her, a huge smile spread across her face. "Darcy! I'm very happy you decided to do this. It means the world to me to be able to get out on my own for a while, knowing Nick will be tended to. He's sleeping now, but come inside."

Darcy stepped into the front hallway. "I brought my computer with me so Nick and I can work on a couple of things."

"Perfect," said Sandy. "Keeping things as normal as possible is a blessing."

"Yes," said Darcy, silently thanking Austin for his advice. "Someone once told me that."

After Sandy left on errands, Darcy quietly set up her computer on the kitchen table and sat down. She was working on some ideas for the paper, and though she didn't want anyone else to know about it, she'd begun making an outline for a novel about two estranged sisters who reunite after their mother dies.

Darcy was still at work when she heard something behind her and looked up to see Nick standing at the entrance to the kitchen.

"So, you're my babysitter?" Nick said, giving her a weak smile.

"No, you're my teacher," Darcy replied with a saucy grin.

Nick laughed. "Don't ever give up that sass, Darcy." He came over to the table and took a seat beside her. "What are you working on now?"

"I've started a couple of articles in response to two letters to the editor my work has received."

"Letters to the editor already?" Nick patted her back. "That's good, Darcy. You're engaging our readers."

"Well, I got one other letter that said I was a fool, that there are no angels, that people had to learn to take care of themselves." Her breath caught. "It really hurt."

Nick gave her a sympathetic smile. "There are always going to be naysayers. Ignore them. Now, let's see what you're doing."

Darcy held her breath as Nick read through the articles. One was about a project in the area for foster kids; the other concerned the need for families to take in exchange students.

"Good, not great, but very good. The greatness comes with more editing, but you're learning that. Right?"

She nodded. She'd never realized that one short column could take so many hours to write.

Nick sighed and gave her a steady look. "I want you to write my obituary. Think you can do it?"

"Oh no! Let's not talk about that now," Darcy protested as shivers raced through her.

"If we don't talk about it now, it might never get done." Nick winked at her. "It might seem morbid to some, but I want to have a say in what is spoken about me."

"Sure," said Darcy, understanding how important it was to him. "Okay, let's get started. Give me some facts."

As she took down what Nick was telling her, she fought tears. She'd thought about it many times, but she sometimes felt as if she and Nick had known each other before. They were so in sync with each other.

They'd just finished a very rough draft of the obituary when Sandy returned.

"What are you two up to?" she asked cheerfully.

"Nothing much," said Nick, giving Darcy a warning look.

"Good to see you working together," Sandy said, placing a bag of groceries on the counter.

Darcy jumped up from her chair. "I'll help you."

She went outside with Sandy and lifted a bag of canned goods as heavy as her heart.

CHAPTER THIRTY-SIX

REGAN

Regan gave herself another inspection in the mirror. Since coming to Florida she'd worn very little makeup, and it suited her. Her skin was lightly tanned, her eyes as dramatic as ever with their violet-blue color. Most times she wore her hair in a ponytail, but tonight, she was wearing it down.

She thought of Sheena describing what it felt like to be with Tony and was searching for the same thing with Chip. Darcy had been very quiet during that conversation. Regan had a feeling that though she swore she wasn't, Darcy was still crazy about Brian Harwood.

Regan shook off the memory of her kisses with Brian. They were fantastic, but why wouldn't they be? She couldn't begin to guess how many women he'd kissed. Lord knew he could choose anyone he wanted from the group of them who all but swooned when they saw him.

"Hey, Regan!" called Darcy. "Chip's here!"

Giving her hair a last pat, Regan picked up her purse and walked into the living area.

Chip let out a long whistle. "You look great, Regan. Very hot."

"Have a good time," said Darcy, waving at them from her seat on the couch where she was involved in one of her computer games.

Outside, Chip put an arm around Regan and lowered his lips to hers, surprising her. "Mmm, good."

Regan's stomach fluttered with anticipation at spending the whole evening with him. He seemed like such a nice guy.

He stepped back and took her hand. "Thought we'd go to Tamales. Okay with you?"

"Sure. It's fun, and I love their fish tacos."

They drove into Clearwater, parked the car, and headed down the sidewalk toward the colorful bar.

"I picked up another client today—a small hotel like yours," said Chip. "I'm working on some special programs for them, and I think they might work for you."

She laughed. "You'll have to speak to Darcy about that because I'm not a computer geek like the two of you."

"That's right," he said. "You're a decorator." He smiled at her, but she caught the dismissive tone in his voice and frowned.

Telling herself she was overly sensitive, Regan said, "Does the hotel need some interior work done? Maybe Mo and I can do it."

Chip caught his lip and studied her. "Who is this Moses Greene you and your family keep talking about?"

"He's someone I met doing some work for the hotel. He's very good at what he does and recently opened his own business. He and I have become good friends and are working together on various projects. I hope to go into business with him one day."

"What about the hotel?"

"Once we've met the challenge, we're going to hire a trained hotel manager. Then, my role with it will be far less."

"Hmmm. But you'll still be an owner. Right?"

"Yes, that shouldn't change. Why?"

"I just think it's pretty cool that you own a hotel. That's all."

Regan grinned. "Yeah, it is cool."

They climbed the outside stairway to the second floor of the bar and looked around for a table.

Regan tugged on Chip's shirt. "Over there, in the corner."

They made their way through the noisy crowd toward the table, escaping sharp elbows and slipping past people ignoring them.

As they neared the table, a guy stepped in front of them and took ownership of it.

"Hey, wait a minute!" Chip began.

"Juan? What are you doing here?" said Regan. "Where's Mo?"

"He's on his way. Who's this?" Juan's dark eyes studied Chip with appreciation.

"Chip, this is Juan Cardoza, Mo's partner," Regan said. "And, Juan, this is Chip Carson. Can we share this table with you?"

Juan and Chip exchanged questioning looks, and then they both nodded.

When Mo appeared wearing a turquoise Hawaiian shirt and khaki Bermuda shorts, his face lit with pleasure when he saw her. As Chip looked on, Mo kissed one of her cheeks, then the other, before giving her a hug.

Regan turned to Chip. "This is Moses Greene or Mo, the most talented, the most dapper man I know."

A scowl formed on Chip's face, but he shook hands with Mo. "Nice to meet you."

"Thanks, you too," said Mo. "What is everyone drinking? The first round is on me." He waved the waitress over to the table.

After they placed their orders, they all took seats.

"What's up, sweetie?" Mo asked her. "Anything new on the hotel front?"

Regan shook her head. "But, Mo, Chip is working on a project for another small hotel, and I think we should approach them for work."

"Okay," said Mo, turning to Chip. "What's the hotel?"

"The Sunshine Inn, not far from the Salty Key Inn," said Chip. "But don't use my name when you talk to them, okay?"

"Why not?" said Regan.

"I don't want to be associated with any other business. That's all," Chip replied, but Regan knew it was more than that, and from the knowing look on Mo's face, he did too.

Disappointment burned through Regan.

Mo patted her hand. "No worries," he said, softly.

Their drinks came, and as they all relaxed, the tension in Regan left her. Mo and Juan were fun to be with. At the end of the evening, the guys shook hands and both Mo and Juan each gave her a kiss on the cheek.

Chip held Regan's hand as they walked back to the car.

"Isn't Mo wonderful?" gushed Regan.

"If I didn't know he was gay, I'd be jealous."

"Really?" Regan wasn't sure whether to be flattered or to feel a little annoyed at the possessive way he'd squeezed her hand.

When they reached Chip's Jeep, he drew her into his arms. "I've wanted to do this all night." He lowered his lips onto hers and kissed her with such intensity she was shocked.

"Hey, get a room!" someone shouted.

Regan pulled away from Chip and stared up into his flushed face. "Whoa!"

"Let's get a room somewhere like the guy says."

Regan shook her head. "I can't. Meaghan is staying with Darcy and me. I don't want her to get the wrong idea."

"Wrong idea? What do you mean? You want me as much as I want you."

"I've promised myself I'd wait until it was right. It sounds totally lame to some people, but I hope you understand. We've only had a couple of dates, and I'm not ready."

Chip rubbed a hand through his blond hair and let out a long sigh. "How long is Meaghan going to be staying with you?"

"Until Sheena and Tony have a place of their own or until we have enough money coming in to renovate the suites." Regan held her breath. If Chip didn't cooperate, she'd walk away.

Chip took several deep breaths. "Okay, we'd better get you back there so I can go home and take a cold shower."

"Thanks." Feeling both wise and foolish, Regan climbed into the passenger seat and waited for Chip to get behind the wheel and start the engine.

CHAPTER THIRTY-SEVEN

DARCY

A few days later, Darcy pulled the van into the parking lot of Publix, hoping to get in and out of the grocery store in a hurry. She was worried about meeting her deadline for her column. Since she'd started doing them, she realized that everyone had a story to tell. Even now, as she walked into the store, she studied the people around her, wondering what lay behind their smiles, scowls, and harried looks.

She was standing in the produce section, trying to decide between a whole pineapple or a container of pineapple chunks when she heard a voice behind her say, "Hello, Darcy!"

She whipped around and faced Bill Blakely. "Hello, Bill. How are you?"

"Doing okay, I guess. The family has gone back home, so I'm here trying to decide what I need to pick up." He looked away and then at her. "Truth is, I had to get out of the house. Seems mighty lonely with Margery gone."

"I'm very sorry, Bill. After being married for so many years, it must be difficult to be alone," Darcy said, aware of his pain. "Have plans for lunch?"

His face brightened. "Not that I can think of."

Darcy grinned. "How about coming to lunch with me at Gracie's, the restaurant at our hotel. It will give you a chance to see the Salty Key Inn."

"Well, now, I'd love that," he said. "I'll wait outside and follow you whenever you're ready."

"I won't be long," Darcy said. "I have just a few things to pick up."

Several minutes later, Darcy met Bill outside. "Ready?"

He nodded eagerly and jumped up from the wooden bench he'd been sitting on outside the store. "I'll meet you at the exit."

Darcy returned to the van and watched with amusement as Bill pulled his car up close, the engine racing as if he couldn't wait to take off.

She led the way out of the parking lot and onto the main road toward the hotel, pleased by Bill's excitement.

When she pulled into the parking lot of the suites building, Bill pulled in beside her.

She got out of her car and waited for Bill to join her. Then she pointed to the carved wooden sign in the distance by the entrance. "When you pulled in, did you notice the sign Austin made? He did a very nice job of it."

"He's good at pretty much everything."

"Hope you don't mind. I'll unload the groceries, and then we can walk across the grounds to the restaurant. This way, you can see what one of the suites looks like before we redo them."

"Sure thing. I'd like a look at the whole deal. Austin was pretty excited by all you're doing."

Regan was nowhere to be found when Darcy entered their suite. She quickly refrigerated what had to be kept cold, and while Bill silently studied his surroundings, Darcy put away the rest of the groceries. "Okay, I'm set. Let's go."

As they crossed the lawn, Darcy explained to Bill how they were opening in stages and told about the changes they hoped to make in the future.

"Sounds good to me. I remember way back when this was a nice family place."

"That's what we hope it will become again," said Darcy. She led the way into Gracie's and waited for a waitress to offer them a table.

As Lynn approached them, her eyes widened. "Bill Blakely? Is that you? How are you doing? I was sorry to learn of Margery's death."

"Hi, Lynn. Thanks. I'm here with Darcy, taking a look around at things."

"Well, now, follow me. I've got a nice spot over here." She led them to a table near the patio and out of the sun.

"Thanks," Darcy said, as Bill helped her into her chair, and then sat down opposite her.

Lynn handed each of them a menu. "I'll be back with water. Anything else to drink?"

Darcy and Bill shook their heads, and she left.

"The food here is delicious," said Darcy. "Order anything you want. It's on me."

"Best date I've had in a long time," said Bill with a twinkle in his eye.

Darcy laughed. "There is a price to pay, though. You once mentioned you were in Vietnam, and I'm wondering if I can interview you sometime for the column I write for the newspaper. The column features different people in the area, with or without naming them, and their different life events."

"Well, now, I think I could do that," said Bill. "You come to my place for lunch, and we'll talk."

"Deal."

They ordered lunch and sat discussing the hotel. Trying not to be nosy, but unable to control her curiosity, Darcy finally asked him, "How do you know Lynn?"

Bill smiled. "Her husband Benny and I used to play golf occasionally before he got sick. I was surprised to see her here."

"She's a valued worker here at the restaurant," Darcy said.

Bill nodded and took another bite of Gracie's famous fried chicken sandwich. "Delicious."

Regan came into the restaurant, saw them, and came over to the table. "Hi, Darcy! And you're Austin's grandfather, aren't you?" At his nod, she continued, "Nice to see you. I was sorry to learn of your wife's death."

"Thank you."

Darcy smiled up at Regan. "We're almost through eating, but do you want to join us?"

"No, thanks. I'm here to pick up some take-out food. I'm supervising the delivery of the bedspreads."

As she walked away, Darcy explained to Bill that they were getting ready to open the hotel on Labor Day. "With construction on the new restaurant likely to be going on and renovations not complete when we open, we're offering special discounts for those who make early reservations."

"Sounds good," said Bill. He took a sip of water, patted his mouth with his napkin and said, "Thanks for lunch. I'd better leave you to your work, but give me a call anytime, and I'll be glad to help you with that column of yours."

She rose with him. "I'll walk you out to your car."

As they crossed the lawn to the suites building, Bill said, "Margery liked you, Darcy. I do too."

A rush of emotion heated Darcy's face. "Thanks."

He gave her a steady look. "Austin is going to be in town this weekend."

Darcy forced a smile that hurt her face. "Say hello. I'm going to be very busy with the hotel."

"Okay. I'll let him know."

When they reached his car, Darcy gave Bill a quick hug. "Thanks for having lunch with me. Goodbye."

Bill started to say something then stopped. "Okay, Darcy.

See you soon, I hope."

Darcy waited until Bill had pulled out of the parking lot before she turned around and went inside.

Sighing deeply, she sank down on the couch, telling herself it would be foolish to cry over a guy who wasn't interested in her.

Meaghan walked into the suite. "Hi, Aunt Darcy. What are you doing?"

"Just catching my breath before heading over to the office. Have you finished your shift at Gracie's?"

"Yes. Now I can meet my friends at the beach. And, Darcy, I think one of the boys likes me."

"Really? Want to bring him to the hotel so we can all meet him?" Darcy barely managed to keep a straight face.

"Uh, no. Not yet," Meaghan said. "Michael and Randy can be so mean."

"I guess most brothers are sometimes that way."

"Yeah, when I get married and have kids, I'm going to have all girls," announced Meaghan before flouncing out of the room.

Darcy laughed. If Meaghan's luck was anything like her own, she'd end up with a houseful of boys. Tears stung her eyes. She'd die of embarrassment if her sisters knew she'd fallen so far as to dream of the children she wanted to have with Austin.

In her office, Darcy stared at the computer screen with disbelief. They had their first reservation request—from her old roommates—Alex Townsend and Nicole Coleman. Darcy's mouth went dry. She wasn't ready for Alex to see the hotel in its present state. In her mind, Darcy could hear Alex's derisive laughter.

Sheena burst into the office, waving a sheet of paper. “We have our first reservation!”

Darcy gave her a glum look. “I know. For Labor Day weekend.”

“What’s the matter with you? Aren’t you excited?”

“It’s from my old roommates. Remember the snobby girl I told you about?”

“Oh, yes. Now I understand. But, Darcy, they, like all our guests, have to understand the property is in transition. We’ll have to make that clear to them.”

Darcy dreaded the thought of telling them.

CHAPTER THIRTY-EIGHT

REGAN

Regan stood back and admired the bedspreads on the bed and the bright-colored pillows atop it. They, along with the drapes, added a certain classiness to the room that she liked. She gazed around the area seeing all the changes. The colors, the fabrics, the finishes worked well together—not ritzy, but very tasteful nevertheless. Keeping to their vow to be honest about the kind of place it was meant to be, she thought she and her sisters had made a wise decision. No one could complain about this room or the other rooms when they were completed. She gazed out the window and frowned. The landscaping needed additional touches. Eventually, they'd make an area for refreshments right next to the pool, but, until then, she was going to speak to her sisters about beefing up the plantings around it.

Sheena came into the room and glanced around. "This looks great. Rosa and Paul are all set to come this evening and test out everything."

"Bernice and her family will come over the weekend. It will give her a chance to see what kind of work it will be to take over the housekeeping department for us."

"I've agreed with Rocky for him to handle the maintenance, and Brian's crew is doing the landscaping. With those cost estimates in place, I have a better idea of the expenses involved with their work. Naturally, I'm concerned about adding the cost of housekeepers."

Regan's stomach churned. "We are going to make it, aren't we?"

"I hope so," said Sheena. "I'm meeting with Holly this afternoon to work out discount deals for the bar. And I thought I'd check into other businesses as well."

"I'm going out with Chip tonight," said Regan. "I can ask at the Pink Dolphin if they're interested."

"That would be great," Sheena said, giving her a steady look. "You're serious about Chip?"

Regan sighed. "I'm not sure."

"Because?"

"I made him mad when I didn't want to get a room with him. I know it seems babyish of me, but I want to be very sure before I do something like that."

Sheena wrapped her arms around her. "Good for you!"

"So, you understand?"

"Yes, I certainly do. I love Tony and I always will, but I wish I'd had more time for me before committing to anyone else."

"I feel the same way. Now that I'm feeling better about myself, I want to see what I can do with Mo, learning from him and working with him."

Regan's cell rang. She checked it and smiled. "Speaking of Mo, here he is."

Sheena gave her a little wave goodbye and left the room.

"Hey, Mo! What's up?" Regan said. At the sound of a sob, Regan felt her eyes widen. "What's wrong?"

"Juan left me," Mo managed to choke out.

"Oh, hon, I'm sorry. What can I do to help you?"

"Can I come over? I need a shoulder to lean on, and you're the best person I know."

Regan's heart melted. "Of course, I'm here for you, Mo."

She disconnected the call and checked the time. Chip was supposed to pick her up in an hour. She punched in his number and was forced to leave a message canceling their date. No way could she leave Mo like this.

Regan was making a list of things she wanted Bernice to note for her newly formed cleaning company when Mo walked into the office and plopped down in a chair next to her desk.

After taking a look at the way his eyes filled, Regan rose from her chair and wrapped her arms around him. “I’m so, so sorry, Mo. What happened between you and Juan?”

“I’m not sure. He says he just wants to play the field for a while.”

Regan hesitated and then blurted out, “You deserve better than that Mo. I saw the way Juan flirted when we were at Tamales.”

“But I loved him,” protested Mo. “I thought he and I had a future together.”

“You’re going to have a better future without him,” Regan said bluntly.

Mo studied her. “You think so?”

Regan nodded.

Her cell phone rang, interrupting them. She picked up the call.

“What are you doing, canceling out on me at the last moment?” Chip’s voice was very low, very tense.

“I’m sorry, but something’s come up with Mo. We’ll have to make it another night.” Regan worked hard to hide her annoyance at his tone. “It’s not a super big deal.”

“Yeah? Is that so?”

“Oh, Chip, I didn’t mean it that way,” said Regan. “It’s just that we can go out another night. Right?”

“I guess I have no choice. I’ll talk to you later.” He hung up the phone.

Regan frowned. Chip had never even asked her what was wrong.

CHAPTER THIRTY-NINE

SHEENA

As she waited for Rosa and Paul to show up at the hotel as their first "practice guests," Sheena's nerves did a little tap dance inside her. Though it was a trial run, she wanted everything to be perfect for them.

When their car pulled into the parking lot, Sheena went right over to them. "Hello, welcome to the Salty Key Inn. May I help you with your luggage?" she said, playing her role.

Paul opened the trunk of the car and pulled out a large, rolling suitcase.

Sheena said, "Let's go to the reception office to get you checked in." As she rolled the suitcase behind her, Sheena took a critical look around. The sidewalk from the parking lot was clean and wide but lacked plantings.

They left the suitcase outside the reception office, and Sheena realized they'd need a dry place to put luggage in case of rain, or perhaps she'd simply have guests keep their bags in their car until they were assigned a room.

Regan was waiting for them inside the small office. She gave them a wide grin. "You must be Mr. and Mrs. Morelli. Welcome to the Salty Key Inn."

Playing along with them, Rosa said, "Yes, it's our first time here. I hope you have a poolside room for us."

Regan checked her computer screen. "Your accommodations are on the first floor looking out to the pool."

"I know we said we'd stay two nights, but we need to

change that to one night. Is that possible?"

"In this case, yes," Regan replied smoothly. "Normally we'd charge a cancellation fee for making the change this late, but we're happy to work with you on this issue."

Sheena smiled at her sister. Regan had handled the situation in such a smooth way. It was obvious her old receptionist job had taught her a lot about dealing with people.

After they were checked in, Sheena handed her mother-in-law a sheet of paper. "I've drawn up this checklist for you to use when evaluating your stay."

Rosa took it and tucked it into her purse. "Thanks, sweetheart. I'll use it. I promise."

Sheena laughed. "I know you will. That's why we wanted you and Paul here." She led them outside and into the Egret Building. "You'll be staying in room number E-105."

As Sheena walked them down the hallway, she decided the walls needed some artwork. When she and Darcy had cleaned the office, they'd found old photographs of what the place had looked like in the seventies. Sheena decided to have enlargements made and framed.

Drawing in a nervous breath, Sheena unlocked the door to the room, handed the key card to Paul and stepped back.

Rosa walked in and uttered her approval. "Oh, this is perfect! I love it!" She turned to Sheena with shining eyes. "You girls have done a wonderful job."

"Regan and Mo decorated it," said Sheena.

"Yes, it has their special touch."

Sheena left them to get settled and hurried back to the reception office. "Good job, Regan. Now, let's hope they have a good visit."

Darcy entered the office breathlessly. "Sorry, I'm late. I got into the middle of an article for the paper and forgot the time.

How'd it go with Tony's parents?"

Sheena gave her a thumbs-up. "They liked the room. But, after seeing it through their eyes, I'm starting a list of all the things I'd like to see changed."

"How are we doing with the money?" Darcy asked.

Sheena's sigh made its own statement. "Let's just say I'm very worried about getting us off to a good start. Like we've talked about, our guests have to understand our situation."

"I tried to talk to my old roomies about holding off until things are in better shape, but they might come anyway," said Darcy, giving them both a worried look.

Sheena placed a comforting hand on Darcy's shoulder. "I understand how worried you are about their reaction, especially Alex's, but we'll just have to do the best we can."

When Sheena returned to the suite, she found a note from Michael on the kitchen counter that read: "Gone out with friends. Be back early."

Unease crept through her. Sheena picked up her cell and called him. No answer.

She was still feeling very unsettled about Michael's note when Tony walked through the door.

"I'm beat," he said, placing his water bottle on the counter. "Want to take a swim before dinner?

Sheena kissed his cheek. "Sounds good. I'm a wreck thinking of your parents' stay here."

In their bedroom, Sheena stripped off her clothes and reached for her bathing suit.

"Hold on! Come here," said Tony. He drew her to him, pressing her up against his bare skin, sending a wave of interest through her that matched his own obvious interest.

"Where's Meaghan?" he murmured into her ear.

"Mmm. Last I saw her she was with your parents in the pool," Sheena replied as desire swirled through her.

Tony left her side to go to the window and look through the blinds. He turned back to her with a grin. "Looks like everyone is having a good time. Give me a second to lock the door and then, Mrs. Morelli, you're mine."

"I thought you were tired," she said playfully, noticing how ready he seemed for a romp.

He laughed. "Not for this." He turned away from the door, swept her up in his arms, and lowered her onto the bed.

Lying next to her, Tony caressed her body with sure but tender strokes. Sheena responded, loving the new, spontaneous way they'd begun making love whenever they could. She wasn't sure whether it was the sunny, warm weather or the fact that Tony wasn't constantly worried about his business, but he'd changed since coming to Florida.

He cupped her breasts and teased them, sending a streak of desire through her. And when his mouth replaced his hands, she let out a groan of satisfaction.

He lifted his head and brought his face closer so their lips could meet. As his tongue thrust inside her mouth, his hands moved lower, caressing her in ways that demanded an even stronger response from her. After playing with and pleasing each other, they moved together in a rhythm that brought them each release.

Chuckling, pleased with himself, Tony wrapped his arms around her. "Think this is how it will be after the kids are gone?"

"I hope so," said Sheena, laying her head against Tony's chest, hearing the strong beat of his heart, wishing they could stay this way forever.

###

Later that evening, Sheena and Tony faced two stoned boys.

Furious that the boys had disregarded their rules, Sheena glared at them. "Why would the two of you do something like this? You both play sports and know the damage drugs can do to both your brain and body. You know better!"

"Drugs? It's just weed," said Randy.

Sheena's nostrils flared. "Like it or not, I consider it a drug, and so do the Feds. And like it or not, the two of you are grounded because we don't allow the use of it."

"What? My mother smokes weed all the time."

"Yeah, you're treating us like babies," groused Michael.

"You heard your mother. You're grounded." Tony said, standing beside her, placing a hand on her shoulder. "You can go to your baseball practices and games, but then you must come right home. Understand?"

"Unless we don't come home at all. Right, Michael?" said Randy.

They exchanged silly smiles.

"We're not even going there," said Sheena, realizing in their state of mind, she couldn't get through to them.

After the boys went into their bedroom, Sheena and Tony sat on the patio talking quietly.

"I didn't realize having Randy staying with us would be this difficult," Sheena said. "We haven't had this kind of trouble with Michael until now."

"We're stuck," said Tony grimly. "We have to show Randy that we're not like his parents, that we'll stick with him until we no longer can. I'll try to have a private talk with him tomorrow. If he still talks about leaving, we'll let him."

"Okay," said Sheena. "Let's see where it leads us."

CHAPTER FORTY

DARCY

Darcy hadn't realized how hard it would be to keep up with weekly newspaper columns. When she talked to Nick about it, he suggested she keep a few columns ahead. With that in mind, she picked up the phone and called Bill Blakely.

"Darcy! Delighted to hear from you. I told Austin I was going to do an interview with you, and he encouraged me to go through with it."

"Great. I'm looking forward to meeting with you. When would you like to schedule our time?"

"Why don't you come to lunch tomorrow? We can do the interview then. Too bad Austin couldn't stick around to be here. But I promised him you'd take good notes and then we can sit down and share them with him."

Darcy paused. The less she had to do with Austin the better, but she owed Bill something in return for the interview. "I'll be happy to email him those notes."

"Yes, you can do that too."

They said goodbye, and Darcy went to work on a column she was writing about Clyde, the youngest member of Gavin's people. Maggie had agreed to sit with Clyde while she interviewed them both about how Clyde with his disabilities had come to be part of Gavin's group.

Looking through the first draft of the column, Darcy understood how easily Clyde could have been someone lost on the streets, uncared for, and without a purpose in life.

Maggie had met Clyde when his mother came to the hospital to die several years ago. Back then, in his early twenties, Clyde had always lived at home. For a few afternoons a week, he'd worked for a neighbor stocking goods in their small grocery store. Knowing she was at the end of her life, Clyde's mother had begged Maggie to take care of Clyde, to find a good place where he could live and work.

Darcy thought back to their conversation.

"Mom said I was to stay with Maggie while Mom is in heaven. Right, Maggie?"

Maggie smiled at him and squeezed his hand. "Yes, we've made it work, haven't we?"

"Yes. We live here," said Clyde proudly. "I help you. I'm good too. Like Mom said."

It had touched Darcy's heart to see their interaction.

Maggie didn't want their names used but agreed that their story could prompt another article on the need for people to reach out to those who were challenged. But when Darcy asked for more information about Maggie herself, Maggie shut her down. Darcy gracefully accepted that Maggie wasn't about to share more details of her life, but she hoped that someday she would.

Once more, Darcy looked through her writing, searching for grammatical errors and a way to write it cleaner, neater, better.

The next morning, Darcy met with her sisters to review the comment sheet Rosa and Paul had filled out for them.

Gathered around the table in Sheena's suite, they studied each answer carefully and exchanged grim looks. Rosa had been fair but direct in her responses.

"Okay, let's make a list of the things we need to do and then prioritize them," said Sheena. "We all agree to go ahead and put in more plantings around the pool, yes?"

Darcy bobbed her head. "It will give a real, tropical feel to the area. Since swimming is the one activity we offer at the moment, I think it's important."

"And do you agree we need a couple of folding beach chairs to offer our guests?" Sheena asked her.

"Only because they're inexpensive."

"And only if we buy just a few," said Regan.

"And the dock area?"

"Now that the dock is fixed and we have the two kayaks, I say wait to do anything else until Brian has his dock in and then combine the two operations," said Regan. "That's what Michael keeps talking about."

"Yes," said Sheena. "Brian is asking him to run the operation when it's ready. And that is only if I don't tie him up to keep him out of trouble. He and Randy got stoned last night."

Darcy couldn't hold back her concern. "I know Michael's a good kid, but Randy seems a bit of a puzzle to me. Do you think you were right to take him in for the summer?"

"Sometimes I'm not sure," said Sheena, "but then I see him react to us in a loving way, and I know it's the right thing to do. But he doesn't like the fact that we're watching him. Randy even suggested to Michael that they might not come home at all."

"Whoa!" said Regan. "I don't like the sound of that."

"Tell you what," said Darcy, "I'll have a heart-to-heart talk with Michael myself. He knows I don't put up with any B.S."

Sheena gave her a steady look. "Yes, I think that might be good. Thanks, Darcy."

A rush of satisfaction filled Darcy. Not long ago, Sheena might have been offended by such an offer, but their growing friendship was changing that.

The subject turned to the coupon they'd offered Paul and Rosa for discounts on food and drinks next door.

"They loved it!" said Sheena. "I think we ought to try and make deals with other restaurants nearby. What do you think?"

"I like the idea," said Regan. "Maybe Darcy can design a flyer listing all the discounts we can come up with."

"What about the flyers you were designing for our special rates?" said Sheena. "I thought we'd have them by now, Darcy."

Darcy held back a defensive reply. She'd been worried about getting that done too. "I'll get on it tonight." She checked her watch. "Right now, I have an appointment with Bill Blakely for an interview for the paper."

Sheena gave her a worried look. "This newspaper business isn't going to interfere with the deadlines you have with us, is it?"

"No," said Darcy. "I won't let it." She remembered reading about writers and deadlines. Now, she had a better understanding of the pressure it placed on them. She stood. "Guess I'd better go. Don't worry. I'll do my part."

On the way to Bill's house, Darcy recalled how his home had seemed so rich, so warm with the affection he'd shared with Margery and the love they both had for Austin. Those feelings had been almost tangible. Being with him in that atmosphere and then sharing that kiss with him, she'd opened herself up to a man in a way she'd never done before by allowing him to see how vulnerable she was. Stunned by the sensations he'd caused in her, she'd toppled like a tree in a storm.

A long, shuddering sigh escaped Darcy. Now that she'd felt such an emotional and physical connection to Austin, she wouldn't settle for less with someone else, even if it meant she'd remain an old maid. Love was so much more than receiving, she now knew. It was giving of oneself to another.

As soon as she'd pulled into Bill's driveway, he came out of the front door to greet her. At his eagerness, she was glad she'd agreed to his invitation. It was obvious he was lonely.

Bill stood by as she got out of the van. "Come on in. I've got lunch ready, and I've found some old pictures of my army days to show you."

"Great!" said Darcy. "I appreciate your willingness to share information with me. My column is supposed to give people in the area a chance to get to know each other by encouraging them to tell their stories."

"Sounds good," said Bill. "I'll have the chance to look at it before you publish it. Right?"

Darcy nodded. "Some people don't want their names used, and that's okay too."

Bill led her inside and into the kitchen. Sitting atop two placemats on the kitchen table were plates holding sandwiches, chips, and pickles.

"Hope you like ham and Swiss," he said.

"I do," said Darcy. "Thanks. This looks very professional."

He laughed. "I've always had a hand in the cooking around here. Comes from working in hotels and then in my business."

Darcy remembered the restaurant supply business he'd once owned and smiled.

They sat down and ate in companionable silence, two people suddenly shy.

"I thought it would be interesting to do a story on a Vietnam vet because many younger people don't have a clue about that war, other than what they've read in history textbooks. My father made sure we girls did."

"So, your father served in 'Nam too?"

"He wasn't badly wounded or anything like that, but he was terribly disappointed by the treatment he and other service members received after they came back to the States. Did you experience that too?"

"Yeah, it was pretty bad. The young people screaming at us were spoiled brats who had no idea the hell we'd gone through. War is an ugly thing and always has been. But being part of a unit, willing to give your life for someone else is something that tells a lot about the human condition. I'm still in touch with some of my buddies. One guy, Joey Barrett, actually saved my life. I'll always be grateful to him."

"Where does he live? Do you get to see him?" Darcy asked.

Bill shook his head. "He committed suicide not too long after we got back. Said he couldn't live with what he'd done."

Darcy's stomach twisted with anguish. "I'm so sorry." Growing up, she and her sisters had dreaded their father's regular bouts of depression.

"On a happier note, there are four of us who live in Florida. A couple of times a year, we get together and shoot the breeze about the old days when we were young. It's a strange group bound together by memories others wouldn't appreciate."

"What would you say to young people today?" Darcy said, probing for a twist to her column.

"That's easy," said Bill. He swiped at his eyes, which had begun to water. "I'd tell them to enjoy the freedoms they have because guys like us, women too, were willing to put ourselves in harm's way to protect those freedoms for them. Today, it's a bigger, more difficult battle."

"The world situation is pretty scary," Darcy said. "I sometimes wonder what would happen if we saw another 9/11. It could happen."

"That's why we need good men and women in the service." Bill shook a finger at her. "If I could, I'd make sure that those who are willing to fight for this country, the greatest country in the world, are honored in every way possible."

Darcy looked up from taking her notes and studied the man who was openly a patriot, a proud American. She hid an urge to salute him. He and others like him were their own kind of angels. She jotted down a quick note and sat back. "You have pictures to show me?"

Bill grinned. "Yeah. Here are some of my buddies and me." He handed her a bunch of photographs.

Darcy looked at the top one. The men pictured sitting among jungle growth, smoking cigarettes, looked like high school kids, so young. "Which one are you, Bill?"

Bill pointed out a skinny guy with a shock of dark hair springing out from beneath a red bandana tied around his head. "Nothing but an innocent baby in that shot. You'll see a change in the later photos."

By the time Darcy had finished studying the half-dozen photos, she had an overwhelming urge to cry. Bill was right. Looking at the photos, Darcy saw the toll taken on these young people by their experiences, their expressions changing from eager to others full of horror. War seemed so fruitless, so tragic.

"Guess I'm making you sorry you came," said Bill, patting her shoulder. "Like I said, there were some good moments. Not many, but some."

"This is a part of our history, the fabric that makes this a great country," protested Darcy. "And you and your friends deserve to be recognized. I just hope I can do you justice."

"Aw, it'll be fine. I just want people to understand how important the members of our armed forces are to this country and others. I tell that to Austin and Jasmine all the time." He smiled. "Austin and his cousin are great kids. They patiently listen to me whenever I get up on my soapbox."

Shock burned the nerve ends in Darcy's body. "Jasmine is Austin's cousin?"

"Yes. I'm sorry you weren't able to stay for the reception following the funeral. You could have spent some time with her and could have met Austin's parents. I've told them about you."

"You have?"

"Yes. I like you, Darcy. And so does my grandson."

"Oh, but ..."

He waved a hand to stop her. "None of my business. How about a cup of coffee before you go? You told me you had to leave by two o'clock, and it's almost that time."

Darcy gathered her things together and stood. "Thanks anyway, Bill. But I promised my sisters I'd complete a project for them. I'm behind on my schedule." She knew she was babbling, but she needed time alone to process what she'd just learned.

Bill walked her out to her car. "Hope to see you again. I'm planning on coming to Gracie's for lunch sometime soon. Lynn asked me to meet her there."

"Very nice." Darcy gave him a quick hug. "Thanks so much for everything. I'll send you a copy of the column before submitting it to the paper."

"Sure thing. And don't forget, Austin wants to see it too."

Darcy nodded and slid behind the wheel of the van. With a last wave to Bill, she backed out of the driveway and headed to the hotel so confused by the situation with Austin that she wanted to cry.

Did Austin really like her? If so, why hadn't he called, or asked to see her, or texted her like they used to do?

Memories of earlier rejections washed through her, erasing

the hope that had begun to grow inside her. Maybe, like others, she just wasn't good enough for him.

CHAPTER FORTY-ONE

REGAN

Regan waited for Bernice, her husband, Dylan Richmond, and their daughter, Mercy, to show up at the Salty Key Inn. They'd agreed to spend the weekend at the hotel to test the property, and for Bernice to see how she'd go about handling the housekeeping duties there.

Of all of Mo's cousins, Bernice Greene Richmond had seemed the most outgoing, the most eager to make friends. Her pretty features, like Mo's, were coated with a self-assurance that Regan liked. Her husband was a tall man with broad shoulders, warm brown eyes, and an easy smile. But it was Mercy who'd captured Regan's heart from the beginning. The little girl had a wistful, sweet way about her that tugged at Regan, reminding her of herself at that innocent, unsure age of six.

Bernice waved to her as they headed for the reception office. Mercy skipped behind her, carrying a doll in her arms and holding onto a pink, plastic purse. Dylan walked confidently behind them.

Regan joined them, eager to see how Sheena handled their reservation.

As they entered the office, Sheena looked up from her paperwork. "Welcome to the Salty Key Inn. Hi, Bernice, and you must be Dylan Richmond." Sheena shook hands with them and smiled at Mercy. "And who is this?"

Mercy swung back and forth on her feet.

"Go ahead and say your name," urged Bernice.

"I'm Mercy Beecher Richmond," she said. "And I'm named after my grandmother Beecher."

"Very nice," said Sheena.

"And I live on Sunset Drive," Mercy added.

"Good to know," said Sheena.

"And my doll is Lotti," continued Mercy.

Bernice laughed. "Okay, that's enough, Mercy. Good job."

Regan and Sheena exchanged smiles. "After Sheena gets you checked in, I'll show you to your rooms."

Regan waited while Dylan filled out paperwork and Sheena told them about the property. "You'll be in room numbers E-111 and E-112," Sheena ended. "We want to be sure those accommodations are every bit as popular as the rooms facing the pool. Please let us know what, if anything, we can do to improve them. We've tried to give their patios a garden feel."

"Regan and Mo have given me strict instructions to be brutally honest about everything." Bernice smiled. "But I'll be kind."

"Thanks," said Sheena. "This is a big help to us. We appreciate it."

"Okay, now I'll give you the tour," Regan said, leading Bernice and her family out of the office. At the side of the pool, she showed them how to use the key to the new gate and indicated where they could pick up towels and chairs for the beach. "Until we make more improvements, we've had a soft drink machine installed so guests can purchase cold sodas."

"What's down there?" Dylan asked, pointing to the waterfront.

"We have a dock on the waterway and two kayaks for our guests' use. Eventually, we'll have other kinds of boats. A bocce ball court is back there as well."

"And the restaurant? Mo says it's fabulous."

"Gracie's is the best, Bernice. She's open for breakfast and lunch. In your room, you'll find coupons for The Key Hole, the bar next door, and a few other places along this stretch of the coast."

"Wonderful. Thanks so much, Regan." Bernice hesitated and then said, "I also want to thank you for being such a good friend to Mo. He's devastated by the breakup with Juan, and your encouragement and support mean a lot to him."

"Honestly, I feel as if I've known Mo all my life," said Regan. "It's like we're siblings as well as friends, you know?"

Bernice and Regan looked at one another and broke out with laughter.

"Well, you know what I mean," said Regan.

Bernice gave her a quick hug. "Yeah, I do."

As they continued on their way, Regan grew nervous about their reaction to the interior.

Mo had helped with accessories for the room, but the basic concept for the décor was hers.

They waited for Dylan to get the suitcases from his truck, and then Regan led them inside. She held her breath as Dylan unlocked the door.

"Nice!" exclaimed Bernice, entering the corner room. She glanced around and gave Regan a smile. "Mo said you were talented, and I agree. This is perfect for this kind of property."

"We'll see how easy it is for your new crew to clean it," said Regan. "We're really glad to have you work with us on that."

"Between you and Mo there was no way for me to say no," said Bernice. "But I'm glad you talked me into opening my own business."

"Me, too," said Dylan.

Regan left them and went back to the reception desk to talk to Sheena. When she entered the office, Sheena greeted her with a little whoop of joy. "Guess what? We have two more reservations for our Labor Day Weekend Special. Someone from Georgia and a couple from Orlando."

"Great!" Excitement curled through Regan. The hotel opening was becoming closer to reality.

CHAPTER FORTY-TWO

DARCY

Darcy's elation at learning that Jasmine was Austin's cousin ebbed and flowed. She decided not to call him. She'd been impulsive about doing that in the past, but she was not about to repeat that pattern with Austin. He was too special to her. Like it or not, she'd have to wait for him to be in touch. That was the only way she could be sure of his interest.

Forcing herself to turn to business, Darcy worked on a story based on her conversation with Austin's grandfather. She'd promised Nick and Sandy a visit, and she wanted to get this column done in time to have Nick look it over. Her heart squeezed at the thought of Nick's condition. When she'd first seen him, he'd looked like St. Nick. But in a matter of a couple of months, that image had been destroyed by a disease that was eating his body.

Darcy took a sip of water and began to type about a time and an issue that many people were still ignoring in the face of the country's current situation. When she finished her first draft, she got up from her chair and walked outside.

The sound of people in the swimming pool drew her closer. A couple was in the pool, teaching their daughter to dive underwater for an object.

"Hi, Bernice! Glad you and your family are here," she called to them.

Bernice waved. "Yes, come meet my husband, Dylan, and

my daughter, Mercy."

Darcy used the key card she always wore around her neck and opened the gate. "How's the water?"

Dylan smiled. "Feels good, thanks." He was a handsome man, thought Darcy. If pressed, she would describe him as looking like Jamie Foxx.

"And who is this little fish?" Darcy said to Mercy, who'd climbed out of the water and stood to face her.

"I'm not a fish," the little girl said laughing. "I'm Mercy Beecher Richmond."

"Well, you swim like a fish. Better watch out, pretty soon you'll be growing gills," teased Darcy.

Mercy frowned, looking worried, and then she laughed. "I told you, I'm not a fish."

Darcy grinned. "Well, you're a smart girl." She turned to Bernice and Dylan. "Have a fun, safe stay."

At her desk once more, Darcy looked through what she'd written. In many respects, she was glad she was writing under the pseudonym of Dee Summers because some readers might be annoyed by her columns. In this particular column, she'd brought up the issue of burning the American flag. It was one of the rights people had in this country, but after listening to Bill talk about some of the things he'd gone through to protect that flag, Darcy thought it must seem like a slap in the face to those who'd served and sacrificed. Her article was bound to bring in a lot of letters, some good, some not so good. But her editor would be pleased. And Nick had warned her that these stories were not hers, but those of the people she'd interviewed.

Sheena came into the office. "What'cha doing?"

"Going through my column again," said Darcy. "Want to take a look?"

"Sure." Sheena accepted the sheet of paper from Darcy and

sat down to read it.

Darcy watched a stream of emotions crossing Sheena's face. Her mouth grew dry. Had she gone over the top with all her thoughts on honoring servicemen?

When Sheena finished reading, she looked up at Darcy with tears in her eyes. "This is beautiful, Darcy. I'm very glad you're doing work like this. When it's time to write a novel, I hope you write something as touching."

"Wow! Thanks, Sheena. I appreciate that," said Darcy. "Some people love my columns; others don't like them at all."

"Just be true to yourself, and the rest will fall into place," said Sheena, giving her a satisfied look. "I'm glad I'm getting to know you better. You have a lot of thought-provoking things to say."

"I'm finding a voice through words. Who'd have thought, huh?"

Sheena rose. "I'm going to check on the new restaurant building. Want to come with me?"

"Sure. I need a break."

They left the office and headed across the property to where the pink house had once stood. Now, it was being reconstructed as a small restaurant.

His tail feathers dragging behind him, Petey strutted toward them as if he owned the place. In some respects, Darcy thought, he did.

They approached the new construction. The slab had been poured, and concrete blocks were stacked nearby, ready to build the walls. That, Darcy knew, was the easy part. The rest was detail work, including the plumbing, which Tony was handling for Brian.

"Do you think we're doing the right thing by turning this into a restaurant?" Darcy said.

Sheena nodded. "It's what Uncle Gavin wanted. And none

of us plans to live here, so we're putting the space to good use."

Darcy checked her watch. "Guess I'd better go. I have to take another look at the column and then send it off to Bill and Austin."

"How is Austin? We haven't heard from him in a while."

Darcy shook her head. "I haven't seen him since the funeral." Unwilling to get into a conversation with Sheena about the guy she couldn't get out of her mind, Darcy left.

In the office, she checked once more for any typos and then, before she could change her mind, she sent it off to Bill and Austin, hoping they'd appreciate what she'd tried to say.

Darcy printed off a copy of it and headed out to Nick's.

Sandy greeted her at the door and held a finger to her lips. "Nick's sleeping, but come on in. I have an appointment and will head right on out. Thanks so much, Darcy."

"Sure thing. I'll just set up in the kitchen like always. Take your time."

After Sandy left, Darcy sat down in the kitchen and pulled out her computer. In the quiet, she could work on another idea she had for a column. She wanted this one to be fun. She'd talked to one of the bartenders at The Key Hole who'd come up with a new recipe for a drink he was calling Davy's Locker. A nice guy, married, with two young children, he was working at night to help pay for his son's baseball camp and his daughter's ballet lessons.

She was deep in thought when she heard a noise behind her. She swiveled in her chair and held back a gasp at the sight of Nick. He looked terrible—drawn, thin, and fragile. She jumped to her feet and helped him to a chair at the table opposite her.

"Hi! Good to see you! Can I get you anything?" she asked

him, working hard to hide her dismay.

He gave her a quick smile. "A glass of water would be nice. I'd get it myself, but I'm too damn weak."

She hurried over to the refrigerator to get him the water, wondering how much thinner Nick could get.

"Thanks." After taking a sip of the water, his cheeks showed a bit of color. He leaned back in his chair and smiled at her. "What do you have for me?"

Suddenly feeling shy, Darcy handed him a copy of the column she'd done on Bill Blakely.

He read through it. "Good. Remember, don't get too preachy. Your readers will hate that." He studied her. "When you write your novel, what's that going to be about?"

Darcy chuckled. "I'm not sure. Maybe something about sisters."

"Ah, Darcy, you have such talent. Too bad I won't be around to see what you do with it."

Tears stung her eyes, but Darcy merely nodded. The truth was, he was fading fast.

Tired, needing a break from the downward spiral of spirits from her visit with Nick, Darcy changed her clothes and headed out to the beach. The late afternoon sun had lost some of its heat, and she looked forward to filling her lungs with fresh, salty air.

Stepping onto the sand, Darcy drew a deep breath and closed her eyes. It always felt to her as if she'd just opened a door into a magical land. The tension in her shoulders melted as she walked along the edge of the water, grinning at the sandpipers skittering ahead of her. Once in a while, one of them stopped and entered the water, intent on feeding on the schools of tiny fish that darted about in the shallows.

Darcy thought back to her first days at the hotel, how shocked she'd been, how disappointed. Now, it seemed like home. She wondered about plans for the future and how she'd fit them into her newly found goals of writing for the paper and beginning a novel.

She picked up her pace and jogged south along the beach, ignoring the others sunbathing, swimming, or searching for shells. The pain she'd felt at the thought of losing Nick eased when she recalled his words to her as she'd left his house. "I'll be fine and so will you."

When she could no longer easily get her breath, she slowed and turned around for the walk back to the hotel. She gazed up at the sky and watched puffy clouds hang above her like dollops of meringue. She reached up into the air as if she could touch them and then chuckled at herself for her foolishness.

As she walked up the boardwalk to the road, Darcy decided to stop off at her office. She wanted to know if Bill and Austin had read the column. She was discovering putting yourself out there with words on paper was sometimes terrifying.

When she entered the office, she found Sheena sitting at one of the desks, her head in her hands.

"What's wrong?" Darcy asked.

Sheena lifted her hand and let out a long sigh. "It's Meaghan. I found some weed in her bureau."

"Whaaat? Meaghan? I don't believe it. I just saw her down at the beach with a group of kids. It looked like they were hanging out, having old-fashioned fun."

"I'm sitting here, wondering how to approach the subject," said Sheena.

"I'd just ask her," said Darcy. "She and I talk pretty often, and I've always found her to be pretty straight-up with me."

"Maybe you're right. I want to speak to her before her father gets home. He's going to be devastated. Meaghan is his darling who can do no wrong." Sheena stood. "I'm going to go down to the beach now. See you later." She headed for the door, stopped and turned around. "Thanks for the advice."

Darcy waved goodbye and took a seat at her desk to check her email. Nothing from Austin or Bill. Disappointed, she jotted down a few ideas she'd thought of at the beach and decided to call it a day.

CHAPTER FORTY-THREE

SHEENA

Fighting anger, disappointment, and fear, Sheena marched out of the hotel property, crossed the street, and walked onto the beach. After moving her daughter to Florida, Sheena had hoped Meaghan would choose her friends and her activities more wisely. But that didn't appear to be the case, and it pissed her off. Still, she didn't want to jump on Meaghan and get her so defensive she wouldn't be truthful.

Sheena recognized Meaghan's auburn hair among a group of kids lying on towels. Drawing a deep breath, she walked over to them.

"Hi, everyone! Meaghan, can I talk to you for a minute?"

Meaghan sat up and frowned. "Yeah."

Sheena waited while Meaghan got to her feet. Then shoulders slumped, Meaghan faced her. "Yeah, what do you want?"

Taking her daughter's arm, Sheena led her away from the other kids. "I need to talk to you about something, and I need you to be honest with me."

Meaghan gave Sheena a quizzical look. "What's this all about?"

Sheena studied her daughter carefully. "In putting away some of your clothes, I found marijuana in one of your bureau drawers. What was it doing there? Is it yours?"

Meaghan backed away from her, shaking her head. "No! It's not mine! I'm not that stupid! I'm going to be trying out for cheerleading with my new friends. And they don't do stuff like that."

"If it's not yours, do you know whose it is?"

Meaghan looked away and kicked at the sand. "Maybe."

"And?"

"And I'm not saying. Randy would kill me!" Eyes wide, Meaghan covered her mouth with her hand. "Oh no! You can't let him know I told you."

Sheena placed a hand on Meaghan's shoulder. "Thank you. I'll bring it up at a family meeting tonight and won't implicate you at all."

Tears filled Meaghan's eyes. "I told him I'd keep it for him. He didn't want you to know."

"Don't worry. We'll work it out," said Sheena, trying to comfort Meaghan while wanting to wring Randy's neck. No doubt Michael was involved too.

Sheena wrapped her arms around Meaghan and gave her a good squeeze. "Honesty always pays."

"Can I go back to my friends now?"

Sheena nodded. "Bring them up to the pool if you want."

Meaghan gave her a little wave and trotted back to the group of kids.

Watching her go, Sheena wondered what else Meaghan had promised to do for Randy and Michael.

That evening at dinner, Sheena said quietly, "We need to have a family meeting right now."

"What's going on?" asked Tony, looking around the table.

"This," said Sheena, pulling out a small baggie of weed from her pocket and holding it up.

"Weed?" said Tony. "Whose is it?"

"That's what we need to talk about. I found it in Meaghan's

bureau when I was putting away her clothing. Meaghan swore it wasn't hers, and it doesn't belong to my sisters. I'm waiting for a response from Randy and Michael."

"Maybe Meaghan was lying," said Randy.

"How can you be sure it doesn't belong to Regan or Darcy? It was in their suite," said Michael. "Don't look at Randy and me."

"Well, actually, I am looking to the two of you to tell me the truth. In this family, truth is the most important thing. Give us good news or bad news, but always tell the truth."

Michael glanced away from her.

"How about you, Randy?" said Sheena. "Is this yours?"

"Why would you think I'd have something like that?" he said, looking scared.

"Sheena asked you a question," said Tony sternly "Now answer it."

"I don't have to answer to you," Randy scoffed. "I'm a visitor."

"A visitor who has been treated like family. And like family, you'll answer truthfully, or you'll be asked to leave," said Tony in a quiet, firm voice that belied the pulsing beat at his temple.

Worried that things would become ugly, Sheena said, "Look, all we want is the truth and then a promise not to bring something like that into the house again. All of you know how we feel about drugs of any kind, and we ask that you respect that and refrain from using while you're under our roof."

"Awww, Mom, we're not big drug users," said Michael. "What's a little weed? States are legalizing it right and left."

Tony slapped his hand on the table. "Enough of this bullshit. Whose is it?"

Michael and Randy glanced at each other.

"Mine," they said at the same time.

"Okay, then," Tony said. "No more using, no more keeping

any of it here or Randy goes home, and Michael stays grounded, understand?"

Sheena knew it wouldn't be the end of it, but she let it go. One day at a time.

The next morning, during a meeting with her sisters, Sheena told them what had happened. "And if you see anything I should know about, please tell me. Until this summer, we haven't had a problem with Michael and drugs, and we don't want it to go any further. He loves sports, and we're hoping he gets a sports scholarship to college."

"I'm glad it wasn't Meaghan," said Darcy. "Her friends seem like good kids."

"Yes, I've told Meaghan she can invite them to use the pool if they want. Okay?"

"Sure, until we have our own hotel guests," said Regan. "Now let's look at Bernice's comments."

They went over a few suggestions that Bernice had offered, relating mostly to the pool and to the area by the bayfront.

When they were through, Sheena gave Regan and Darcy a worried look. "We're not going to be able to do any more work on the upstairs rooms in the Egret Building. And we can't even think of starting on the suites until we bring in enough money to do them the way we want."

"All we need to do is get the hotel up and running, right?" said Darcy. "We'll be doing that come Labor Day Weekend when we have our official grand opening. Let's not worry about it."

"Okay. The small amount of money we have left after all the upgrades to landscaping will be for emergencies only," said Regan. "We'll have a soft opening the week before Labor Day to again test things out. All we have to do is keep the hotel running and bring money in."

Sheena hated sentences that started with the words: "All we have to do ..." They usually meant trouble.

CHAPTER FORTY-FOUR

DARCY

After the meeting with her sisters, Darcy went to her computer to update the website with a list of discounts available to guests. No matter how you counted, twenty rooms would not produce enough income to do more than float along.

She pulled up the website on her screen and studied the logo Austin had helped design. It was simple but stunning. She looked at the photograph of the wooden sign he'd carved for them and admired the clean, easy lines of it. No doubt about it, Austin was a talented artist.

She sat back in her chair and sighed. Bill Blakely had replied to her regarding the column she was doing on him, praising her effusively. No word from Austin.

Lost in thoughts of him, Darcy jumped when the phone on her desk rang. She answered it, hoping for another reservation.

"Darcy? It's Austin. I'm going to be in town tomorrow and wondered if we could get together for lunch. There's something I want to talk to you about."

"Okay. I can free myself up for that." She didn't add that she'd do almost anything to see him or that she almost felt faint with relief.

"Let's do lunch at The Pink Dolphin. We'll have privacy there. Want to meet at one o'clock?"

Privacy at the Pink Dolphin? "Okay," said Darcy,

wondering at the strangeness of his invitation. The Pink Dolphin was a busy place.

"Good. See you then."

Austin hung up before Darcy could find out anything more. She chafed at the idea that she'd have to wait another day to find out what Austin wanted to talk about, but she was glad he'd called.

The next day, Darcy took special care with her hair, allowing her red curls the freedom to form a softness around her face. The new blue, sleeveless top she'd bought for the occasion matched the color of her eyes and offset her white skirt.

Sheena came into her bedroom and stared at her. "Wow! You look great! Where are you going?"

"I'm meeting someone for lunch," Darcy said, trying to evade the question.

But Sheena was having none of it. Placing her hands on her hips, she stared openly at Darcy. "Better spill. Who is it?"

Sisters! Darcy emitted a sigh. "If you must know, I meeting Austin. I sent him a copy of the column I wrote about his grandfather, and he wants to discuss it."

"Hmmm, you're getting all dressed up to discuss a newspaper column?"

Darcy turned away from her. Feeling sick with apprehension, she had no way to respond.

Sheena's arms came around her. "Sorry. I didn't mean to make you upset." She turned Darcy around to face her. "Oh my Gawd! You really like him, don't you?"

Darcy nodded numbly, wishing she could melt away. She didn't want anyone to know how she felt about Austin, especially when she had no idea if he felt the same way about her. Until she heard that directly from him, she wouldn't believe it. And after their last conversation, she wasn't sure of anything.

"Oh, hon!" said Sheena. "I didn't mean to upset you. I'm just so surprised. You've always said that Austin wasn't anyone you were interested in." She beamed at her. "He's a wonderful guy. I hope it works out for you."

"Please don't say a word to Regan or anyone else because I don't know if he feels the same way," said Darcy. Her body turned cold at the thought of being in another situation where she wasn't good enough.

"I promise I won't." Sheena placed a hand on Darcy's shoulder. "I mean it. I'd love to see the two of you together."

"Thanks." Darcy drew an unsteady breath and picked up her purse. "Guess I'd better go."

"Good luck," Sheena called to her, making Darcy feel as if she was a teen going on her first date. She was that nervous.

Walking into the restaurant, Darcy told herself to act natural. This was, after all, merely a lunch with a guy—a guy she thought of constantly.

She noticed Austin sitting at a table on one of the outside decks and went to join him. When he saw her, he smiled and stood to greet her.

"Hello," she said in a breathy voice that betrayed her nervousness.

He helped her into her chair and took his seat opposite her. "Good to see you. I've ordered a beer for myself. What do you want?" He waved a waitress over to the table.

"I'll have a coke with lemon," she told the waitress.

After she left, Darcy said, "You wanted to talk to me?"

Austin nodded. "I liked the article you did on my

grandfather. He was pleased with it. My parents too. They're traveling again, but I sent it on to them."

"Thank you. That was nice of you to do," she said politely.

"I'd wanted to introduce you to them at the funeral service for my grandmother, but you took off before I could." His light-blue eyes pierced her gaze.

"I'm sorry I ..." Darcy stopped talking when the waitress delivered her Coke, along with a couple of menus.

"And Jasmine? You were rude to her, Darcy, and I don't know why." A puzzled expression crossed his face, forming lines on his brow.

"You don't?" she asked, both relieved that his grandfather hadn't mentioned her misconception and worried about it.

"When Drew Chaplin was here, he made it seem as if Jasmine was your girlfriend ..."

Austin held up a hand to stop her. "I thought we had a connection. Was that just in my head?"

Darcy shook her head. "No, I felt it too."

"I hope you don't think I'm one of those guys who jumps around from one hot girl to another."

Hot girl? "I haven't had a whole lot of luck with relationships, and I didn't know what to think." Admitting her failures of the past, she'd never felt so vulnerable, so exposed.

"Darcy, I'm not the kind of guy who fools around. Understand?"

"Me either. I've been hurt by someone who dumped me because I came from the wrong side of town, among other things. I need to know that the interest someone shows in me is sincere."

He gave her a steady look. "Are you ready to work with me on this?"

"What do you mean?"

His lips curved. "I think we need to start dating again."

Her surprise turned to delight. "Yes, oh yes. That would be perfect."

He reached across the table and took hold of her hand. Lifting it to his lips, he kissed it. "I think so too."

That night, just as he'd promised, he picked her up at seven o'clock to take her to dinner.

Instead of visiting the usual bar scenes, they chose to eat at a seafood restaurant in Indian Rocks Beach.

Sitting opposite him at a table next to a wide, glass window overlooking the marina, Darcy wanted to pinch herself. Her dreams of him hadn't been foolish after all. He was as good-looking, as nice, as fabulous as she'd remembered. And the magic between them? Her body still tingled from the kiss he'd given her in the parking lot of The Pink Dolphin after arranging this date.

He returned her smile. "It's good to spend some time together like this—alone and away from your hotel and my responsibilities with my grandfather. I know I've been busy with school and family issues, but, Darcy, I didn't forget you. I've already told my parents how I feel about you and me together."

"You have?" Darcy swallowed nervously. "What if they don't like me?"

He chuckled. "They already do. My grandfather talks about you all the time. In fact, he told me I'd be a fool if I ever let you go."

Tears sprang to Darcy's eyes. She turned to the window so Austin wouldn't see.

"Darcy? You don't believe me?"

She turned back to him. "I want to ..."

Pain filled his eyes.

"Oh, Austin, it's just that I can't believe it's true. I've dreamed about us together."

A smile replaced his look of concern. "I have too, Darcy, and now it's up to us to make it real."

Later, exiting the restaurant, Austin turned to her with a grin. "Are you going to write a review on the restaurant?"

Darcy stopped in her tracks, realizing she couldn't begin to describe the food she'd had, that her whole focus had been on Austin and how much she loved him.

She laughed happily. "Not this time."

A few days later, Austin finished his final class at summer school and moved to his grandfather's house while he prepared to start his internship in St. Petersburg. For the next few weeks, Darcy's days were happily filled by her growing relationship with Austin. When texts and phone calls were not enough in a day, they met for lunch, or dinner, or one afternoon, a simple stroll along the sandy beach.

Walking hand in hand along the shore, they moved in unison.

Darcy looked over at Austin and couldn't stop her lips from curving.

"What?" said Austin.

"You, just you," she replied.

He stopped walking and turned to face her. "I'm moving to St. Petersburg at the end of the month, and I want you to help me choose a condo. It's important to me that you like it because I want us to spend a lot of time there together. I've said it before, but I love you, Darcy. More than you'll ever know."

Darcy blinked with confusion. *Was he asking her to marry him?*

"How about it? Will you help me pick out a place to live? I'm tired of staying at my grandfather's house and want to have some privacy with you."

She let out a nervous little laugh at her misconception of his intentions. "Sure. I'd be glad to."

That night, after Austin and his grandfather had prepared a meal for her, Austin and Darcy sat on the porch talking.

Austin took hold of her hand and gave her a steady look. "With your sharing a suite at the hotel with your sister and my staying here, we haven't had a real chance to be together like we want. There's an inn up the coast that is supposed to be nice. How about going there with me tomorrow night?"

Darcy was touched by his look of uncertainty. She squeezed his hand. "I'd love it."

Austin grinned. "Good. I was hoping you'd say that."

The kiss he gave her was full of promises of better things to come.

CHAPTER FORTY-FIVE

DARCY

As Darcy was packing for their overnight trip, she thought of Austin. Handsome in his own way, his presence filled her with a loving security she'd never known. Seeing the earnestness on his face as he'd asked her to come away with him, she was surer than ever that his feelings for her were real. And there was no question about the magic between them when he'd kissed her goodbye last night. Even now, she almost swooned thinking of it.

Sheena came into the room, followed by Regan. "What are you doing?"

"Austin and I are going up the coast to a little B&B he knows." Overwhelmed by a rush of anticipation, she grabbed hold of their hands and forced them to do a little dance with her. "He loves me! He loves me!"

Regan threw her arms around Darcy. "I'm so happy for you."

"Group hug," Sheena announced, joining them.

Laughing, they stood together, caught up in the moment.

When they heard the sound of a car pulling into the parking lot, they looked out the window.

"Oh my Gawd! Austin's here. Better go keep him busy while I finish packing," said Darcy. "And don't you dare say anything to him about what I told you."

"We'll see," teased Sheena, following Regan out of the bedroom.

Darcy carefully folded a dress for dinner and lay it atop the sexy nightgown she'd hurried to Jenna Lynch's store to buy that morning. When the last of her things were in her suitcase, she wheeled it out to the living area, where Austin stood talking to her sisters.

"I've signed up with a dental office in St. Petersburg and will begin an internship there right after Labor Day," he was explaining to them.

"Good, you'll be nearby," said Sheena.

"We're officially going to open the hotel that weekend," Regan said. "You can help us celebrate. Right, Darcy?"

Darcy smiled. "I hope so."

"Ready?" said Austin, holding his hand out for the suitcase.

"Yes," said Darcy, as ready as she ever would be for what she was sure would be a deliciously romantic time.

Darcy climbed out of Austin's car and stood a moment looking at The Sandy Beach Inn. It was a pretty, yellow-clapboard house with a sweeping porch that stretched across the entire front of the house and wrapped around the wings on either side. The Inn nestled among palm trees and a variety of live oak trees Darcy couldn't name. A gabled dormer above the front entrance had multi-paned windows that peered out at them like the eyes of curious children.

"Wait until you see the inside, both modern and with an Old-Florida touch you'll love. Or maybe it's the wooden trim and moldings that I naturally like," said Austin.

Darcy smiled. He was such an interesting person—an artist as well as a practical man, who was eager to help his family and others.

"Shall we?" he asked, turning to her with a sexy grin.

Darcy's heart pounded with anticipation. "Sure."

"We'll have time before dinner to take a walk or something," he said, grabbing hold of their suitcases.

She knew he was waiting for a response, and liked the fact that he was leaving choices up to her. She gave him a quick kiss. "Or something."

He chuckled. "That's what I was thinking."

They entered the house.

The older couple who greeted them introduced themselves as Lila and Jack Pierce. Jack explained that they were retired but loved opening their house to others.

"And Lila here is a fabulous cook," said Jack. "What time shall we plan on serving dinner for you? The house is empty tonight, though two couples arrive tomorrow."

"How about eight o'clock?" said Darcy, receiving a nod of approval from Austin.

"Okay, then. Do either of you have any allergies?" said Lila.

Darcy and Austin shook their heads.

Jack led them upstairs to a pale-pink door. "This is what we call our honeymoon suite. It's my favorite room in the house, and very private."

He gave them a key and left them in the hallway.

"I'm not going to carry you over the threshold," said Austin with a straight face.

Darcy laughed. "You're not?"

He shook his head. "Let's see what it's like."

They opened the door to a room with white walls and dark green carpeting. A large, four-poster bed was covered in a white, quilted spread with a vibrant pattern of hibiscus blossoms in bright pink. A small, pink couch sat in front of a gas-lit fireplace that would be pleasant during winter months, perhaps, but would remain off for now. French doors opened onto a small balcony that overlooked the front lawn and, in the distance, they could see the shoreline.

"This is lovely," said Darcy, wishing Regan could see the décor. She'd adore it. Maybe later, Darcy decided, she'd snap a couple of pictures to show her.

Austin set the suitcases down and turned to her. "It's good to get away and have time just for us to get to really know each other."

As Austin approached her, Darcy's pulse sprinted. He seemed so big, so confident, so ready to take the next step.

Austin seemed to sense her hesitancy. Lifting her chin, he lowered his lips to hers.

A soft moan escaped her as he drew her closer to him. And then all nervousness fled as his arms wrapped tighter around her. It felt so good to be in his embrace. His strength, his gentleness, his kindness were things she'd been looking for all along, she thought, wanting to melt into him.

When they drew apart, he smiled down at her. "I imagined this."

"I wanted this so badly. When you kiss me, I feel whole." Afraid of being foolish, she gazed at him. "You know what I mean?"

"Yeah," he said quietly.

Still clothed, they lay on the bed, facing each other.

Austin cupped her cheek in his hand. "You're beautiful, you know."

She shook her head. "Not like Regan or Sheena."

His eyebrows shot up. "Why are you saying that?"

"Because that's what everyone always says," Darcy answered.

He had the audacity to laugh. "You're kidding!" He pulled her closer. "Come here, my beauty."

He kissed her with such tenderness that tears stung her eyes. His hands caressed her breasts, sending a pulse of desire through her. And when he moved his hips, letting her feel his arousal, she reached for him.

The dam of hesitancy between them broke, and in a flurry of motion they undressed and lay looking at each other. Darcy loved Austin's broad chest, the way his chest hairs tapered to a V that led to his sizeable manhood. He was more than the Teddy Bear Regan had once called him. He was magnificent.

After proving how generous and exciting a lover he was, Austin lay beside her.

He smiled with satisfaction. "Ah, Darcy, like I thought, there's a fire in you that's so ... sexy."

"Oh?" Darcy gave him a challenging look.

"Yeah. I felt it that first time we kissed."

She fingered his mouth and then lowered her lips on his. When she pulled back, she studied him, and her eyes filled. "It's the first time I've ever given my soul away."

"God, you have no idea how long I've waited for you."

Languid and satisfied, Darcy lay her head on his chest, listening to the slowing of his heartbeat. Her thought as she fell asleep was of Sean Roberts' parents, whose disapproval had broken them up. *Bless you,* she thought, *for leading me to this moment, this man.*

CHAPTER FORTY-SIX

DARCY

Darcy was roused from sleep by the ringing of her phone. Dazed, she propped herself up on one elbow and studied Caller ID. *Sandy Howard.* Her heart pounded with alarm as she clicked on the call. "Hello?"

"Darcy? It's Sandy. I want you to know that hospice is here and they're telling me it won't be long now before Nick leaves us. I thought you'd want to know."

"Tell him to hold on. I'm out of town, but I will try to get there as soon as I can."

Austin sat up beside her as she clicked off the call. "What's going on?"

"It's Nick. He's dying. Hospice is saying it won't be long." She climbed off the bed and stood to face him. "I've got to get to him."

He climbed out of bed and walked over to her. "I understand. Let's get dressed, and then we'll take off."

Darcy reached for him, and he took her in his arms. "I'm sorry, Darcy. I really am."

She gave him a worried look. "This doesn't change anything between us, does it?"

His smile was sad. "No, of course not." He gazed into her eyes, cupped her cheek with his hand and leaned forward to brush his warm lips against hers.

Darcy hugged him, certain she'd never met anyone as special as he.

###

They dressed quickly, efficiently, and then went downstairs to explain the situation.

"No problem," Jack said. "Come back again, and we'll give you a special rate."

"Do you want me to pack you a sandwich?" Lila asked.

Austin nodded. "That would be great. We can eat it on the way."

Moments later, Darcy was settled in the passenger's seat of Austin's car, and they headed out.

Austin broke the silence between them. "I'm sorry about Nick, Darcy. I know how close you became to him."

"Thanks." She turned to him. "And thanks for setting up this visit to the inn. I'm sorry it's ending this way."

He gave her a tender look. "But it's not ending. It's just beginning. Right?"

Darcy felt a happy smile slide across her face. "Right. Has anyone ever told you how fantastic you are?"

"Well, not exactly like you did," he said, giving her a roguish grin.

She laughed. "I mean it, Austin. You're a great man. Some guys would be furious at me for wanting to go home to see Nick."

Austin frowned. "That's pretty selfish, don't you think?"

Darcy thought back to some of her experiences with Sean. "You're right. Guess I haven't made such good choices in the past."

Austin reached over and gave her hand a squeeze. "Darcy, you're better than you think you are. Prettier too."

Her heart warmed. She lifted his hand and pressed her lips to it. "You make me feel that way. Thanks."

It was dark when Austin pulled into the parking lot behind

the suites building. "Are you sure you don't want me to go with you to visit Sandy and Nick?"

Darcy hesitated. "Yes, but I need you to be with me for the funeral. I promised Nick I would deliver a eulogy and I'm already nervous about it."

"Don't worry. I'll be there." Austin leaned over and gave her a kiss. "Let's try for another time at the inn." His eyes twinkled with humor. "I liked it."

She laughed. "Me too. You were ... well, wonderful."

As they gazed into each other's eyes, Darcy felt a stirring inside. She'd said she loved Sean, but compared to her feelings for Austin, she hadn't really known love at all.

When Darcy rolled her suitcase into the suite she shared with her sister, Regan jumped up from the couch. "What are you doing home?"

Darcy let go of the suitcase and, gazing at Regan, felt her eyes fill. "It's Nick. He's dying. I have to go see him. Austin said he'd go with me, but I don't know how long I'll be gone. I need the keys for the van."

"Oh, hon, I'm sorry," said Regan. "I know how much he means to you."

Darcy felt tears roll down her cheeks and tried to swipe them away.

Regan gave her a hug and handed her the keys to the van. "Call if you need us."

"Okay, please tell Sheena what's going on."

Regan nodded. "I'm sorry you didn't get to enjoy the inn with Austin."

Darcy's lips curved. "Oh, but I did." She sighed, momentarily lost in the memory. The ring of her cell phone brought her back to the present with a shock. She checked the number. *Sandy*.

Feeling sick, Darcy clicked on the call. "Is it Nick? Is he gone?"

"No, but you'd better come quickly. He's asking for you."

"I'm on my way." Darcy waved goodbye to Regan and raced out the door, her pulse sprinting with alarm.

Pulling into Nick and Sandy's driveway, Darcy couldn't count the times she'd come to the house to spend time with Nick—times in which she'd held out hope that he'd somehow survive the onslaught of this terrible disease. She realized how foolish that had been, especially after her last visit with Nick. But the thought of his dying had been too painful to contemplate.

Now, she got out of the van and hurried up the front walk.

Sandy greeted her at the door. "Thank God you're here. He's been calling for you."

Darcy's throat was dry as she entered the bedroom, Nick lay in bed, looking like a skeleton of his former healthy self. Amazed that a body could still live like that, Darcy hurried to his side and took hold of his cold hand.

"Nick? It's Darcy. I'm here."

His eyes flickered open, and his mouth stretched over his teeth in an eerie smile. "Good. Like a daughter to me. Wanted to tell you so you'd understand."

"Understand what?"

Sandy gave her a gentle look. "He's leaving you all the first-edition books he's collected over the years. He thought you, an author, would appreciate them."

Tears flooded Darcy's eyes and made a burning trail down her cheeks. She leaned over and kissed Nick's cheek. "Thank you. I will treasure them."

"We both wanted you to have them. They're worth a lot of money, but it's right that they go to you. He's been talking about it for some time."

Darcy continued to hold Nick's hand. Sandy took hold of Nick's other hand. Standing above his body, they gazed at one another with sorrow and heard him take his last breath.

"I'm so sorry," Darcy whispered. "What can I do to help you?"

"Just being here with me, with Nick, it means more than you know," said Sandy. "Hospice and I will take care of the rest. I'll see you later at the service."

"I'll be there to do what he asked," said Darcy, shaken by all that had happened. "Call if you need anything."

A hospice nurse approached her as she left the room. "Are you all right, hon?"

"Yes," Darcy said, knowing she wasn't all right at all. She'd lost one of the best friends she'd ever had.

CHAPTER FORTY-SEVEN

SHEENA

Two weeks before Labor Day and the hotel's opening, Sheena and Tony sat in the reception area of Gatto and Ryan, waiting for Gregory Ryan to meet with them. A partner of Blackie's, he specialized in business law. Noting the soft, green, Oriental rug she'd always liked, Sheena was anxious to meet the man who'd helped build the company into such a very successful one. It was an interesting combination: Blackie as a financial advisor and Greg as the lawyer.

"Excited?" Sheena asked Tony in a soft whisper.

Tony eyes shone and matched the glowing smile on his face. "Not every day I sell my business."

Her smile was sincere. "I'm glad you're handing it over to a long-time worker and your brother-in-law. And I'm really happy that doing so means you'll be in Florida full-time."

He grinned. "Me too."

The receptionist walked over to them. "Mr. and Mrs. Morelli, Mr. Ryan can see you now."

She led them down a hallway and stopped outside the door of a large office.

They stepped inside a room with a wall of glass that overlooked the inlet below.

A short man with sparkling, blue eyes and faded red hair rose from behind his desk and held out his hand. "Greg Ryan. Glad to meet you. Looks like we have some interesting business to take care of today."

After shaking hands and making their introductions, Sheena and Tony took the seats Greg indicated.

Greg sat back in his chair behind the desk and steepled his fingers. "So, you're going to set up business here in Florida, Tony?"

"Yes, after meeting all the regulations. In the meantime, I'm working for Brian Harwood's company."

"Ah, yes. Brian's a good guy. Smart and motivated." Greg shifted in his chair and opened the folder of papers sitting in front of him. "This looks like a pretty straightforward deal. The valuation seems a little low to me, but if everyone is satisfied, I suggest you go ahead and sign the papers. As we discussed on the phone, there's nothing to be unhappy about. Everyone can get along with their lives."

"I have my truck and my tools and all the things I need to work here," said Tony.

Greg looked at her. "And you're happy with these arrangements, Sheena? As co-owner of the company, you need to approve the deal and sign off on it."

"I'm very pleased with the sale. It means Tony is here with our children and me ." She loved seeing the smile that crossed Tony's face.

"All right then, let's get your signatures, and we'll send the papers up to Boston." Greg handed them each a blue pen and sat back.

As Sheena wrote her signature, she was relieved. Now, maybe with the sale of the business, she and Tony could think of buying a house.

When they completed their business , they shook hands with Greg and left the office.

Outside, Tony said, "Want to celebrate? How about lunch at the Don CeSar?"

"How about lunch at the Key Pelican instead? It's

something I've wanted to show you for a long time. Regan, Darcy and I are basing a lot of decisions on the design and construction of our restaurant on it because that's what Gavin envisioned."

"Sounds fine with me. So far, I've looked over the blueprints for only the plumbing in the place, but it's a good idea to get an actual visual of what you want."

They left St. Petersburg, crossed Boca Ciega Bay onto the barrier beach, and drove along the shore, pulling into a driveway south of Indian Rocks Beach.

"Isn't it cute?" said Sheena. They pulled to a stop by the turquoise and pink trimmed house. "We haven't decided on the color we want, but I'd like something as bright and welcoming as this."

Tony gazed at the building. "Let's see the inside."

When they entered the restaurant, the hostess gave her a puzzled look. "Aren't you Blackie Gatto's friend?"

"Yes, both my husband and I are friends of his. Why?"

"No reason; I simply recognized you."

After they were seated, Tony said, "Care to celebrate with a drink?"

"Sounds great," said Sheena.

When the waiter came to their table, Sheena ordered a glass of white wine and Tony ordered an imported beer.

After their drinks arrived, Tony turned to her. "I know you want to buy a house and get the kids settled before school, but I've been thinking that the smarter thing to do is to build a house in the same neighborhood where Brian is building a number of homes. By doing a lot of the work myself and using Brian's discount on materials, we could save a lot of money. He'll sell a lot to us for a good price. What do you think? You've seen the neighborhood. It's great."

"But it means staying at the hotel. What will we do about

the kids and their schools?"

Tony grinned. "I have it all planned out. Michael can drive himself to the high school by the new neighborhood, and we can take turns getting Meaghan to her school."

Sheena's brow furrowed with worry. "But if Michael has the car, what will I use?"

"Either the hotel van or this." Almost shyly Tony handed her a fob for a car.

Sheena studied it with shock. "What's this?"

His eyes sparkled with mischief. "The key to your new car. A little VW convertible, just for you!"

Sheena's eyes widened and then filled with tears. "Really? How wonderful!" She rose from her chair and fell into his embrace. "I can't wait to see it. Where is it?"

"At the hotel. I made arrangements for Regan to pick it up."

"Oh, I'm so excited! Let's finish our drinks here and then leave."

He laughed. "Okay with me. We can have lunch at Gracie's."

He signaled the waiter and paid for their drinks.

As she took a final sip of her wine, Sheena studied the man she thought she knew. The old Tony, the one who constantly worried about his business in Boston and was always too tired to do anything fun, would never have done anything this frivolous. "Where'd you come up with this idea?" she asked him.

"I saw one the other day and thought of you. You once told me you'd love a convertible." "How can we afford this with the house and everything else?"

He smiled. "After renegotiating the sale for some extra money, it should be pretty much as we talked about."

"And Michael gets my old car? I bet he's thrilled to have wheels as he says."

Tony nodded and then grew serious. “I told him he could use the SUV as his own for as long as he and Randy don’t get into any more trouble.” He stood. “Ready to go see your new car? We’ll talk about the house another time. I’m still working on plans to show you. Then we can decide what we want to do.”

Sheena followed Tony out to his truck, wondering what other surprises were coming her way.

CHAPTER FORTY-EIGHT

REGAN

Regan drove Sheena's new car into the parking lot behind the suites building, parked it in the shade, and, as promised, tied a big pink bow to the steering wheel.

Standing back to admire her work, she smiled, thinking of Sheena's surprise. Tony didn't seem the kind of guy who'd spring for such a nice gift, but after living and working in Florida for the past couple of months, he'd become a whole lot more fun. And it probably was a good thing that Sheena would now have her own car. The hotel van wasn't always available, and Gertie, Gavin's old 1950s Cadillac, was being held in reserve for emergencies only.

Regan left the car and went into the reception office where Chip was working on the computer. It apparently needed upgrading of some sort.

"How are you doing?" she asked Chip when he emerged from the back hallway where he'd worked on the system. "Is it all fixed?"

"I think so." He smiled at her. "I installed a new program and set up a better backup system." He studied her. "Want to go out tonight? There's a new band playing at The Pink Dolphin?"

Regan hesitated.

"C'mon!" Chip coaxed. "It'll be fun."

"Okay," she said. "Let's give it a try."

"Great. I'll pick you up at seven."

Regan watched him cross the hotel lawn. Then she noticed Brian Harwood, who'd stopped to speak to him. Her pulse raced at the sight of him. She was doing her best to stay away from him, but there was an excitement about being with Brian that she couldn't forget.

CHAPTER FORTY-NINE

DARCY

Following Regan's phone call, Darcy hurried outside. She was as excited as the others standing by the parking lot, waiting to see Sheena's reaction to the cute, little white convertible. It was, she thought, such a sweet gesture on Tony's part, but more than that, it had brought the group together in a wholesome new way. Even Gracie and the others on Gavin's team were here to share the moment. And with Nick's upcoming funeral, Darcy needed as many heartening events as possible to lift her spirits.

After lunch, she was going to meet Austin at his grandfather's, and then they were going to spend the evening at a restaurant close to Sarasota, farther down the coast. Darcy was anxious to see Austin. He'd been a huge support to her as she grieved for Nick and worried about giving the eulogy at his service. Being in his arms would feel good.

Tony's truck came into view, and Darcy, like the others, held her breath as he pulled up beside the white car.

Sheena jumped out of the truck and ran over to the car. "It's mine? All mine?" She surprised them all by jumping up and down, clapping her hands like a child.

Laughing, Tony reached her and swung her around in his arms to applause from the group.

Meaghan rushed to her mother's side. "It's so cool, Mom! Can I have a ride?"

Sheena held up the fob in her hand. "Get in! We'll go for a

spin." She faced the group. "Thanks so much! I've never had anything like this, and I love you all so much!"

"Hurry up, Mom!" called Meaghan from the passenger seat.

Sheena slid behind the wheel, took off the pink bow, and waved it in the air. At the sound of the engine, Darcy watched Sheena's face light with excitement. Unexpected tears misted her vision. She'd never realized how disappointed Sheena had been to miss out on college and how hard it had been for her to strive to be the perfect mother and wife after getting pregnant and marrying Tony.

When Sheena drove back into the parking lot, Darcy went over to where she'd pulled in.

"Congratulations, Sheena, on everything—the sale of the business, the car, everything." She leaned over and gave her sister a hug and a kiss. "I've got to go now. See you later."

"Want me to drop you off?" Sheena said, grinning like a kid with the best birthday present ever.

Darcy smiled. "That would be great. I was going to ask Regan, but this is even better. Austin will bring me home."

Meaghan got out of the car, and Darcy slid into the passenger seat.

As they drove away, Darcy waved to Regan. The two of them had done a lot of late-night talking about Austin. Regan was thrilled that Darcy had fallen for him and couldn't wait to see what would happen next.

Sheena turned to Darcy. "So, this is serious between you and Austin?"

"I know it seems very sudden, but I truly love him." Even now Darcy could remember how shocked, how thrilled she'd been over that first kiss. And then, later, when they'd finally admitted their feeling for one another and then had made love, she'd felt as if she was giving her soul to Austin. And he'd responded in kind.

She loved him. It was as simple as that, as deep as that, as wonderful as that. It had taken her a while to see it, but now that she felt it, she couldn't imagine a day without him. It was frightening to think of how she'd once declared she wanted someone more exciting. How shallow she'd been!

Sheena grinned. "I'm happy for you. He's a great guy—super nice, super smart, and super talented."

After Sheena dropped Darcy off at Bill Blakely's, Darcy and Bill shared cool drinks in the kitchen while waiting for Austin to get back from an errand.

"I'm glad you and Austin are serious about each other," said Bill, offering Darcy a cookie from a box he pulled out of the cupboard.

She shook her head at his offer and smiled. "Yes, me too."

Bill took his seat across from her again and gave her a steady look. "We Blakely men fall fast and hard and forever. You're not going to hurt him, are you?"

Darcy reeled back in surprise. "No, I'd never do that. He's the first man I've dated who really knows me, and the first one I honestly trust not to hurt me."

Bill nodded his head with satisfaction. "Good."

They heard Austin enter the house and abruptly ended their conversation.

Austin walked into the kitchen and grinned at the sight of her. Coming to her side, he leaned down and gave her a lingering kiss on the lips that sent waves of pleasure through her. She couldn't help responding, and when he pulled back, they looked at each other and laughed with pure delight.

"Guess I didn't need to worry after all," said Bill, beaming at them.

Austin frowned at his grandfather. "Worry about what?"

"The two of you together. Looks like the Blakely magic is working, same as it did for Margery and me."

Darcy exchanged glances with Austin and turned to Bill. "She was a lovely woman."

Bill reached across the table and gave her hand a squeeze. "So are you, Darcy." He rose. "Now I'm going to leave the two of you alone."

Austin stood and held out his hand. "Want to take a walk? We can head down to the park and talk there."

Darcy rose and took Austin's hand. They went outside and walked to the little park in the middle of the neighborhood, as they'd once done at what now seemed ages ago.

The sun was gently playing with floating clouds, hiding behind them and then bursting forth with brightness. A family of ducks waddled down to the pond, quacking loudly as if protesting anyone intruding on their territory. Darcy laughed when the littlest one hurried to catch up to the others.

They sat on a bench in the shade, and Austin turned to her with an earnest expression. "Darcy, you and I share something special, don't you agree?"

Darcy grinned. "Oh, yeah, I knew it from that first kiss."

Her heart pounded as he lowered himself on one knee in front of her. "I know it may seem too soon to others, but I don't want to wait. I love you and want you to be with me for the rest of our lives. Without you by my side, I'll never know all that life may be. Darcy, will you marry me?"

Darcy stared at him for a moment, wanting to pinch herself to see if this was real or something she'd dreamed. Then she realized he was waiting for her reply. "Yes, oh yes!" she cried, clasping her hands together.

Austin pulled a small, square, black velvet box from his pocket. "I designed this ring for you." He opened the lid, exposing three large diamonds of the same size in a wide platinum band. Still on one knee, he looked up at her with such tenderness, her heart caught. "Its simplicity symbolizes to me how I love you—with all my heart, body, and soul."

Tears spilled down Darcy's cheeks, washing them with a joy she'd never known.

He got to his feet, slipped the ring on her finger and wrapped his arms around her.

"Let's not wait too long to get married, okay?"

She smiled."How does a winter wedding sound?"

"Perfect," he said. "You should be through your challenge at the hotel and will be able to do some traveling with me."

Darcy felt her eyes widen.

He laughed. "Remember, my parents are in the business, so you choose where you want to go for our honeymoon, and we'll make it happen."

"Now I *am* dreaming," said Darcy. "You, the ring, traveling." Suddenly she was sobbing.

"My God! What is it?" Austin said, giving her a worried look.

"It's fabulous, that's what it is," she said, sniffling.

When they returned to the house, Bill looked up from the book he was reading. "Well?"

Austin laughed. "She said yes."

"Your parents called to say they'll be here as soon as they can to celebrate. Guess you told them all about marrying our Darcy."

Darcy turned to Austin. "Really? They knew?"

A grin spread across Austin's face. "I called your father for permission too."

"Oh my Gawd! What did he say?"

"He told me to keep you in line and to make certain you're happy."

Darcy laughed. "Sounds just like him."

Later, after a fancy dinner at a restaurant where they ordered champagne and talked for hours about their plans, Austin drove Darcy back to the hotel. Climbing out of the car, Darcy stood under one of the lights lining the parking lot and stared at the ring on her finger. It glittered and glowed like a magical firefly.

"Guess you like it, huh?" said Austin, coming over to her and wrapping his arms around her.

"I like you better, but, yeah, I like it a lot. C'mon, let's tell my sisters the good news."

Darcy led Austin inside, and when she found her own suite empty, she went and knocked on the door to Sheena's suite.

Tony opened the door. "Hi, come on in!"

Sheena got up from the couch where she was reading and came over to them. "What's up?"

Grinning, Darcy held out her finger. "Notice anything?"

"Oh, my word!" Sheena cried. "You're engaged? How wonderful! What a nice surprise!"

Sheena wrapped her arms around Darcy and then hugged Austin. "Congratulations to you both!"

As Tony was shaking hands with Austin, Meaghan rushed into the room. "Darcy's engaged? When is the wedding? Can I be in it?"

Darcy laughed. "Sure. We're thinking of a winter wedding, after the challenge date."

"Sounds good," said Sheena, looking up when Regan entered the room.

"What's going on?" Regan asked. She took a look at the

hand Darcy was waving in front of her and shrieked, "Oh my Gawd! You're engaged?"

Feeling as if she were the luckiest girl in the world, Darcy hugged her sister and then watched as Austin received more congratulations.

CHAPTER FIFTY

DARCY

On an unusually cool August day, Darcy sat in a pew beside Austin in the crowded community church, her body taut with nervousness, about to make one of the most important speeches of her life. Light shone through the stained-glass windows, sending shards of color throughout the interior.

She bent her head and prayed she'd do justice to Nick. He'd given her a new life, just as Austin had given her new love.

The service became a blur of words and singing. When it was time for her to stand, her knees felt wobbly.

Austin gave her hand a gentle squeeze. At his silent encouragement, Darcy drew a deep breath and climbed the short stairway to the pulpit at the front of the church.

Looking down at the audience, she focused on Sandy and her family and turned to gaze at the people from *West Coast News*. Jeremy McCarthy and Bruce Gilman sat with their wives. Lainey Edwards, as flamboyant as ever, sat with Ed Richardson, the editor.

Her mouth dry, Darcy glanced at her family, here to support her. They knew how much she'd cared for Nick, how nervous she was about giving a speech that would do him and their friendship justice. Randy and Michael sat with the others, giving her a respectful look.

Darcy drew a deep breath and then she cleared her throat and began to talk.

She and Nick had worked on the eulogy together, but she

couldn't hold back from writing words of her own. Just as she sometimes felt when she was writing her column, the words seemed to flow through her from someplace else. She talked about Nick's kindness, the way his personality fit his appearance, how he wanted to be remembered, and what he hoped for the future of his family and friends.

"Nick regretted he had no children of his own and worried he wouldn't leave a legacy behind." Darcy shook her head. "He had no idea how he'd touched my heart and those of the people around him. Having you here, honoring him, can in no way begin to do him justice. I, for one, will be forever grateful for the wings he gave me in the form of words. To say farewell to Nick Howard would be wrong. He will remain a part of us and the future forever." She stopped talking, looked up at the ceiling, and whispered, "Thank you."

The silence that followed was disconcerting until Darcy realized that people were crying.

As she returned to the pew, Austin rose to help her to her seat. She clung to his hand, needing his presence to steady her.

Soft organ music filled the church.

Darcy looked once more at the colors in the stained-glass windows and imagined they were the changing colors in her life. She'd come to Florida a woman uncertain of herself and her role in life. After finding her way through her friendship with Nick and with Austin's love, she'd learned to love others in a different way and had come to know that she, herself, was worthy of love.

Filled with tenderness, Darcy leaned against Austin's strong, steady shoulder and took hold of the hand he offered her, excited for their future together.

Thank you for reading *Finding My Way*. Please help other readers discover it by leaving a review on Amazon, Goodreads, BookBub, or your favorite site. It's such a nice thing to do. And be sure to read the other books in The Salty Key Inn Series: *Finding Me, Finding Love,* and *Finding Family*.

Enjoy an excerpt from my book, *Finding Love,* Book 3 in The Salty Key Inn series.

CHAPTER ONE

REGAN

Regan Sullivan crossed the grounds of the Salty Key Inn to the pool, stopping to gaze at the bougainvillea that was recently planted around its perimeter. Lifting a blossom-laden branch, she studied the vibrant pink color of the petals and drew a deep breath, allowing herself a moment to embrace its beauty. No matter how often people tried to capture color like this in fabric or paint, Regan thought they could never quite succeed. Mother Nature would always win out.

Regan looked up at the sky. Streaks of pink broke through the early morning gray, promising another hot, early September day along the Gulf Coast of Florida. She gazed at a nearby hibiscus bush whose pink blossoms were opening to the sun and thought about all the changes in her life. Growing up in Dorchester, Massachusetts, she would never have dreamed she would be part owner of a hotel. She'd already begun to think of her life in two sections—before Uncle Gavin's will, and after.

The far-fetched challenge their Uncle Gavin had given her

and her sisters was like something out of a comic book, Regan thought, reviewing it in her mind. They were to live and work together for one whole year to restore the hotel and get it up and running. If they met that requirement, they'd each inherit a third of his sizeable estate. But it was no easy matter. Living together, working together, and coming up with creative ideas to accomplish this were the real challenges.

Their uncle had wanted this experience to be a life lesson for each of them. At the bottom of the letter he'd left for her, he'd written an ambiguous message: "Beauty is in the eye of the beholder." When she'd read it, she'd been upset, thinking he'd been referring to her appearance, which she felt was the only thing people noticed when they met her. Now, she was beginning to suspect that when he'd given her that message, he'd had something entirely different in mind.

She had these thoughts as she gazed around feeling as if she was in a tropical painting. Nothing quite as exotic as a Paul Gauguin, but scenery she liked a lot better than what she'd been used to seeing in New York City or her hometown of Boston.

Because of age differences, she hadn't known her sisters all that well. Sheena, the oldest at thirty-six, was always considered the "perfect one." At twenty-six, Darcy, her middle sister, was sometimes outspoken and impulsive, but in the last few months, she'd grown into a softer version of her former self. At twenty-two, Regan was also changing as she discovered more about herself.

She caught sight of Brian Harwood and returned the wave he gave her before he entered Gracie's, the restaurant at the hotel. Drawing a deep breath to stop her racing heart, she vowed to keep her promise to herself to avoid getting involved with him. No matter how easily he played with her emotions, she was sure he was someone who would hurt her. Women all but drooled over his handsome face, his buff body, and the dark eyes that drew people in. He almost always responded to them with interest, proving to her that he was Trouble with a capital T.

Regan hurried to the hotel's reception office beside the pool. Their opening was about to take place and she wanted to be on top of things. Sheena was dealing with issues in her family, and Darcy was writing her weekly column for the *West Coast News*, a local newspaper.

She entered the office and went right to the computer to check the reservations system. They were opening only the twenty ground-floor rooms in the Egret Building. The top-floor twenty rooms would remain unfinished until they had enough revenue to complete them. The eight suites in the separate building where she and her sisters were temporarily living would be the last rooms to be renovated.

Her eyes scanned the list of people due to arrive for the Labor Day Weekend. Twelve couples were taking advantage of the special renovation rates. For a stay of two days or more, they'd receive a discount off their room rate for two days anytime within the next four months, when Uncle Gavin's challenge would end.

Regan's cell rang. She checked caller ID and smiled. *Moses Greene*. In a very short time, Mo had become one of her best friends. They'd met when he'd helped her select furniture for the hotel. Colorful and sweet, he was a very talented interior decorator. She hoped to be his partner one day.

"Hi, sweetie," he said. "I called to wish you and your sisters a successful weekend at the hotel. It should be a good beginning. By the way, Bernice is excited about having her business up and running for you."

"She's doing fine," Regan said. She and Mo had talked his cousin into opening a cleaning business to handle the

Housekeeping department at the hotel.

"You're going to the Keys for the weekend as planned?" Regan asked him.

"Yes, I figure it's time to get out and meet some new people. After the holiday, I've got a busy schedule coming up. Sheena's mother-in-law has done a great job promoting me. I've got a number of houses to work on."

"Let me know when I can help. Hopefully, after the holiday, things will settle into a calmer routine with fewer guests."

He chuckled. "I know how much you want to come into my business, but I think you're supposed to hope for more and more business at the hotel, not less of it."

Regan's eyes rounded, and then laughter burst out of her. "Gawd! Sheena and Darcy would kill me if they'd heard what I just said."

"Kill you for what?" said a voice, and Regan turned around to face Darcy.

"Gotta go, Mo," Regan said. "Have fun, and call me when you get back. I'll want to hear all the news."

"Deal," said Mo, and hung up.

"What's going on?" Darcy's blue eyes penetrated Regan's violet-blue ones, challenging her for an answer.

"I told Mo I hoped things would settle down here at the hotel, and he reminded me that as a hotel owner, I shouldn't want that."

Darcy shook her head, tossing her red curls. "I know how you feel. Between the newspaper work and trying to organize a small wedding, I sometimes wish ...

Sheena entered the office. "Sometimes wish what?"

Regan and Darcy exchanged amused glances. *Sisters!*

"Well?" Sheena prompted.

"I sometimes wish this whole challenge was over. I'm busy with other things, and so is Regan," said Darcy.

Sheena studied each of them and then sighed. “Okay, pep talk time. We have to focus. We’re down to four months to meet the challenge of getting the hotel up and running and pulling in some revenue. You know and I know that this could mean a lot of money to us if we succeed. More than that, we can make this hotel the kind of place Uncle Gavin envisioned. I, for one, want to stay on and help run the hotel if, and right now it’s a big IF, we can pull this off. Don’t let anything keep you from making this happen. Agreed?”

Chastised by the determined tone in Sheena’s voice, Regan nodded. Her big sister was sometimes bossy, but she had a good heart, and they all had good reasons to want to beat the challenge. For Sheena, it would be to help her husband, Tony, set up his own plumbing business in Florida and to help educate their two teenage children, Michael and Meaghan. For Darcy, it would be the chance to write a novel and to have a life with Austin Blakely, her fiancé. And for herself? Regan would go into the interior decorating business with Mo, combining childhood wishes for both recognition of her skills and acceptance for who she was as a person.

“Okay, then,” said Sheena. “Let’s see who we’re talking about as guests.” She looked over the list. “Sorry, Darcy, but your old roommates from Boston are still coming. I thought you told them not to.”

Darcy made a face. “I tried to tell them to wait until we’ve had time to do more renovations, but nobody can tell Alex Townsend anything. I’m sure she wants to come here just to make nasty remarks. You know how snobby she is.”

“We need to make our guests understand that we’re in transition, working to make the hotel better,” said Sheena. “You’ve made that clear in our advertising campaign, Darcy.”

“You don’t know Alex like I do,” griped Darcy.

“Nicole Coleman is nice though,” Regan said, offering

Darcy a smile of encouragement.

"She's the whole reason I roomed with them in Boston," Darcy sighed. "I guess we'll have to do our best with Alex."

"Now that Sheena is here, let's grab a cup of coffee," Regan said to Darcy. "It's going to be a busy day."

"Bring me back a cup," said Sheena. "I think I'm going to need an extra jolt of energy. With Randy's summer stay with us ending, Michael and Meaghan are at each other, fighting over every little thing. It has everything to do with their being nervous about entering new schools, not that they're about to admit it."

The phone rang, and as Sheena answered it, Regan and Darcy left.

As they entered Gracie's, Brian was leaving. He smiled at Darcy. "Congratulations on your engagement. Austin is a great guy. I'm happy for both of you."

A flush crept up Darcy's cheeks. At one time, she'd thrown herself at Brian, going so far as to even proposition him. Now, it seemed so foolish. "Thank you. I'm a very lucky woman."

Brian grinned at her. "And talented too. I read your columns, you know."

The look of surprise on Darcy's face was telling. Regan squeezed her sister's hand, proud of all that she'd accomplished.

Brian's gaze swept over Regan, causing goose pimples to do a tap dance across her shoulders. "Heard you and Chip were at The Pink Dolphin last night. Sorry I missed you. I wanted you to meet Jill."

Regan ordered her raised eyebrows to lower. "Jill?"

"She's an old girlfriend who's moved back here. We're together again."

The pit in Regan's stomach filled with acid. She told herself it was nerves from their opening weekend, but as Brian exited the restaurant, she felt the sting of tears.

Darcy elbowed her. “What’s the matter?”

“I think it might be allergies,” Regan said. “I love all these new flowering bushes, but it’s a little much.” As she said the words, Regan was amazed by how easily she’d just lied.

# # #

About the Author

A ***USA Today* Best-Selling Author,** Judith Keim is a hybrid author who both has a publisher and self-publishes. Ms. Keim writes heart-warming novels about women who face unexpected challenges, meet them with strength, and find love and happiness along the way—stories with heart. Her best-selling books are based, in part, on many of the places she's lived or visited, and on the interesting people she's met, creating believable characters and realistic settings her many loyal readers love.

She enjoyed her childhood and young adult years in Elmira, New York, and now makes her home in Boise, Idaho, with her husband, Peter, and their lovable miniature Dachshund, Wally, and other members of her family.

While growing up, she was drawn to the idea of writing stories from a young age. Books were always present, being read, ready to go back to the library, or about to be discovered. All in her family shared information from the books in general conversation, giving them a wealth of knowledge and vivid imaginations.

Ms. Keim loves to hear from her readers and appreciates their enthusiasm for her stories.

"I hope you've enjoyed this book. If you have, please help other readers discover it by leaving a review on Amazon, BookBub, Goodreads, or the site of your choice. And please check out my other books and series:

The Hartwell Women Series
The Beach House Hotel Series
The Fat Fridays Group
The Salty Key Inn Series
The Chandler Hill Inn Series
Seashell Cottage Books
The Desert Sage Inn Series
Soul Sisters at Cedar Mountain Lodge
The Sanderling Cove Inn Series
The Lilac Lake Inn Series

ALL THE BOOKS ARE NOW AVAILABLE IN AUDIO on Audible, iTunes, Findaway, Kobo, and Google Play! So fun to have these characters come alive!"

Ms. Keim can be reached at **www.judithkeim.com**

And to like her author page on Facebook and keep up with the news, go to: **http://bit.ly/2pZWDgA**

To receive notices about new books, follow her on Book Bub:

https://www.bookbub.com/authors/judith-keim

Sign up for my newsletter and get a free story. I keep my newsletters short and fun with giveaways, recipes, and the latest must-have news about me and my books. Welcome! Here's the link:

https://BookHip.com/RRGJKGN

She is also on Twitter @judithkeim, LinkedIn, and Goodreads. Come say hello!

Acknowledgements

And, as always, I am eternally grateful to my team of editors, Peter Keim and Lynn Mapp, my book cover designer, Lou Harper, and my narrator for Audible and iTunes, Angela Dawe. They are the people who take what I've written and help turn it into the book I proudly present to you, my readers! I also wish to thank my coffee group of writers who listen and encourage me to keep on going. Thank you, Peggy, Lynn, Cate, Nikki Jean, Mel and Megan. And to you, my fabulous readers, I thank you for your continued support and encouragement. Without you, this book would not exist. You are the wind beneath my wings.

www.ingramcontent.com/pod-product-compliance
Lightning Source LLC
Chambersburg PA
CBHW061555190726
48288CB00007B/2044

* 9 7 8 1 9 5 9 5 2 9 9 4 1 *